THE

Aunt Daisy

COOKBOOK

EDITED BY BARBARA BASHAM

Hodder Moa

National Library of New Zealand Cataloguing-in-Publication Data
Daisy, Aunt, 1879-1963.
The Aunt Daisy cookbook / edited by Barbara Basham.
Previous ed.: Hodder & Stoughton, 1968.
Includes index.
ISBN 978-1-86971-184-9
1. Cookery. 2. Home economics. I. Basham, Barbara. II. Title.
641.5—dc 22

First published by Hodder & Stoughton in 1968
Reprinted 1970, 1971, 1973, 1974, 1976, 1977 (twice), 1978, 1979, 1981 (twice), 1982 (twice),
1984, 1985, 1986, 1988, 1989, 1991, 1992, 1994

This edition published in 2009 by Hachette New Zealand Ltd
4 Whetu Place, Mairangi Bay
Auckland, New Zealand

Designed and produced by Hachette New Zealand Ltd
Printed by Everbest Printing Co Ltd

Contents

Preface

This heritage collection of well-loved, tried and true Aunt Daisy recipes was originally read over ZB radio to housewives, mothers and cooks all over New Zealand from the 1930s to the 1960s.

Armed with pen and paper, many of our grandparents waited eagerly by the wireless to scribble down the latest great recipe for a succulent roast meal, a really good pavlova, or a moist golden syrup pudding to impress their families and friends. They knew that, with Aunt Daisy testing every recipe, they could be counted on to work.

It was a different time and, many will argue, a different world, but this is the kind of food most of us love to remember. It's comfort food in the best sense — wholesome, nutritious, and with a taste that never fails to make us recall the best family dinners.

Aunt Daisy's late daughter Barbara Basham lovingly researched and compiled this extensive collection as a tribute to her mother. Before Barbara died, she arranged to establish a charitable trust under her Will to which all sale proceeds from this book will go.

The Barbara Basham Medical Charitable Trust is managed by Guardian Trust to fund world-class medical research in New Zealand. The Trust has already enabled the completion of ground-breaking stroke research on improving treatment outcomes.

If you would like to support the Barbara Basham Medical Charitable Trust in this aim, donations are tax-deductible and can be made at any branch of Guardian Trust, or by cheque (payable to the Barbara Basham Medical Charitable Trust) to PO Box 1934, Auckland.

We hope you and your family enjoy these recipes that little bit more, knowing that the sale proceeds of this collection will fund ongoing medical research in New Zealand.

Guardian Trust

About The
Aunt Daisy Cookbook

The Aunt Daisy Cookbook is one of New Zealand's bestselling recipe books. It was first published in 1968. Although Aunt Daisy's recipes themselves stand the test of time, some ingredients, terminology, measurements and methods have changed since 1968.

INGREDIENTS

There are no unusual ingredients in *The Aunt Daisy Cookbook*. Here is an explanation of some ingredients that, while mostly still available, are not used as widely today as when the cookbook was first produced.

dripping is melted fat and residue that is left in the pan after meat has been cooked. It is used as a cooking fat and can therefore be substituted for other cooking oils or fats.

lard is rendered pig fat. It's not used as widely today because of health concerns posed by its saturated fat content. Pure lard is useful for cooking because it produces little smoke when heated, but can be substituted for other cooking oils or fats.

ratafia essence is made from bitter almonds or the kernels of peaches or apricots. It has an almond flavour, so almond essence can be easily substituted.

suet (the hard fat from around the kidneys of cows and sheep) is sometimes called for in Aunt Daisy's pudding recipes. Because suet has a high melting point, it serves as a 'place holder' in puddings when the dough has begun to set (and long after other fats would have melted). As a result, the structure of the pudding is already set by the time the suet melts, leaving thousands of tiny air holes that give the pudding a light texture. You can substitute suet with solid vegetable shortening in most recipes.

Some recipes ask for a suet crust but do not give instructions for the pastry. Make suet pastry by combining 225g self-raising flour, 110g shredded suet and ¼ teaspoon salt. Add enough water (about 150ml) to mix to a stiff dough. Knead until smooth. (Makes about 450g.)

top milk is the milk that used to sit at the top of the milk bottle, i.e. thick and creamy. We have substituted either cream or full-cream milk, depending on the recipe.

MEASUREMENTS

All recipes have been metricated. Pounds and ounces have been changed to grams, quarts and pints to millilitres, and inches to centimetres.

Breakfast cup and teacup measures remain unchanged. A breakfast cup is a little larger than a standard cup; about 280ml or ½ pint. A teacup is smaller than a standard cup; about 140ml or ¼ pint (similar to 1 gill). A rough conversion is:

1 breakfast cup = 1 standard cup + 2 tablespoons
1 teacup = ½ standard cup + 1 tablespoon

Here are some common breakfast cup and teacup measurements and their approximate gram equivalents.

Ingredient	1 breakfast cup	1 teacup
flour	160g	80g
mixed fruit	150g	75g
sugar	250g	125g
brown sugar	230g	115g

COOKING INSTRUCTIONS

Some of Aunt Daisy's recipes presumed the cook had a good amount of know-how, and so give instructions such as 'cook as usual' or 'bake in the usual way'. In the recipes that were particularly sparse and where we felt today's cooks would have difficulty, we've added some extra instructions to clarify.

Either oven temperatures or cooking times were frequently omitted. We've added these to most recipes to make life easier for the modern cook.

OVENS

In Aunt Daisy's recipes the oven temperature is often not given in Celsius or Fahrenheit but described as 'a quick oven' or 'a slow oven'. For today's cook cooking in a modern oven we have converted these descriptions as follows:

slow oven	120°C
moderate oven	180°C
quick oven	220°C

Aunt Daisy's recipes usually do not tell you how to tell when something is done. Heavier cakes and puddings are cooked when a skewer pushed into the centre comes out clean. Lighter cakes are cooked if they spring back when pushed gently with your finger.

Aunt Daisy's Cookery Books

Aunt Daisy's Cookery Book of Selected Recipes,
    Whitcombe & Tombs, Auckland, 1933.
Aunt Daisy's Cookery Book of Approved Recipes, D. Basham,
    Auckland, 1934.
*The N.Z. "Daisy Chain" cookery book containing over 800 recipes
    and hints, No. 2*, Mrs. D. Basham/Harvison & Marshall Ltd.,
    Auckland, 1935.
*Aunt Daisy's Book of Selected Special Recipes: From California,
    Canada, France, Australia and New Zealand (Volume No. 3)*,
    Whitcombe & Tombs, Auckland, 1935.
Aunt Daisy's Cookery Book of Selected Recipes (Cover title:
    Aunt Daisy's Radio Cookery Book), Whitcombe & Tombs,
    Christchurch, 1939.
Aunt Daisy's Cookery Book of Selected Recipes (Cover title: *Aunt
    Daisy Cookery No. 4*), Whitcombe & Tombs, Christchurch, 1939.
Aunt Daisy's Cookery Book of 1,150 Selected Recipes (Cover title:
    Aunt Daisy Cookery, No. 5 Limited Edition), Whitcombe &
    Tombs, Christchurch, 1942.
Breakfasts For Everybody: 280 Appetising Recipes, Whitcombe &
    Tombs, Christchurch, 1945.
*Aunt Daisy's Pickles and Sauces, Jams and Jellies: 383 Proved
    Recipes*, Whitcombe & Tombs, Christchurch, 1949.
Aunt Daisy's New Cookery No. 6, Whitcombe & Tombs,
    Christchurch, 1951.
Aunt Daisy's Favourite Cookery Book, Whitcombe & Tombs,
    Christchurch, 1952.
Aunt Daisy's Ultimate Cookery Book, Whitcombe & Tombs,
    Christchurch, 1959.
The Aunt Daisy Cookbook with Household Hints, Hodder &
    Stoughton, Auckland, 1968.

Foreword

'Good *morning* everybody!'

Three generations of New Zealanders responded to that radio greeting from Aunt Daisy every morning at 9 o'clock. Thousands of tiny children learned to repeat it after her, and later their own children did the same. Her listeners were cheered by her unquenchable optimism — she could always find a patch of blue sky on the stormiest morning.

Each session began with a 'scrapbook piece' and a chat about things in general. She had a strong Christian philosophy and was never afraid to speak of it. In the session she passed on to the housewives — the 'Daisy Chain' as some called it — new recipes, new ideas, new hints. She never prepared a script, but just 'talked'. Shortly after 7.30 each morning she would arrive at the studio, select the recipes and hints, and decide which particular virtues of her sponsors' products she would extol that day. She advertised only those products she believed in. Then at 9 o'clock came the four chimes, the 'Bicycle Built for Two' theme, and then, 'Good *morning* everybody', and away she'd go, non-stop. And during that morning half-hour Aunt Daisy was a friend, visiting everyone's home — the busy city mothers, the sick, the isolated, the 'shut-ins', the lonely, the sad and the happy — and many a man listened too, and enjoyed it.

Her first advertising session was on Friday, 20 October 1936 from 1ZB Auckland. By 1937 her programme was heard from the four main commercial stations in link, originating in Wellington; and so it continued for nearly thirty years. Before that she had broadcast similar programmes from 1ZR, the 'Friendly Road'. But this does not explain the 'Aunt'. That goes back originally to the late 1920s when she relieved 'Cinderella' with the children's session at the old

1YA. In the early 1930s she became 'Aunt' to Wellington children from 2YA, with a group of youngsters who came along to sing, a group called 'The Cheerful Chirpers'.

Aunt Daisy managed to travel a little during her days of broadcasting. An early trip to America from the proceeds of her first cookery book during the Depression gave her new recipes and topics. But no one could have received a more triumphant farewell than she did in 1938. The Wellington Town Hall was filled at least two hours before the appointed time, and the crowd overflowed outside. On the way to Auckland, when the train stopped at a station, a group of admirers would be on the platform singing, 'Daisy, Daisy, give me your answer do'. And the Auckland Town Hall was filled, too.

Though she was away for six months, her voice was heard every day, for she sent recordings back from overseas. Today it is commonplace to fly tapes round the world. Then, cumbersome 15-inch acetate discs had to be sent by sea; so it was indeed a pioneering trip. One idea she brought back was the Easter Sunrise Service which she organised on the top of Mount Victoria in Wellington.

But the Second World War put a stop to that. And for the next few years her courage and cheerfulness were needed to keep strength in the hearts of thousands of households where husbands, sons and daughters were overseas with the Forces. And she could indeed sympathise, for her own daughter was serving on the hospital ship *Oranje*. During the war she went on a semi-official visit to America, on a blacked-out Liberty ship, to tell the mothers there how their sons were faring in the Pacific and in New Zealand.

Only the most serious sickness prevented Aunt Daisy from giving her morning broadcasts. Twice she had such bad influenza that she lost her voice — and what is a broadcaster without a voice? Once she broadcast with an eye so black and blue and swollen she could hardly see the microphone, let alone her notes. A gust of wind had blown her into a building on the way to the studio.

Then one Friday at the end of June 1963, she unknowingly made her last broadcast. On the Sunday morning she became ill. As she returned to consciousness later that day, she struggled up and said: 'I have to do the session tomorrow morning.' But she had no more strength, and quietly let her life slip away — a life that had begun in London nearly 84 years before. She had several careers during that long life — a brilliant scholar, a school teacher, singer, mother, singing-teacher, journalist, broadcaster, and 'universal aunt'. She had her sorrows, her problems, her fun; lived every minute of her life with zest. And perhaps the great secret of her success was — enthusiasm and sincerity, tempered with humility.

During these many years of broadcasting, and writing for the *Weekly News* and *Listener*, Aunt Daisy gathered up thousands of tried recipes and handy hints. She published ten cookery books and a hint book, as well as some of her favourite 'scrapbook pieces'. I have selected many of her most popular recipes, and have revised the hints. In the years she wrote the 'Ask Aunt Daisy' page in the *Listener*, a highlight was the illustration each week, by Russell Clark. His widow, Mrs Rosalie Clark, has given me permission to use some of them in this book. I am grateful to her, and to the *Listener*, for their cooperation.

May this book help you in your housekeeping, and may it help you to remember your friend Aunt Daisy — or to give her her proper name, Mrs Daisy Basham, M.B.E.

Barbara Basham

SAVOURY DISHES

BATTER FOR FISH (1)

115g flour • 1 egg yolk • tepid water • 1 egg white • pinch of salt •
fat for frying

Put flour in a basin. Drop in the egg yolk, and beat in. Add a little
tepid water and make a smooth batter. Leave 10 minutes. Beat the
egg white stiff with a pinch of salt and add. Dip fish in, and fry in
boiling clean fat.

BATTER FOR FISH (2)

1 egg yolk, beaten, in 1 dish • breadcrumbs or flour • 1 egg white,
beaten, in another dish

Dip the fish first in the egg yolk, then in breadcrumbs or flour, then
in egg white. Fry.

BACON AND EGG PATTIES (Devon)

flaky pastry • bacon, finely chopped • parsley, finely chopped •
2 eggs, beaten • ⅓ cup milk • dash of pepper

Line patty tins with flaky pastry. Put in 2 or 3 layers of bacon and
parsley. Pour over 1 dessertspoon of beaten egg, milk and pepper to
each patty. Do not cover. Bake in hot oven (about 210°C).

BACON AND EGG PIE (Devon)

flaky pastry • 225g streaky bacon, chopped finely • plenty of finely chopped parsley • a little milk for basting • 2 eggs • ⅓ cup milk • dash of pepper

Line a shallow dish with flaky pastry. Put 2 or 3 layers of bacon and parsley on pastry. Put pastry lid on top with a 12mm square hole cut neatly out of the centre. Wash over with milk and bake in hot oven at 210°C for 20 minutes. While this is cooking, beat the eggs with the milk and pepper. Take pie from oven and pour egg mixture in through prepared hole. Return to oven for another 20 minutes. Take out of tin, turn upside down and return to hot oven for 5 minutes, to make bottom crisp. Serve in thin pieces for savouries (hot) — or as a hot dish at a meal — or in thin wedges for morning or afternoon tea or supper.

BEEF OLIVE PUDDING

suet crust (see page 7) • 1 thin slice of steak • bacon rashers • sliced kidney • ~~a few~~ • pepper • 1 small cup water flavoured with tomato sauce • flour for sprinkling

Line a pudding basin with a suet crust. Add steak, bacon rashers, kidney ~~~~. Roll up and put in a basin. Pour over flavoured water and sprinkle with flour. Cover and steam for 3 hours.

BOBOTIE (South Africa)

900g fresh mutton • 1 large slice white bread • 1 cup milk •
███████, chopped finely • 2 tablespoons butter or fat •
juice of 1 lemon • 2 tablespoons vinegar • 8 chopped almonds •
4 drops almond essence • 1 tablespoon strong curry powder •
1 tablespoon sugar • a few bay or lemon leaves • salt and pepper •
2 eggs, beaten • rice for serving

Mince the meat, soak the bread in milk and squeeze. ███████████
████████████████. Mix all ingredients except 1 egg and milk.
Beat egg, add the milk. Put mixture into a pie dish. Pour over beaten
egg and milk. Stick leaves into top of meat. Bake until 'custard'
is set and meat is well done. Serve with rice. May be made with
cooked meat.

BOLOGNA PUDDING

suet crust (see page 7) • equal amounts of minced bacon, pork,
beef and veal • salt and pepper • sage • small amount of stock or
water • ██████████████████████████

Line a pudding basin with suet crust and fill centre with meat
seasoned with salt, pepper and sage. Moisten with a little stock or
water. Put suet on top. Cover and steam for 2 to 3 hours. ██████████
██████████████████████████

BRAINS AND BACON

sheep brains • salted water • bacon strips • pepper •
parsley sprigs for garnish

Boil brains in salted water, break each one into 4 pieces and roll in
a strip of bacon. Skewer with a toothpick or match, sprinkle with
pepper and grill until bacon is cooked. Garnish with parsley.

CALIFORNIAN MEAT BALLS

225g minced pork • 225g minced steak • 1½ cups grated breadcrumbs • ¼ cup cold water • 2 tablespoons salad oil • 2 tablespoons finely chopped green pepper • 1 clove garlic, minced fine • ▬▬▬▬▬▬ • 1 teaspoon salt • ½ teaspoon pepper • 2 tablespoons chilli powder (if liked) • 2 tablespoons fat • flour • 2½ cups cooked tomatoes • ½ cup grated cheese

To meat add breadcrumbs, water, oil, peppers, garlic, ▬▬ and seasoning. Melt fat in a frying pan, roll balls in flour and brown in pan. Remove balls from pan. Thicken fat with flour. Add tomatoes and cheese. Add meat balls. Cook slowly on top of stove or in oven for 30 minutes.

CELERY AND EGG SAVOURY

60g butter, melted • 1 heaped tablespoon flour • cold milk • 2 tablespoons grated cheese • 2 or 3 hard-boiled eggs, chopped • 1 head celery, washed, scraped, cut into 25mm long pieces and boiled • breadcrumbs, browned in oven • extra grated cheese

Melt butter in saucepan and blend with flour. Gradually add milk to keep smooth. Add cheese, then celery and eggs until creamy. Place in casserole dish or individual pie dishes. Cover with breadcrumbs and extra cheese. Place in oven to brown and melt the cheese.

FLUFFY CHEESE BALLS

fat for frying • 3 egg whites • pinch of salt • 115g finely grated cheddar cheese • cayenne pepper

Heat fat in a pan. Whisk egg whites into a stiff froth and add salt. Fold cheese into egg whites, flavour with cayenne pepper and mix all together. When fat smokes slightly drop in a teaspoon of the mixture. The little white lumps will puff up into a large ball, turn golden brown and float. Take out with a fish slice and drain. Reheat fat and fry remaining balls, 3 or 4 at a time. Pile on a paper dish and serve at once.

CHEESE DUMPLINGS

60g shredded suet • 115g wholemeal flour • 85g sharp cheese • ½ teaspoon baking powder • pinch of salt • dash of pepper • milk or water

Mix suet into flour, add cheese, baking powder, salt and pepper, and mix to an elastic dough with milk or water. Divide into small pieces, roll in flour, then drop into boiling soup or stew and simmer for 15 minutes. Serve with vegetables.

CHINESE OMELETTE

4 tablespoons butter • ▮▮▮▮▮▮▮▮▮▮▮▮▮▮ • 1 teaspoon salt • ⅛ teaspoon pepper • 1 tablespoon flour • 1½ cups chopped cooked chicken, pork or veal • 4 eggs • melted butter for frying

Melt butter, add a pinch of sugar. When butter is melted, ▮▮▮▮▮▮▮▮. ▮▮▮▮▮▮▮▮▮▮▮▮▮▮▮▮▮▮▮▮. Add salt, pepper and flour. When well mixed, add meat. Beat eggs until light and combine with hot onion mixture. Drop generous tablespoonfuls into a heavy, heated frying pan containing enough melted butter to barely cover the bottom. Fry one side, then the other, like pancakes, and serve very hot. Chopped cooked or canned crayfish or lobster may be substituted for meat.

CHINESE PORK WITH ALMONDS

¼ cup almonds • 2 cups diced carrots • 450g green peas (frozen
or fresh, not tinned) • 450g lean pork, cut into 13mm cubes •
1 teaspoon salt • 2 cups diced celery • ½ cup chicken broth
(may use package or cube) • 2 tablespoons cornflour •
2 teaspoons soy sauce • ⅓ cup cold water • cooked rice to serve

Blanch and chop almonds, fry until golden brown, then drain and set aside. Boil carrots and peas for about 5 minutes until almost tender. Preheat a thick shallow 25mm pan. When hot add 4 tablespoons oil or fat plus salt. Add the pork and cook over a moderate heat until golden brown. Add celery and chicken broth then the carrots and peas. Cover with lid and cook on a low heat until meat is tender, about 5 minutes. Mix cornflour with soy sauce and water, add to the pan and stir until juice thickens and is very hot. Stir in the almonds and serve immediately with hot boiled rice.

COLONIAL GOOSE

2 small cups breadcrumbs • ~~1 parboiled onion, finely chopped~~ •
1 teaspoon salt • ½ small teaspoon pepper • chopped parsley,
sage, thyme • 1 teacup shredded suet, or 2 tablespoons butter or
dripping • a little minced lean bacon or ham • a little milk or 1 egg •
1 leg of mutton, boned by the butcher • flour for dredging

Mix the first seven ingredients together into a forcemeat, using less suet if the bacon is fatty. Bind the forcemeat with milk or an egg. Fill the space in the mutton that the bone occupied with the forcemeat. Sew up the openings. Dredge with flour and bake at 180°C.

CRAYFISH CONTINENTAL

1 large cooked crayfish • melted butter • salt and pepper to season •
2 tablespoons white wine or lemon juice • 1 or 2 egg yolks •
1 spoonful cream • chopped chives or parsley to serve

Slice meat from crayfish and put in a saucepan with butter. Cook for a few minutes, add seasoning to taste and wine. Add egg yolks and cream. Stir until this thickens but do not boil. Serve hot or cold with chives and parsley.

FAGGOT LOAVES

225g raw liver • ▓▓▓▓▓▓▓▓▓ • 2 rashers of bacon •
2 or 3 slices of bread • milk • 2 eggs • 2 tablespoons flour •
salt and pepper to taste • herbs (if liked)

Mince liver, ▓▓▓ and bacon, catching juice; soak bread in milk. Make a batter from eggs, flour and milk, add seasoning and herbs. Mix all, blend with batter. Put into greased tins with covers, or in pie dish. Cook in oven in a pan of water. Serve hot or cold in slices.

FARM TOAST (Shropshire)

bacon • bread • thick slices of apple • thick slices of cheese •
salt and pepper

Fry bacon crisp. Fry bread in the bacon fat. Fry slices of apple. Put cheese slices on bread, melt cheese under the griller. Now lay on bacon, then apple, sprinkle with salt and pepper. Serve hot.

GOLDEN GARNISHES

Hot peach halves — fresh or canned, make accompaniments for meats and meat dishes, chicken, etc., fish and egg dishes.

- Heat peaches in own syrup, and serve plain.
- Fry drained peach halves in a little butter or dripping for about 10 minutes, turning as necessary. Sprinkle with brown sugar and a dash of cinnamon while cooking.
- Bake: Put a little peach syrup into a baking pan, put in peach cut side up. Dot with butter, bake about 20 minutes in a hot oven (200°C). Fill up cavities with jelly or relish. Those filled with relishes (chutney, chilli sauce, ketchup or French dressing) are good with steaks, roasts, fish or croquettes.
- Stick with whole cloves, fill cavity with sugar mixed with a dash of cinnamon, bake. Nice with ham or pork.
- Roll drained peach halves in melted butter, then in finely chopped crushed nuts or flakes, and bake gently. Serve with any meat.

HAM — WHOLE

See Christmas Cookery section

HAM AND ASPARAGUS ROLLS WITH CHEESE

thin slices of uncooked ham • tinned or fresh cooked asparagus

Grill ham on both sides. On each slice of ham place several stalks of asparagus. Then roll up the ham slices. Serve covered with a generous amount of thin rich cheese sauce.

Cheese Sauce:

¼ packet processed cheese (60g) • ⅓ cup milk

In the top of a double boiler melt the cheese. Gradually add the milk, stirring all the time until smooth.

HAM SOUFFLÉ

4 egg yolks • 1½ cups thick white sauce (see page 123) • 2 cups cooked minced ham • salt and pepper • 4 egg whites, beaten

Beat egg yolks, and add to hot white sauce. Add ham and seasoning. When sauce is cool, fold in egg whites. Pour into a buttered baking dish, set in a pan of hot water, and bake in a moderate oven (180°C) for about 50 minutes. Serve at once.

HAM AND PINEAPPLE

6 x 6mm slices cooked ham • 6 slices pineapple • 6 pork sausages • ½ cup brown sugar • ¼ cup pineapple juice • parsley for garnish

Arrange ham slices in a grill pan. Place drained rounds of pineapple on each, then add a sausage cut in two lengthwise. Sprinkle with sugar, pour over pineapple juice, and place under grill. Grill for 8 minutes, turn sausages, and grill for another 8 minutes. Sprinkle with parsley.

INKY PINKY FISH PIE

4 large potatoes • milk • butter • salt and pepper to taste •
1 medium-sized can salmon or 450g boiled white fish •
1 cup parsley sauce • pinch of ground mace or curry powder •
½ teaspoon vinegar • melted butter

Boil and drain, then mash potatoes until smooth. Add hot milk and butter to taste. Beat until fluffy then season with salt and pepper. Remove any bone or skin from fish. Flake fish, add to parsley sauce and season with mace or curry powder, add salt and pepper, flavour with vinegar. (If liked, stir ½ teaspoon anchovy essence or 1 teaspoon minced capers into sauce before using.) Place mixture in a greased pie dish. Cover with mashed potatoes. Ornament with a fork. Brush with melted butter. Bake in a moderate oven (180°C) until golden brown.

KABOBS

1. Put on metal skewer a piece of chicken liver, a slice of bacon, ▬▬▬ ▬▬▬, 1 or 2 raisins, or stoned prunes. Repeat 2 or 3 times, and grill. Or sprinkle with curry powder and serve with curry sauce.
2. Season pieces of lamb, kidney, bacon ▬▬▬▬▬ with salt, ground ginger and curry powder. Leave an hour or two. Put on skewers and bake in oven. Serve with boiled rice and curry sauce.
3. Alternate on skewer, pieces of lamb, or mutton, a bay leaf, slices of sheep kidney, bacon and sausages. Grill or fry. Serve with tomato or curry sauce.

KIDNEY TURBIGO (Lambs')

For 6 people allow:

6 kidneys • 18 slices of bacon, cut into strips • 3 sausages •
fat for frying • salt and pepper • mashed potatoes • chopped
parsley to garnish

Cut kidneys in half lengthways, and skin. Wrap each in a strip of bacon, fasten with a toothpick. If no pick, lay with fold underneath. Skin sausages (put in cold water for a few minutes). Roll sausage meat into balls, fry in hot fat until coloured. Fry wrapped kidney in same pan for a minute or two, until bacon is coloured. Put kidneys and sausage balls in clean pan. Pour off surplus fat in frying pan, and make gravy. Pour this over kidneys and sausages, bring to boil, and cook for about 10 minutes. Season to taste. Arrange mashed potatoes around edge of dish, pour kidney and sausage mixture into middle. Fry remaining bacon and arrange over the kidneys and sausages. Sprinkle with parsley and serve hot.

KEDGEREE

2 cups cooked fish (smoked may be used) • 1 cup white sauce (see page 123) • 2 cups boiled rice • salt and pepper • 1 egg • pinch of nutmeg • chopped parsley to garnish • hard-boiled egg to garnish

Mix all together except parsley and egg. Make very hot in a saucepan, season and pile on to a hot dish. Garnish with parsley and egg (egg yolk sieved and egg white cut into fancy shapes).

KROMESKIES (Fish Roes)

fish roes • salted water • dash of vinegar • rashers of bacon • batter • fat • fried bread

Simmer roes for 10 minutes in salted water with vinegar. Then cut roes into slices, wrap a rasher of bacon around each piece, and fasten with a skewer. Dip into batter and fry in boiling fat. Remove skewer, and serve on slices of fried bread.

LEFTOVER MEAT AND VEGETABLE LOAF

3 cups leftover meat • 1 cup celery • ▪▪▪▪▪▪▪▪▪▪ •
1 cup cooked potatoes • 1 cup carrots • ¼ teaspoon red pepper •
2 teaspoons salt • 1 teaspoon pepper • 2 eggs • 1 cup milk •
tomato sauce to serve

Mince meat and vegetables. Add salt and pepper and mince again to make it light. Add eggs and milk and mix well. Pack into loaf tin, bake about one hour. Serve with tomato sauce.

LIVER PIE (Scottish)

thin slices of liver • seasoned flour • tomatoes, sliced •
▪▪▪▪▪▪▪▪ • sliced raw potatoes • bacon fat or dripping

Roll liver in flour and lay in a casserole dish. Cover with a layer of tomatoes, ▪▪▪▪▪▪▪▪▪, and a layer of potatoes. Add dabs of bacon fat or dripping and bake slowly until done.

MEAT BALLS AND MACARONI

450g lean minced beef • ½ cup soft breadcrumbs • 1 egg •
2 tablespoons currants or sultanas • 2 tablespoons grated cheese
• 1 dessertspoon chopped parsley • ½ teaspoon salt • pepper to taste • olive oil

Mix all ingredients together. Take dessertspoons of mixture and form into balls. Cover bottom of frying pan with thin film of oil and fry balls until brown; add more oil if necessary.

Sauce:

██████████ • 1 x 290g can tomato purée • macaroni • grated cheese to serve • green salad to serve

██████████ in a saucepan ████████████. Add can of tomato purée, and ¼ the can of water, stir and cook until a rich colour, about 30 minutes. Add meat balls and cook 30 minutes. In the meantime have a saucepan of boiling water ready with salt to taste. About 10 minutes after you have placed the meat balls in sauce, put macaroni in water and boil about 20 minutes. Strain water off macaroni and place in basin. Take meat balls out of tomato purée and pour tomato purée over macaroni. Serve with grated cheese. The meat balls are served separately with green salad as an extra course. Spaghetti may be substituted for macaroni, but cook it for a little shorter time (about 10 minutes).

MEXICAN RAREBIT

30g butter or fat • ½ green pepper • 170g grated cheese • 1 egg, beaten • 115g tinned sweet corn • 60g breadcrumbs • 1 medium tomato, chopped • salt • bread for toast

Melt butter, add green pepper and stew gently. Add cheese and stir until it has melted. Stir egg into mixture with corn, breadcrumbs and tomato. Season with salt. Stir well, pour on to slices of toast and serve very hot.

MUSHROOMS WITH BEEF (Chinese)

Note that nothing is ever strained away or wasted in Chinese dishes.

2 tablespoons oil or fat • 1 teaspoon salt • dash of pepper • ▪ ▪ ▪
450g flank or round steak, cut into 3mm thick slices •
▪▪▪▪▪▪▪▪▪▪▪▪▪▪▪▪▪▪▪ • 1 clove garlic, finely diced • ½
cup beef bouillon (or 1 stock cube in hot water) • 450g fresh
mushrooms, sliced • 2 teaspoons cornflour • 2 teaspoons soy
sauce • ¼ cup water • rice to serve

Heat oil or fat in a preheated, heavy 25cm frying pan, and add salt
and pepper. Add meat, ▪▪▪▪, garlic and cook over a moderate heat,
stirring constantly until meat is brown. Add bouillon and mushrooms.
Cover pan tightly and cook over a low heat for 10 minutes. Blend
cornflour, soy sauce and water, and add to pan. Cook a few more
minutes, stirring constantly, until juice thickens and mixture is very
hot. Serve immediately with hot boiled rice.

MUSSELS IN WINE

2 dozen mussels • butter • salt and pepper • ▪▪▪▪▪▪▪▪▪▪
▪▪▪▪▪▪▪▪ • ¼ cup sweet sherry or sauterne •
2 slices of bacon, cut in half • grated cheese

Clean mussels and place in a buttered casserole. Add salt and pepper
to taste ▪▪▪▪▪▪▪▪▪▪ Pour over the sherry. Cover with bacon and
put lid on. Bake for 15 to 20 minutes in a moderate oven (180°C).
Remove lid, sprinkle all over with cheese, and return to oven to
brown nicely.

MUTTON BIRDS

Mutton birds are rich in oil containing some vitamins, iodine, and bone-making material. The oil is of high medicinal value. The flesh is tender and, when cooked, resembles the flesh of wild duck, the flavour being more akin to that of fish.

To cook mutton birds:
Wash in warm water. Simmer in sufficient water to cover. Simmer slowly for 30 minutes, remove from the water and drain. Place bird on a hot grid-iron or frying pan, with fat part uppermost. Cook slowly until fat is crisp and golden brown. No extra seasoning is required. Serve with sliced lemon and plain boiled or baked potatoes.

NORMANDY STEAK

900g blade steak, trimmed of fat and cut into 5cm pieces •
1 dessertspoon sugar • 2 tablespoons flour • ▮▮▮▮▮▮▮ •
1 clove garlic, finely chopped • sprig each of parsley, thyme
and sage • 1 tablespoon Worcestershire sauce • 2 tablespoons
tomato sauce or purée • 2 tablespoons vinegar • ½ cup stock •
2 or 3 rashers bacon, cut into strips (rind removed) • salt and pepper •
tomato wedges and parsley sprigs to garnish

Coat steak with sugar and flour. Line an ovenproof dish with ▮▮▮▮ garlic and herbs, and place meat on top. Pour sauces, vinegar and stock over. Stand 6 to 8 hours, uncovered, in a cool place. Top with bacon strips and season with salt and pepper. Cover and bake in a moderate oven (180°C) for 2 to 2½ hours. Garnish with tomato and parsley.

ONION RINGS (French Fried)

3 large Spanish onions • ½ cup milk • ¼ cup flour •
½ teaspoon baking powder • ⅓ teaspoon salt • 1 egg yolk •
½ tablespoon melted shortening

Peel onions and cut across into slices 6mm thick. Separate into rings. Make batter by beating together milk, flour, baking powder, salt, egg yolk and shortening, using an egg beater. Dip onion rings into batter and fry until browned in deep fat, hot enough to brown a cube of bread in a minute (180°C). Drain on crumpled paper towels, dust with salt and serve with fish or baked tomatoes.

Alternatively, the onion rings may be dipped first in milk and then in flour and dropped into deep smoking hot fat. They are cooked in 3 to 4 minutes. Remove with a perforated spoon, drain and serve.

OYSTERS (Scalloped)

milk • oyster liquor • chopped parsley (optional) •
fine breadcrumbs • oysters • pepper • butter

Make a rich white sauce using half milk and half oyster liquor, and add parsley if desired. Butter a deep pie dish and line with breadcrumbs. Add a thin layer of sauce, then a thick layer of raw oysters. Add pepper. Add another layer of white sauce (a little chopped parsley in it is good) and then a layer of breadcrumbs. If the dish is big enough, repeat with sauce and oysters. Finish with a layer of breadcrumbs. Dot generously with butter. Bake in a hot oven (220°C) for 15 minutes.

POOR MAN'S GOOSE

parboiled potatoes, sliced • lamb or sheep's fry, sliced thickly •
chopped bacon (optional) • 1 small teacup water or sage ▬▬

Stuffing:
225g breadcrumbs • ▬▬▬▬▬▬▬▬▬▬▬
60g butter • 12 sage leaves, chopped finely (or 1 teaspoon
dried powdered sage) • pinch of ginger • salt and pepper •
1 egg, beaten (or milk)

Mix all stuffing ingredients with egg or milk. In a greased casserole
put a double layer of potatoes, then a layer of liver slices, then a
layer of stuffing. Repeat until dish is full, finishing with potatoes.
Add bacon if liked. Pour over water or gravy, cover with greased
paper, and bake in a moderate oven (180°C) for 1½ hours. Serve with
apple sauce.

PORK POT ROAST

1.8kg shoulder pork • 1 cup water or stock • 1½ teaspoons salt •
6 medium apples, peeled and cored • ½ cup seedless raisins •
4 tablespoons flour

In a saucepan with a well-fitting lid, brown meat on all sides in a
little fat. Add salt and water or stock. Cover tightly and cook slowly
on top of stove until tender, about 2¾ hours. Add apples and raisins,
and cook until apples are done and raisins are plump. Remove from
stove, thicken with flour and add water to make about 2 cupfuls.

SALMON LOAF AND CHEESE SAUCE

450g tin salmon • 1 cup breadcrumbs • ▓▓▓▓▓▓▓▓▓▓ ▓▓▓▓▓▓▓▓▓▓ • ¼ cup milk • 2 eggs, beaten • salt and pepper

Bone and flake the salmon. Mix with breadcrumbs ▓▓▓▓▓. Moisten with milk and eggs and season with salt and pepper. Bake in moderate oven (180°C) until firm in a buttered dish.

Cheese Sauce:

115g cheese, grated • ½ cup milk

Put cheese in a saucepan with 1 tablespoon milk. Heat and stir until smooth. Pour remainder of milk in, slowly cooking and stirring constantly. Pour sauce over hot Salmon Loaf. Serves 6 to 8 persons.

SARDINE SAVOURY

1 tin sardines • 1 teaspoon Worcestershire sauce • 1 teaspoon anchovy sauce • 2 eggs • 1 teaspoon butter • 1 teaspoon flour • salt and pepper • buttered toast to serve

Put all into a large saucepan and stir until thick. Spread on hot buttered toast. This is really delicious and goes a long way.

SAUSAGE AND PINEAPPLE BUTTERFLIES

pineapple slices, halved • sausages • mashed potato • chopped parsley • ▓▓▓▓▓▓▓▓

Fry pineapple until light brown. Fry sausages. Place sausage on plate, mashed potato each side, stand pineapple in potato to resemble butterfly wings. Sprinkle potato with parsley ▓▓▓▓▓▓▓.

SEAFOOD COCKTAIL

6 tablespoons mayonnaise • 4 tablespoons tomato sauce •
2 teaspoons Worcestershire sauce • chopped parsley •
~~juice of 1 onion~~ • prawns, oysters, crayfish or any other fish liked

Mix ingredients smoothly ~~and add 1 or 2 drops of onion juice~~. Mix in fish and serve in cocktail glasses with a little parsley on top.

SEA PIE

900g steak or gravy beef, cut into 50mm pieces • dripping • ~~1 large~~ ~~onion, thinly sliced~~ • 1 carrot, thinly sliced • 4 potatoes, sliced thin • salt and pepper • 2 cups water • 225g suet paste

Fry meat in small quantity of dripping until brown. Place vegetables on top of steak, add salt and pepper and the water. Make a suet pastry and roll out in a round to fit inside the saucepan. Place suet on top of the vegetables when boiling and simmer for 2 to 3 hours. Lift out suet pastry. Place meat, vegetables and gravy on a hot dish. Cut the pastry into nice pieces and put them around edge of the dish.

SHIRLEY FRITTERS (Special)

1 cup flour • 1½ teaspoons baking powder • ½ teaspoon salt • 1 egg, well beaten • ½ cup milk • ½ cup cold, cooked, minced leftover meat • 2 teaspoons chopped parsley • ~~1 teaspoon~~ ~~grated onion~~ • pinch of mixed herbs (optional) • fat for frying • gravy and vegetables to serve • thick slices of grilled tomato, to serve

Use any leftover cooked meat, or cooked mince. Chicken is nice, and bacon and kidney may be added. (Meat must be cooked.) Sift flour, baking powder and salt. Add milk to egg and mix with dry ingredients only until flour is moist. Then add other ingredients. Fry in fairly deep fat in dessertspoon lots, about 2 minutes each side. Serve with gravy and vegetables, or grilled tomato. Makes a lot.

SNOW FRIED WHITEBAIT

whitebait • fat for frying • lemon wedges, to serve

Wash whitebait well. Dry thoroughly then toss in flour and toss into batter. Try to keep them separate, and using a big fork, put a few at a time into smoking fat. They should be very pale brown. Stir in fat to keep them separated. Remove from fat with perforated spoon, drain and serve with lemon.

Batter:

1 egg, lightly beaten with fork • ½ teacup milk • flour • pinch of salt • baking powder

Add milk to egg with enough flour to make a thick cream. Add salt and a little baking powder.

SOUSED FISH

900g fish • ▬▬▬▬▬▬ • a few peppercorns and cloves • 1 bunch of herbs • cayenne pepper to taste • ¼ teaspoon spice • ½ teaspoon salt • 3 teacups vinegar • lemon for garnish • cucumber to serve

Put prepared fish in a flat baking dish, cover with ▬▬▬▬ other ingredients and pour in vinegar. Cover with greased paper and bake in a moderate oven (180°C) for about 20 minutes. Leave until cold, lift out carefully, garnish with lemon and strain the liquor over. Serve with cucumber.

STEAK (Savoury)

steak, beaten well on both sides • vinegar • ▬▬▬▬▬ • pepper • salad oil or lard • mashed potato • sliced fried onions • flour • water

Put steak in a dish with vinegar, ▮▮▮▮ and pepper. Leave to soak for a while. Take meat out and dry it. Rub over with salad oil or lard. Lay out, spread on a layer of mashed potato and onions. Roll up, tie, sprinkle with flour and put in a baking dish. Pour on a little water to come halfway up. Baste occasionally while cooking in a hot oven (220°C) for about 1 hour or so. Make gravy from the liquid.

STEAK AND OYSTER PIE

3 dessertspoons flour • salt and pepper to taste • 900g rump steak, trimmed of fat and skin, cut into cubes • 2 tablespoons melted butter • 1 dozen fresh oysters and liquor • 1 teaspoon vinegar • ▮▮▮▮▮▮▮▮▮▮▮ • 1 bay leaf or a little grated nutmeg • puff pastry • 1 egg, beaten

Mix flour, salt and pepper and rub steak in it. Fry steak on both sides in butter until brown and tender. Add oysters and their liquor, vinegar, ▮▮▮▮, bay leaf or nutmeg. Turn into a pie dish and leave until cold. Cover with rough puff pastry. Make a hole in the centre and ornament with pastry leaves. Brush top lightly with egg, avoiding the edges. Bake in a hot oven (220°C) until brown and cooked.

TOHEROA FRITTERS

2 dozen fresh toheroas or 1 tin toheroas • 1 egg, beaten with a little milk • flour • salt and pepper • 1 teaspoon baking powder

If using fresh toheroas, do not boil to open as you lose half the flavour. Wash the tongues to free from sand, then mince. Stir the toheroas into egg and milk with sufficient flour to make a fairly stiff batter, season with salt and pepper, and add baking powder as this makes the fritters lighter. Fry until nice and brown. Delicious with Worcestershire sauce. If using tinned toheroas be sure to save the liquor to add to batter.

TONGUE CASSEROLE

sheeps' tongues • butter • breadcrumbs • parsley, chopped • a little thyme • salt and pepper • 4 slices lean bacon • 1 cup milk • mashed potato

Boil the tongues until they peel easily. Slit in half lengthwise. Grease a casserole with butter, sprinkle with breadcrumbs, half the parsley, thyme, salt and pepper to taste. Layer tongue, then bacon, then remainder of the tongue. Pour milk over and cover with breadcrumbs and remainder of parsley. Cover and cook slowly in a moderate oven (180°C) for 1 hour. Remove lid. Spread a good layer of mashed potato on top and cook again until nicely browned.

TRIPE (Stuffed)

675g tripe • ▓▓▓▓▓▓▓▓▓▓ • 1 cup breadcrumbs • salt and pepper • powdered or chopped sage • 2 cups milk • dab of butter • parsley sauce

Cook tripe until tender — do not cut it up. ▓▓▓▓▓▓▓▓▓▓. Mix with breadcrumbs, salt, pepper and sage, and bind with milk. Spread on to cooked tripe, roll up and tie with thread. Put into casserole, pour over milk, dab butter on top, cover and bake in a hot oven (220°C) for ½ to ¾ hour. Remove thread, serve with parsley sauce made with milk in casserole.

WAFFLE OGILVIE

waffle mixture (see pages 201–202) • sausages • pineapple slices • butter

Make waffles and fry sausages. Fry pineapple in butter. On a hot waffle, lay a sausage cut in half lengthwise, then a slice of pineapple, then another waffle. Serve steaming hot.

WELSH RAREBIT (Real)

1 cup cold milk • 1 tablespoon butter • 1 tablespoon flour •
1 teaspoon mustard • ½ teaspoon salt • few grains of pepper •
115–225g grated cheese • 6 slices of buttered toast

Heat milk. Melt butter and add it to flour, mustard, salt and pepper. Drop into the milk and stir until thick. Add cheese, and beat and cook until all is melted. Serve hot on toast.

Or, melt butter, add flour and cook a little. Gradually add cold milk and stir until thick and smooth. Add cheese, beat and cook until all is melted. Serve hot on toast.

WHITEBAIT FRIED

whitebait • flour • fat for frying

Wash and dry whitebait thoroughly in a clean cloth. Shake well in flour to separate them. Put into deep, hot smoking fat and fry until crisp (2 or 3 minutes). This is a delicious way to cook whitebait, but they do not go as far when they are done in batter.

A GRADELY PRAYER

Give us, Lord, a bit 'o sun,
A lot o' work, and a bit o' fun;
Give us all, in th' struggle and splutter,
Our daily bread, an' a bit o' butter.

Give us health, our keep to make,
An' a bit to spare for poor folk' sake.
Give us sense, for we're some of us duffers,
An' a heart to feel for all that suffers.
Give us, too, a bit of a song,
An' a tale, an' a book to help us along;
An' give us our share o' sorrow's lesson,
That we may prove how grief's a blessin'.
Give us, Lord, a chance to be
Our gradely best, brave, wise and free;
Our gradely best for ourselves and others,
Till all men learn to live as brothers.

Doidge's West County Annual

CONFIDE YE AYE IN PROVIDENCE

Confide ye aye in Providence, for Providence is kind,
And bear ye all Life's sorrows wi' a calm and steadfast mind.
Tho' pressed and hemmed on every side,
ha'e faith and ye'll win through,
For ilka blade o' grass keeps it ain drop o' dew.

POULTRY AND GAME

CHICKEN A LA KING

1 tablespoon butter • 1 tablespoon flour • dash of white pepper •
¼ teaspoon salt • ½ teaspoon paprika • 1 cup milk • ¼ cup cream •
1 cup cooked chicken, cut into pieces • 2 olives, chopped •
1 pimento, chopped • toast or baking powder biscuits to serve •
1 tablespoon sherry (optional)

Melt butter in top of a double boiler. Blend in flour and add pepper,
salt and paprika. Add milk and cream gradually, stirring constantly
until thickened. Beat well. Add chicken, olives and pimento. Cook
for 15 minutes and serve on toast, baking powder biscuits or in patty
shells. Sherry can be added, or omit olives and add ½ cup cooked
mushrooms and 1 tablespoon chopped green pepper.

CHICKEN CHOP SUEY

2 cups cold chicken, cut up • 1 cup cooked celery • 1½ cups
cooked rice • 1 teaspoon salt • pepper • 1 tablespoon butter •
2 tablespoons flour • 1½ cups chicken stock • parsley for garnish

Cut chicken and celery into thin strips, mix with rice, and add salt
and pepper. Melt butter, add flour and mix well. Add stock slowly
and bring to boiling point, stirring constantly. Add chicken mixture
and heat thoroughly. Serve with a garnish of parsley.

CHICKEN HAWAIIAN (Or Rabbit)

1 tin sliced pineapple, juice reserved • 4 tablespoons vegetable oil • ~~onion, finely chopped~~ • 3 slices bacon, chopped • 1.8kg chicken, cut into joints • flour, seasoned with salt and pepper

Fry the pineapple pieces in hot oil until pale brown. Cook ~~onion and~~ bacon in the same fat for 5 minutes. Roll chicken joints into seasoned flour and brown in the pan with ~~onion and~~ bacon. Lay slices of pineapple on chicken. Add pineapple juice which has been made up to 2 cups with water. Cover tightly and cook slowly (120°C) for 1 hour. Serve on plate around a mound of rice and garnish with parsley.

CHICKEN IN ASPIC

1 veal knuckle • 2.7kg chicken, cut into joints • 3 cups stock (from boiled meat), chilled and fat removed • ~~1 onion, grated~~ • juice of 1 lemon • salt and pepper • 1 tablespoon gelatine • ¼ cup cold water • 1 cup chopped celery • 3 eggs, hard-boiled • olives, stoned and sliced, to serve • mint leaves to serve

Cover veal with cold water and bring to the boil. Add chicken. Boil until tender and season. Remove the meat. Slice the chicken and mince the veal coarsely. There should be about 1½ cups of chopped veal. Boil stock and season if necessary. Add ~~onion~~, lemon juice and check seasoning. Soak gelatine in cold water, and add with celery and veal. Mix well. When cool, just cover the bottom of a mould with this liquid. Let it nearly set, decorate with hard-boiled egg slices, olives and mint. Add a layer of chicken and 1 cup of liquid, and chill. Repeat until all is used. Chill.

CHICKEN PIE (Bombay)

chicken (or rabbit), cut into joints • salt and pepper • tomatoes, sliced • 1 hard-boiled egg, sliced • ▊▊▊▊▊▊ • curry powder • small amount of garlic • 2 cloves • 2 green chillies, finely chopped • 1 cup stock • short or puff pastry • 1 egg, beaten

Parboil chicken in seasoned water. Drain, and put in a pie dish with alternate layers of tomato, egg ▊▊▊▊▊▊. Season with salt, curry powder, garlic, cloves and chillies. Add stock. Cover with pastry. Make a hole in the centre, brush with egg and bake in a moderate oven (180°C).

CHICKEN SALAMIS (With Wine)

1 cooked chicken cut into pieces, or leftover pieces from 2 chickens • 2 tomatoes • ▊▊▊▊▊ • 3 tablespoons red wine • 2 tablespoons water • sprigs of parsley, thyme and sage, tied together • 2 tablespoons madeira wine • 1 large teaspoon red currant jelly • a few sliced mushrooms • cornflour

Simmer gently in a saucepan the chicken, tomatoes, ▊▊▊▊▊, wine, water, and herb sprigs for 10 minutes. Remove chicken and herbs. Add madeira wine, red currant jelly and mushrooms. Bring to the boil and thicken with a little cornflour. Cook for 3 minutes. Put back pieces of chicken, and simmer gently for about 10 minutes or so.

CHICKEN SOUFFLÉ (California)

2 cups milk • 3 tablespoons butter • 2 heaped tablespoons flour • salt and pepper • ¾ cup stale breadcrumbs • 2 cups cut up cooked chicken • 1 tablespoon minced parsley • 3 egg yolks, beaten well • 3 egg whites, stiffly beaten

Sauce:

chicken stock • mushrooms

In a saucepan, make a paste with milk, butter, flour and salt and pepper. Add breadcrumbs and simmer for 15 minutes. Remove from the heat. Stir in chicken, parsley, egg yolks, and fold in egg whites. Place in a pan of boiling water and bake in a slow oven (120°C) for 30 minutes. Serve with mushroom sauce.

Make a rich sauce using chicken stock and add mushrooms.

CHICKEN STUFFED WITH OYSTERS

1 chicken • salt and pepper • raw oysters

Prepare chicken as for roasting. Sprinkle inside and out with salt and pepper. Stuff with oysters, fasten securely, and put in steamer with close-fitting lid. Steam until chicken is tender, then keep in hot oven on dish.

Gravy:

1 tablespoon butter • 1 tablespoon flour • minced parsley • 1 blade of mace • ½ cup cream or milk • 3 hard-boiled eggs, cut up

Heat butter in a pan until hot, then stir in flour until mixture bubbles. Add parsley and some of the liquor in the pan below the steamer in which chicken was cooked. Add mace and cream or milk. Stir until boiling, and boil for 5 minutes. Add egg and pour over chicken.

CURRIED CHICKEN (Malayan)

60g butter or good fat • ▮▮▮▮▮, finely chopped • 1 tablespoon curry powder • pinch clove powder • pinch cinnamon powder • 1 chicken, cut up •1 teaspoon salt • 2 cups cocnut cream

Melt butter in a pan. Add ▮▮▮▮▮curry powder, cloves and cinnamon. Fry, stirring constantly, until brown. Add chicken and fry until brown. Add salt and warmed coconut cream. Cover saucepan and simmer gently until chicken is tender.

FRIED CHICKEN (Maryland)

1.35kg chicken, cut up • flour seasoned with salt and pepper • ¼ cup fat • ¼ cup hot water

Wipe chicken pieces with a cloth and roll in seasoned flour. Make flour coating thick so that pieces of chicken will be covered with a thick brown crust. Heat fat in a pan and fry chicken joints until well browned all over. Remove to a casserole or oven dish and add the hot water. Cover tightly and cook in a slow oven (120°C) for about 35 minutes or until tender. Remove lid and cook for 10 minutes longer.

Sauce to Serve with Fried Chicken:

▮▮▮▮▮▮▮▮▮▮▮▮▮▮ • 1 large green pepper, sliced thin • 1 cup chopped celery • 1 tablespoon butter • 1 teaspoon paprika • a pinch of cayenne pepper • 1 cup sliced tomatoes • 2 cups chicken stock • flour • a few mushrooms, cut up and fried in butter

Cook all sauce ingredients except flour and mushrooms for 30 minutes. Thicken with flour and add mushrooms.

BRAISED DUCK (French)

1 duck • butter or good fat • 2 tablespoons flour • 1 to 2 cups
boiling water • salt and pepper • 1 sprig parsley • thyme •
1 bay leaf • stoned olives (optional)

In a saucepan, fry duck whole in butter or fat until a nice golden
brown — about 20 minutes. Take out duck. With fat in pan, mix in
flour. When smooth and brown, stir in gradually the hot water to make
a thick sauce. Add salt, pepper and herbs. Let cook a few minutes,
replace duck, cover pan, and finish cooking gently until tender. If
liked, add stoned olives to sauce and cook another 5 minutes. Serve
duck on dish surrounded by olives, and sauce poured over.

CHINESE PINEAPPLE DUCK

1.5–2kg duckling, cut into 4 pieces • boiling water • 2 tablespoons
oil or fat • 1 teaspoon salt • dash of pepper • 4 slices canned
pineapple, cut into 6 pieces • 1 green pepper, cut into 8 pieces •
2 tablespoons cornflour • 2 teaspoons soy sauce • ¼ cup water •
hot boiled rice to serve

Cook duckling until tender in boiling water (enough to cover), about
45 minutes. Remove from broth. In a preheated, heavy 25cm stewing
pan place oil or fat, salt and pepper. Place duck in pan. Cook over a
moderate flame until brown, turning frequently. Add 1½ cups duck
broth, pineapple and green pepper. Cover pan tightly and cook over
a moderate flame for 10 minutes. Blend together cornflour, soy sauce
and ¼ cup water. Cook for a few minutes, stirring constantly, until
juice thickens and mixture is very hot. Serve immediately with hot
boiled rice.

ROAST DUCK AND
ORANGE SAUCE (Hotel St George)

1 cleaned duck • 3 tablespoons butter • 1 glass of wine •
1 orange, cut into very fine strips and thinly sliced • long spirals
of orange peel • round pieces of orange, cut like buttons •
maraschino cherries • extra orange slices and peel for garnish

Place duck in a pan over a high heat, watching to see it doesn't burn, until most of the fat has been extracted. Throw away fat and repeat. Add butter to pan and place in a hot oven (220°C). Baste constantly and turn frequently for 1 hour. Remove duck from pan and add wine and orange slices to the remaining butter and juice. Reduce this mixture over a high heat to consistency of marmalade. Place duck on a large platter and surround it with orange peel spirals. Down the centre of the breast, place orange buttons with a maraschino cherry on top of each. Arrange half slices of orange with the peel in scallops around edge of platter and garnish the duck with the sauce.

ROAST DUCKLING (Good)

1 duckling • whole soaked prunes • apples, cored and quartered •
walnut-sized piece of butter • 2 or 3 rashers of bacon • 1 cup or
more boiling water • cream

Stuff bird with prunes, apples and butter. Place in a roasting pan and put bacon on breast. Allow to brown for 20 minutes in a hot oven (220°C). Remove fat from pan. Add the boiling water. Cook in moderate oven (180°C) for another 30 to 40 minutes, basting every 10 minutes. Remove bacon from breast for last few minutes to brown meat. Make a good gravy (see page 119), and add a little cream to this.

ROAST MALLARD DUCK

1–1.5kg mallard • 1½ teaspoons salt • ⅛ teaspoon pepper • ½ apple, pared and cored • ~~small onion, peeled~~ • 2 thin slices salt pork

Wash duck inside and out, and dry. Sprinkle salt and pepper on outside of body. Place apple ~~and onion~~ in body cavity. Truss bird; place on wire rack in covered baking pan. Lay slices of salt pork over breast. Place in very hot oven, 260°C, and roast 15 to 20 minutes for rare, or 30 minutes for well done (on the basis of 20 minutes per 450g).

ROAST WILD DUCK (Using Milk)

wild duck • milk • forcemeat (see Stuffings, pages 52–54), with heart and liver of bird minced in • salt and pepper • flour • butter • 1 glass port wine • 1 dessertspoon red currant jelly

Do not tear the skin when plucking. After having plucked and wiped the birds, leave in milk for at least 1 hour. Stuff with forcemeat. Do not over-season. Roll in flour and brown in butter, then put in oven (not very hot, about 180°C) and baste with the milk used for soaking the birds. When nearly done, lift out the birds and place in casserole. Make gravy with equal parts of flour and butter, browned and broken down with the liquid in which the birds have been cooking. Strain and add port wine and red currant jelly. Pour over the birds in the casserole and cook slowly until quite tender.

WILD DUCK (American)

1 duck • 1 carrot, scraped • salt and pepper • flour • 2 slices fat salt pork (or bacon) • 2 tablespoons fat • 1 cup water • cranberry jelly • 1 orange, sliced for garnish

Prepare and truss duck, tucking back the wings. Put carrot inside bird. Put bird in a pot of boiling water and let it simmer for 10 minutes. Remove, and dust with salt, pepper and flour. Put in baking tin, cover breast with slices of fat salt pork or bacon. Add fat and water and bake in a hot oven (220°C) for 15 minutes, then reduce heat. Do not overcook wild duck. Make brown gravy in tin with cranberry jelly, and serve with slices of orange.

GOOSE (Roast)

450g breadcrumbs • a little warm water • ▬▬▬▬▬▬▬ • 1 dessertspoon finely chopped sage • 1 teaspoon thyme • salt and pepper • 1 egg, beaten • 30g melted butter • 1 goose • flour • dripping

Soak breadcrumbs a few minutes in a little warm water, then squeeze dry. Mix with ▬▬▬, sage, thyme and seasoning. Add egg and butter. Wipe goose inside and out with a damp cloth, stuff then dredge with flour. Put into a lightly floured baking dish. Cover with plenty of dripping and bake at 190°C for 2 or 3 hours, according to size. Turn bird over after first hour. If it cooks too quickly, cover with greased paper. Duck is cooked the same way allowing 1½ to 2 hours.

TO MAKE GOOSE TENDER

Stuff as usual, but bake it slowly in milk instead of dripping. Baste often, and it will cook a lovely brown, and the toughest birds should be delicious and tender.

GUINEA FOWL

1 guinea fowl • 5 slices fat bacon • 2 tablespoons flour •
2 cups stock or water • ¼ teaspoon pepper • 1 teaspoon salt •
1 dessertspoon red currant jelly

Prepare fowl, and cut into joints. Fry bacon in pan until most of fat is extracted. Brown joints of fowl in bacon fat. Take out fowl, add flour to saucepan and brown it. Add stock or water, bring to the boil, and stir all the time. Put back joints of guinea fowl, season with salt and pepper, and stir in the jelly. Put lid on tightly and simmer until bird is tender.

JUGGED HARE DE LUXE

1 hare or rabbit, cut into joints • ▪▪▪▪▪▪▪▪ • 2 or 3 cloves •
2 sprigs thyme • 1 teaspoon grated nutmeg • ½ cup port • ½ cup
madeira wine • flour • fat • 2 or 3 slices bacon •
1½ to 2 cups water (or stock) • red currant jelly to serve

Put joints of hare in a deep casserole with ▪▪▪▪ cloves, thyme, nutmeg and wines. Allow to stand in marinade for 4 to 6 hours. Remove the joints, flour them lightly, and brown in hot fat. Pour off fat, add bacon and cook for a minute or two. Return to casserole. Add the water or stock and cook all together in casserole in oven until tender. Serve from the casserole and pass red currant jelly.

ROAST PHEASANT

1 pheasant (retain liver) • ordinary fowl stuffing (see pages 52–54) •
bacon, chopped and cooked, fat reserved • flour • bread sauce •
fried breadcrumbs • clear stock • watercress to garnish

Stuff bird with stuffing, add liver and bacon. Place in a roasting pan, breast downwards. Add bacon fat and roast in moderately slow oven (160°C) for about 45 minutes. Ten minutes before bird is cooked, turn over on its back, sprinkle with a little flour and baste to brown the breast. Serve with bread sauce (see page 116) and fried breadcrumbs. Make gravy by adding a little clear stock to roasting pan, mix well with fat and serve gravy in a sauce boat. Garnish with watercress. Guinea fowl is cooked in the same way.

STEWED PUKAKI [Pukeko]

bacon, thinly sliced • pukaki, cut in pieces • ▓▓▓▓▓▓▓ • thyme • salt and pepper • 2 cups water • grated rind and juice of ½ lemon • mashed potatoes to serve

Put bacon in casserole. Add pukaki, ▓▓▓, thyme, salt and pepper, and the water. Slowly cook for several hours. Take out the bird, thicken the gravy a little, and add lemon rind and juice. Serve with mashed potatoes.

RABBIT FRICASSEE

1 rabbit, cut into neat pieces • milk • water • ▓▓▓▓▓▓▓▓▓▓ 2 cloves • bunch of herbs • salt and pepper

Wash rabbit well in warm water. Soak in milk and water to whiten the meat then place in a pan with enough milk or water to cover. Add ▓▓▓▓▓▓ cloves, herbs, and salt and pepper. Simmer 1 hour or until tender.

Make 2 cups white sauce:
½ milk and ½ stock from rabbit • 2 teaspoons capers • 1 teaspoon vinegar from capers • 1 teaspoon sugar • 1 dessertspoon butter • salt and pepper • cooked rice • lemon slices to garnish

Strain stock from rabbit, and pour white sauce over rabbit. Serve in a border of rice. Garnish with lemon slices. Keep surplus stock for soup. Parsley or onion sauce can be used instead of caper.

RABBIT HAWAIIAN

1 tin sliced pineapple (juice reserved) • butter • ~~onions, chopped~~ •
rabbit, cut in joints • cornflour, seasoned • fat • bacon slices •
curry powder (optional)

Fry pineapple in butter until light brown. Remove ~~and fry onions in the same butter.~~ Roll joints of rabbit (or chicken) in seasoned cornflour and fry in fat. Put in casserole with bacon and onion, with pineapple slices on top. Make up the pineapple juice with water to 2 cups and add. Cover and cook 1 hour. Add curry powder if liked.

RABBIT AND MUSHROOM PUDDING

1 rabbit • vinegar • water • suet crust (see page 7) •
~~onions, chopped~~ • sage • mushrooms, peeled • salt and pepper •
cornflour

Joint rabbit and soak in vinegar and water. Line a pudding basin with suet crust. Add a layer of rabbit, ~~onion~~ and sage, layer of mushrooms and salt and pepper. Repeat until basin is full. Sprinkle with cornflour, nearly fill with water, put on the suet crust lid and steam for about 3 hours.

SWAN

1 swan • sage ~~and onion stuffing~~ (see page 53) • flour • dripping

Immerse swan in dish of scalding water (not quite boiling) for about 5 minutes. Pluck feathers off and cut wings off at first joint. Stuff with stuffing. Put in a large pot, half full of boiling water, and steam for 2 hours. Take out of pot, flour well and put in oven with dripping in a baking dish. Bake for 1 hour until nicely brown. If you do not possess a large enough pot, use a baking dish filled with boiling water and some dripping, and put into oven. Cover bird with greased paper, and baste well. Cook at 190°C for 3 hours approximately.

ROAST TURKEY

1 turkey • veal stuffing (see page 54) • fat or bacon fat • bread
sauce to serve • brown gravy to serve

Stuff turkey with the veal stuffing. Put breast side down in baking
tin with plenty of fat (bacon fat may be smeared over the bird). Put
into a hot oven (220°C) for first 15 minutes, then reduce to 150°C
and cook slowly near bottom of oven for about 3 hours for a bird
weighing 3.6 to 4.5kg. Turn over on to its back when half done. Baste
several times. Cover with greased paper if getting too brown. Slow
cooking is best. Serve with bread sauce and brown gravy.

TURKEY SOUFFLÉ

2 cups leftover turkey, cut fine • 1 cup medium white sauce (see
page 123) • ~~1 tablespoon minced onion~~ • 2 tablespoons parsley •
½ teaspoon salt • ½ teaspoon pepper • ½ teaspoon paprika •
3 egg yolks • 3 egg whites • buttered crumbs • mushroom gravy
to serve • cranberry sauce to serve

Add chopped turkey to white sauce with seasoning and egg yolks.
Beat the egg whites and fold into mixture. Turn into a buttered
casserole, sprinkle with crumbs and bake. Serve with mushroom
gravy and cranberry sauce. Any leftover poultry may be used. Bake
25 to 35 minutes at 190°C.

VENISON

1 joint venison • flour • pieces of fat, or dripping • 1 cup boiling
water • salt and pepper • red currant jelly to serve

Wipe and trim a joint of venison. Dredge with flour and put on rack
of baking dish with pieces of fat or plenty of dripping in pan. Put
in hot oven (220°C) for 15 minutes, reduce temperature, and pour
boiling water into pan. Cook until tender, allowing 15 minutes for
every 450g and basting every 15 minutes. Add salt and pepper when
half cooked. Serve with red currant jelly.

VENISON (Braised)

venison • breadcrumbs • ▓▓▓▓▓▓▓ • thyme • salt and pepper •
1 egg, beaten • carrots • sherry • red currant or quince jelly
to serve

Make a pocket in the venison and stuff with breadcrumbs, ▓▓▓▓,
thyme, salt and pepper. Moisten with egg. Brown thoroughly all
over in fat in a saucepan, then add a little water, and cover with a
well-fitting lid. Leave over low heat for 3 hours, depending on size.
Add carrots when venison is half cooked. Baste venison at intervals.
Add a little sherry to the gravy and serve with red currant jelly or
quince jelly.

VENISON (Flemish)

venison • 2 cups white wine • 1 cup vinegar • 3 tablespoons oil • ▓▓▓▓▓▓▓▓▓▓▓▓▓▓▓▓ • 1 shallot, chopped • parsley • thyme • 1 bay leaf • salt and pepper • a little butter • 2 tablespoons white wine • 2 tablespoons stock

Mix well but do not cook the first quantity of wine, the vinegar, oil, ▓▓▓▓▓▓▓, parsley, thyme, bay leaf, salt and pepper. Wipe venison with a cloth then put in an earthenware dish. Cover with the mixture, and stand in a cool place for 24 hours. Baste 2 or 3 times. For meat from a very young animal, steep for 12 hours only. Put venison in a casserole with a little butter, white wine (second amount) and stock. Cook with lid on in a moderate oven (180°C). Serve in slices on long dish with Duchess Potatoes, cooked Brussels sprouts, parboiled white cabbage and apple slices.

VENISON STEAK (American)

1 venison steak • salad oil • lemon juice • butter • cranberry jelly • cracker crumbs, rolled into a powder • fat • 1 tablespoon flour • 1 tablespoon cranberry jelly • 1 cup boiling water

Leave venison soaking for 2 hours in marinade of salad oil and lemon juice. Drain, and grill over a high heat, turning often to avoid scorching. Serve on a hot dish, spreading both sides with a mixture of butter and cranberry jelly (half as much jelly as butter).

If fried, take venison from marinade and cover both sides with cracker crumbs, and fry each side rich brown in fat. Make gravy with a little fat left in pan, flour, cranberry jelly and boiling water.

STUFFINGS

INTRODUCTION

Stuffing does not necessarily need to be baked in the fowl or meat. If the bird is small or there is some stuffing left over, it may be baked or steamed in a greased ring mould, loaf pan or individual moulds. Croquettes of stuffing may be served around bird.

APPLE AND RAISIN STUFFING
(For Duck)

~~¼ onion, minced~~ • 1½ cups peeled, cored and diced apples • 3 cups lightly packed day-old breadcrumbs • ½ cup seeded raisins • ¾ teaspoon salt • dash of pepper • 1 tablespoon sugar • 4 to 5 tablespoons melted butter or good margarine or fat

Mix all well, and stuff duck, not too tightly.

POTATO STUFFING
(For Duck or Pork)

2 cups mashed potato • 1 cup stale breadcrumbs • 1 egg • ~~1 onion, finely minced~~ • ¼ cup melted fat • 1 teaspoon salt • ¼ teaspoon pepper • 1 teaspoon sage

Mix all well together.

POTATO AND CELERY STUFFING
(For Duck or Chicken)

8 medium-sized potatoes, boiled • 1 cup hot milk • salt and pepper •
2 eggs, beaten • 4 tablespoons butter or margarine or fat •
~~1 large onion, minced~~ • 2 cups fine breadcrumbs • 2 cups minced
celery • 4 tablespoons chopped parsley

Mash potatoes with hot milk and salt and pepper to taste. Add eggs
and beat until light and creamy. In a saucepan melt butter, ~~add onion
and cook until tender~~. Add breadcrumbs, celery and parsley. Blend
this all well, and finally mix it thoroughly with the mashed potatoes.
A very substantial stuffing.

SAGE AND APPLE STUFFING
(For Pork)

2 cups soft breadcrumbs • 2 tablespoons melted fat • 1 small
teaspoon salt • ¼ teaspoon pepper • 1 cup finely chopped tart
apple • ~~1½ tablespoons minced onion~~ • 1 teaspoon powdered
sage (or chopped sage leaves) • boiling water or 1 egg, beaten

Moisten all to a rather dry paste with boiling water, or a beaten egg.

SAGE AND ONION STUFFING
(For Duck, Pork or Goose)

~~450g onions, peeled and quartered~~ • boiling salted water •
1½ teaspoons crushed sage • salt and pepper •
225g breadcrumbs

~~Drop onions into~~ boiling water with a little salt and parboil for 15
minutes. Drain, chop, add sage, salt, pepper and breadcrumbs. Use
for stuffing pork, ducks, geese, etc.

SAGE AND ONION STUFFING

~~3 or 4 onions~~ • 9 sage leaves • 1 teaspoon salt • 1½ large breakfast cups breadcrumbs • 45g butter or dripping • 1 teaspoon pepper • 1 egg, beaten

~~Boil onion for about 5 minutes, strain and chop finely~~. Scald sage leaves and chop them. Mix everything, using the egg to bind.

SAUSAGE STUFFING
(For Turkey, Veal or Pork)

450g sausage meat • 1 cup diced celery • ~~1 cup minced onion~~ • 7 or 8 cups fine breadcrumbs • parsley, chopped

Fry together first 3 ingredients, for about 10 minutes over a medium heat. Mix thoroughly with breadcrumbs, and plenty of parsley.

STUFFING FOR TURKEY

10 breakfast cups lightly packed day-old breadcrumbs • 1½ teaspoons salt • 1 tablespoon powdered sage • 2 tablespoons diced celery • 2 tablespoons minced parsley • ¼ teaspoon pepper • ¾ cup butter or shredded suet • ~~½ cup minced onion~~

Combine breadcrumbs, salt, sage, celery, parsley and pepper. Melt butter in pan, ~~add onion and simmer until tender~~. Add seasoned breadcrumbs and heat well, stirring. Should stuff a bird of about 3.6kg.

STUFFING FOR WILD DUCK

1 large apple, grated • ~~1 medium onion, grated~~ • breadcrumbs • salt and pepper • small piece of butter

Mix apple, ~~onion~~ with enough breadcrumbs to make it stiff. Add salt and pepper and a small piece of butter.

CHRISTMAS COOKERY

CHRISTMAS CHICKEN PIE

3 or 4 large chickens • 1 onion • herbs • ham or bacon, sliced • 3 or 4 eggs, hard-boiled and sliced • sausage meat (optional) • salt and pepper • nutmeg • mace, pounded • extra hard-boiled eggs, sliced • 1 cup strained stock • puff pastry • 1 cup or more hot gravy (see page 119) • gelatine

Stew chickens gently until tender with onion and herbs. Strain off liquor and remove meat from bones and cut in neat pieces. Make a good forcemeat (see pages 52–54) or use sausage meat if preferred. Arrange in a pie dish a layer of chicken, ham or bacon, a layer of forcemeat, layer of egg, and so on, with seasoning of pepper, salt, nutmeg and mace between each layer. Pour in stock, cover with puff pastry and bake until pastry is nicely cooked. Leave a hole in the top, and when done, add hot gravy. If to be eaten cold, dissolve a little gelatine in gravy before adding. A rabbit may be used instead of chicken if preferred.

CHRISTMAS TURKEY

The directions for cooking a turkey may be found in the Poultry and Game section.

HAM (To Bake)

ham • cloves • spiced vinegar (see page 227) • brown sugar • crisp browned breadcrumbs

Wrap the ham in 2 thicknesses of greaseproof paper to keep in the juice and flavour. Put into baking dish with a little hot water. Bake very slowly, allowing 20 to 25 minutes for each 450g. Leave in oven to cool, after turning off heat. Remove paper and skin, and score the fat into small diamond shapes. Stick a clove in each. Pour over a thick syrup of vinegar and sugar and put back in oven for about 20 minutes at 220°C. Sprinkle with breadcrumbs.

Instead of spiced syrup you can spread the ham with 1 cup brown sugar mixed with 1 cup juice from spiced peaches, or pour canned pineapple juice over and keep ham basted with this for 20 minutes. You could also baste with cooking sherry.

HAM (To Boil)

Put ham into hot water to cover. Bring slowly to the boil and simmer. Allow 20 to 25 minutes for each 450g. Test with a metal skewer. Leave in water to cool. Skin and glaze as above.

HAM GLAZES

As a variation, try these glazes:

Honey Glaze:
Spread with 1 cup liquid honey.

Orange Glaze:
Combine 1 cup firmly packed brown sugar, ⅓ cup orange juice and 1 tablespoon grated orange rind.

Cider Glaze:

Combine 1 cup brown sugar with 1 teaspoon dry mustard. Spread on ham, then baste with cider every 15 minutes during the last hour of cooking.

CHRISTMAS CAKE (1ZR Special)

900g fruit • 285g flour, sifted • 225g butter • 225g sugar • 5 eggs • ½ teaspoon each of essence of: vanilla, lemon, pineapple, brandy, cherry, almond or any other of choice • ¼ to ½ teaspoon curry powder • 1 teaspoon baking powder

Prepare fruit and sprinkle with a little flour. Place in a warm place while creaming butter and sugar. Have flour in a warm place. Add eggs, one at a time with a little flour to prevent curdling, to creamed butter and sugar. Add essences, curry powder, then fruit and flour alternately, and baking powder last. Quickly turn mixture into a well-greased tin, and bake in a moderate oven for 3½ hours approximately — 180°C to begin with and after the first 45 minutes, the heat may be lowered.

CHRISTMAS OR BIRTHDAY CAKE (Keeps Well)

450g flour • 1 teaspoon baking powder • 340g light brown sugar • 340g butter • 6 eggs • 450g currants • 450g raisins • 450g sultanas • 115g almonds • 115g cherries • 115g mixed peel • 1 large cup milk • 4 tablespoons golden syrup

Mix flour with baking powder. Beat sugar and butter to a cream, add eggs one by one, and beat well after each egg. Add fruit and nuts, a little at a time, and still beat well until all fruit is used. Warm the milk and golden syrup and add. Add the flour and baking powder. Bake at 150°C for about 4 hours.

CHRISTMAS CAKE (Ginger Ale)

450g currants • 450g sultanas • 115g cherries • 450g raisins •
225g peel • 1 bottle ginger ale • 665g butter • 450g sugar •
12 eggs, well beaten • 675g flour • 1 teaspoon cinnamon •
1 nutmeg, grated • pinch of salt • 115g ground almonds •
2 tablespoons brandy • 1 tablespoon glycerine

Cut up fruit very fine, cover with ginger ale and soak overnight. Cream the butter and sugar, and add eggs little by little so as not to have the mixture curdle, and beat well. Add flour and spices, fruit and almonds, then brandy and glycerine.

Cook about 3 hours at 140°C.

CHRISTMAS CAKE (Mangatainoka)

12 soft prunes • 225g flour • ¼ teaspoon grated nutmeg •
¼ teaspoon baking soda • 225g currants • 225g raisins •
225g sultanas • 115g candied citron peel, cut very thin •
1 teaspoon grated lemon rind • 225g butter • 225g sugar •
4 eggs, beaten to a stiff froth • ½ cup brandy or wine •
60g ground almonds • 1 tablespoon icing sugar

Stew prunes just long enough to remove stones, drain well. Sift flour with nutmeg and soda. Clean and dry the fruit (except prunes). Cream butter and sugar. Add eggs, fruit (except prunes) and lemon rind. Lastly add flour, then brandy or wine. Mix thoroughly. Put half the mixture in a prepared tin, lay on prunes, strew with ground almonds and icing sugar. Add remainder of mixture. Cook at 180°C for 2½ hours.

CHRISTMAS CAKE (Moist)

450g fruit (or more) • 1 cup hot water • 115g butter • 1 small cup
sugar (brown preferred) • 3 eggs • 1 tablespoon golden syrup •
1½ cups flour • 1 teaspoon baking powder • essence (if liked)

Simmer fruit in water until all water is absorbed. Allow to cool. Cream butter and sugar, add eggs and syrup, then the flour, baking powder and fruit. Bake approximately 1½ hours in moderate oven (180°C). For a larger cake, double quantities.

CHRISTMAS CAKE (£100 Prize)

170g almonds • 60g citron peel • grated rind of 1 orange • grated rind and juice 1 lemon • ½ cup brandy • 450g butter • 450g sugar • 8 eggs • 675g sultanas • 225g seeded raisins • 450g currants • 115g glacé cherries • 565g flour, sifted • 1 salt spoon of salt • 2 tablespoons orange marmalade • ½ teaspoon baking powder

Blanch almonds and cut in two lengthways. Shred citron peel, add orange and lemon rinds, place in a bowl and pour over lemon juice and brandy. Cover tightly and leave overnight. Blend butter and sugar until quite smooth. Add eggs, one at time, using a little flour to prevent curdling. Add fruit and flour mixed with salt, a little at a time. Have oven tin ready with four layers of paper lining. Pour in mixture, hollow slightly, and bake slowly (120°C) for 6 hours. When thoroughly cool, wrap in greaseproof paper and leave for 3 weeks before cutting. Ice 1 week before cutting.

Icing:
450g icing sugar • 115g ground almonds • 1 egg yolk • 2 teaspoons lemon juice and water • 1 egg white, beaten

Sift icing sugar and mix with almond meal. Add egg yolk and lemon juice and water. Keep it stiff and knead well. Roll out to fit cake and brush cake with egg white. Brush crumbs off cake, press icing gently on to it, and allow to stand 2 days before covering with Royal Icing.

Royal Icing:
225g icing sugar • 1 egg white • squeeze of lemon

Mix icing sugar with egg white and lemon. Make very stiff and spread on cake with a knife dipped in hot water. Decorate according to taste.

WHOLEMEAL CHRISTMAS CAKE

225g butter • 225g raw sugar • 2 eggs, beaten • ½ heaped teaspoon baking soda • 1 cup hot milk • 2 level teaspoons curry powder • 2½ breakfast cups fine wholemeal flour • 225g sultanas • 225g currants • 225g raisins • 60g peel • pinch of salt

Beat butter and sugar. Add eggs. Put soda in hot milk with curry powder. (Hot milk and curry powder has the same effect as brandy and improves the flavour.) Sift the wholemeal flour and mix with fruit. Add salt. Add milk and flour, little by little, alternately until all is mixed in. Bake 3 to 5 hours at 160°C for 30 minutes, then at 140°C for 1 hour, and turn to 130°C until cooked.

YULE BREAD

45g compressed yeast • warm milk to mix • 900g flour • 340g butter • 340g sugar • 3 or 4 eggs, beaten • 450g currants • 225g sultanas • 115g mixed peel • 1 teaspoon cinnamon • ½ small nutmeg, grated • 2 teaspoons salt

Crumble yeast into a little lukewarm milk with a pinch of sugar and let rise. Warm flour in basin and rub in butter. Add sugar. Pour yeast into centre, mix and let rise for 15 minutes. Stir in eggs, and as much warm milk as will make a light dough. Beat well and leave to rise about 1 hour. Add fruit, cinnamon, nutmeg, and let rise another hour. Put in tins lined with paper and let rise again. Bake in moderate oven (180°C), time according to size of loaf.

CHRISTMAS PUDDING

225g butter • 225g brown sugar • 4 eggs, beaten • 115g breadcrumbs • 115g flour, sifted • ¼ teaspoon salt • 3 teaspoons mixed spice • 450g sultanas • 225g raisins • 225g mixed peel • 2 tablespoons chopped almonds • ¼ cup brandy

Cream butter and sugar, add eggs, breadcrumbs, flour, salt and spice, fruit, peel and nuts. Add brandy and steam for 5 hours. (Prevent Christmas Pudding from going mouldy by untying the knots in the cloth and thoroughly drying it before re-tying and hanging.)

CHRISTMAS PUDDING (Family)

1 large cup breadcrumbs • 1½ cups flour • 1 cup shredded suet •
¾ teacup brown sugar • 450g mixed fruit • 1 teaspoon baking
powder • ½ teaspoon soda • 1 teaspoon spice • 1 teaspoon
cinnamon • ½ teaspoon nutmeg • 1 teaspoon caramel essence •
¼ cup milk • 2 eggs, beaten

Mix all dry ingredients in a basin. Add essence to milk. Add eggs to the milk and flavouring, and mix all together well. Put into a greased basin and steam for 3½ hours. Makes good large pudding.

POORMAN'S CHRISTMAS PUDDING

1 cup flour • 1 small teaspoon baking powder • 1 cup raisins •
1 cup breadcrumbs • 1 cup currants • 1 cup sugar • 1 teaspoon
mixed spice • 1 cup suet • 115g chopped almonds • 2 eggs •
pinch of salt • milk to mix

Sift flour and baking powder together. Add other ingredients, eggs and the milk last. Boil in basin for 3 to 4 hours. Serve with sauce.

BABY CHRISTMAS PUDDINGS (English)

340g chopped dates • 340g fine breadcrumbs • 170g sugar •
115g shredded suet • 1 teaspoon ground cinnamon • 1 teaspoon salt •
3 tablespoons marmalade • juice of 2 oranges • 2 eggs, well beaten

Prepare fruit and mix all dry ingredients together. Stir in marmalade, orange juice and eggs. Mix well and let stand a few hours. Turn into buttered moulds or small cups and steam for 1½ hours.

MINCEMEAT MERINGUE PIE

Pastry:

115g butter • 115g sugar • 1 egg • 225g flour • 1 teaspoon baking powder

Cream butter and sugar. Add egg, then dry ingredients. Roll out to fit sponge roll tin. Prick bottom well and bake in moderate oven (180°C) for 10 minutes.

Topping:

1 small tin crushed pineapple, drained • fruit mincemeat • 2 egg whites • 4 tablespoons sugar • glacé cherries • angelica (optional)

Mix pineapple with mincement and spread over pastry. Cover with meringue of egg whites beaten with sugar. Decorate with cherries and angelica. Bake in a slow oven (120°C) until meringue is crisp and pastry properly cooked.

CHRISTMAS FRUIT PIE

340g short pastry • 450g cooking apples, peeled and sliced • 6 tablespoons chopped glacé cherries • 3 large tablespoon fruit mincemeat • 85g chopped almonds • 2 tablespoons sherry • 1 egg, beaten

Prepare short pastry and line a plate with half the pastry. Mix together apples, glacé cherries, fruit mincemeat, almonds and sherry. Spread on pastry, cover with remaining pastry and decorate edges. Brush with egg and bake at 200°C for 40 to 45 minutes. Serve with custard or cream.

BAKED MINCEMEAT (English)

900g apples • 225g butter • 450g brown sugar • 450g currants •
450g sultanas • 225g chopped and stoned raisins • 225g stoned
prunes • 115g cup mixed peel • 115g cup finely chopped citron •
rind and juice of 2 lemons • ½ teaspoon salt

Put all in a covered earthenware dish and put in oven on very low
heat (120°C). Cook until apples are soft. Mix occasionally with a
wooden spoon. When making mince pies, take out sufficient and
warm in a basin.

BLACKBERRY MINCEMEAT

1.8kg blackberries • juice and rind of 2 lemons • 1 teacup cold
water • 8 large cooking apples, cored, peeled and chopped •
orange rind, grated • lemon rind, grated • 225g raisins •
225g currants • 225g sultanas • 225g peel • 225g almonds •
15g ground ginger • ½ teaspoon cinnamon • ½ teaspoon ground
cloves • 450g sugar

Put blackberries in a pan with lemon juice and water. Simmer until
tender, and sieve. Stir all other ingredients into blackberry pulp, put
in jars and seal airtight.

GOLDEN MINCEMEAT (English)

900g sweet apples, peeled, cored and diced • butter to butter pan •
900g golden sultanas • 115g shredded lemon peel •
1 teaspoon ground ginger • ½ teaspoon nutmeg •
pinch of mace • 4 cups water • juice of 1 lemon • 675g sugar •
1 teaspoon ratafia or almond essence

Butter a preserving pan and add all ingredients except sugar and ratafia
essence. Boil for 30 minutes. Add sugar and boil again for 15 minutes,
stirring. Set aside until nearly cold. Add ratafia essence. Mix well and
put into warm jars. Cover like jam when cold (see page 229–230).

MINCEMEAT

450g raisins • 450g currants • 115g mixed peel • 225g sultanas •
450g apples, peeled • 225g shredded suet • grated rind and juice
of 1 orange • grated rind and juice of 1 lemon • 450g brown sugar

Mince all fruit and suet (except orange and lemon). Add juice and
rind of orange and lemon. Add sugar and mix well. Put into jars and
tie down.

MINCEMEAT (Old Fashioned)

1 cup chopped currants • 1 cup chopped raisins • 1 cup chopped
apples • 1 cup chopped suet • grated rind and juice of 1 lemon •
30g chopped candied peel • 30g chopped almonds • a little
nutmeg • a little spice • 1 cup brown sugar • brandy or rum

Mix all with brandy or rum and keep in airtight jars.

MINCEMEAT (Quick)

450g raisins • 225g sultanas • lemon peel • ½ teacup orange or
lemon juice • ½ teacup brown sugar mixed with spice • a little
shredded suet, or a good lump of butter • 1 apple, peeled, cored
and grated (if required)

Put in a double boiler and simmer for 20 minutes. If using straight
away, spread over pastry, cover with apple and sprinkle with sugar.
If not using straight away, put in a screw top jar. Will keep for a few
weeks. Do not put apple in when making mince, add when using.

COLD SWEETS

ANGEL'S FOOD

30g gelatine • 4 cups cold milk • 3 egg yolks, beaten •
1 cup sugar • juice of 1 lemon • 3 egg whites, stiffly beaten •
essence of choice to taste

Dissolve gelatine in a little milk. Add remaining milk. When thoroughly dissolved, add egg yolks, sugar and lemon juice. Bring all to the boil and stir. Let cool and when nearly cold stir in egg whites. Add essence and let set.

APPLE FOAM

4 apples, peeled and cored • 2 cups water • sugar to taste •
1 packet red jelly (red currant, cherry, etc.) • 1 egg white,
stiffly beaten

Stew apples in sugar to taste. Make up jelly with the juice drained off the apples and made to amount stated on packet. When jelly is about half set, stir in the apples and egg white. Whip together and put in a glass dish to set. Lovely for kiddies. Is much improved when covered with whipped cream, sliced bananas and grated chocolate.

APRICOT MERINGUE

900g apricots, stewed with syrup retained • 225g stale sponge cake crumbs • 2 egg whites • sugar

Beat apricots to a pulp and put in a casserole. Saturate the crumbed sponge cake with syrup. Put on top of apricots. Make a meringue with the egg whites and sugar, put on top and brown in a cool oven (120°C).

APRICOT WHIP (With Gelatine)

apricots • sugar • 15g gelatine • ¼ cup cold water • ¼ cup boiling water • 2 tablespoons sugar • squeeze of lemon.

Stew sufficient apricots, with sugar to taste, to make 1½ cups pulp when sieved. Soak gelatine in water until soft, then add boiling water. Stir together over hot water, until dissolved, adding sugar. Remove from heat. Mix together mixture and apricot pulp. A squeeze of lemon is an improvement. Leave until just beginning to set. Whip with a strong egg whisk until light and frothy. Set in a mould previously rinsed with cold water.

BAKED ALASKA

3 egg whites, beaten until stiff • 6 tablespoons sugar • ½ teaspoon vanilla • 1 litre block of ice cream

Add egg whites to sugar, beating continuously. Add vanilla. Place ice cream on a thick board and completely cover with egg white mixture. Bake at 200°C until a delicate brown.

For a variation of Baked Alaska, sprinkle coconut over meringue before baking. Or partly bury the small half of an egg shell in centre top of meringue before baking. When dessert is removed from oven, fill shell with rum or brandy. Light the liquor and bring to the table flaming.

BANANA CREAM

2 cups mashed banana (to a creamy consistency) • 1¼ cups milk •
3 tablespoons orange juice • 3 tablespoons honey • pinch of salt •
1 dessertspoon gelatine, dissolved in ½ cup hot water • whipped
cream with a little nutmeg to garnish

To mashed banana add milk, orange juice, honey and salt. Blend
thoroughly. Stir in gelatine and mix. Pour into wetted mould to set.
Turn out on to a pretty dish and garnish with whipped cream. If you
set the mould in the refrigerator you need a little less gelatine.

BANANA LOGS

bananas • raspberry jam • coconut or cornflakes •
whipped cream to serve

Peel bananas and spread with raspberry jam. Roll in coconut or
cornflakes. Serve with whipped cream or custard. Cut point off ends
of bananas.

BOSTON PUFFS

cream puffs • ice cream • powdered sugar • hot chocolate sauce
to serve

Cut tops off cream puffs and fill with ice cream. Replace tops and
sprinkle with powdered sugar. Serve with hot chocolate sauce.

BUTTERSCOTCH SPONGE PUDDING

2 tablespoons butter • 1 cup sugar • 1¾ cups hot milk •
3 egg yolks, beaten • 3 teaspoons gelatine dissolved in ¼ cup hot
water • few drops of vanilla, almond, ratafia or caramel essence •
3 egg whites • pinch of salt

Make a thick paste of butter and sugar, and pour hot milk over. Pour all over egg yolks. Heat until smooth like custard, but do not boil. Leave until cold. Add gelatine and essence. Beat egg whites stiff with salt and whisk in. When beginning to set, put in wetted mould.

CAPE GOOSEBERRY SPONGE

cape gooseberries • sugar • hot water • 1 packet jelly crystals

Stew cape gooseberries gently with sugar. Strain off syrup, and make to just under 2 cups with hot water. Make up a jelly with it. Leave to get cold. As it is setting, whip and then add the cape gooseberries and let it set.

CARAMEL CUSTARD

6 tablespoons sugar • 8 tablespoons water • 2 cups milk • 2 or 3
eggs • sugar to taste • pinch of salt • essence of choice • mock
cream or real cream to serve

Make a caramel with sugar by browning over a gentle heat. Add water and cook until a nice syrup. Coat a basin or mould with the syrup, which will set. Make custard with milk, eggs, sugar, salt and essence. Pour into basin carefully, cover, and steam in saucepan of boiling water with lid on, until set. Lift out and, when cold, turn out onto a glass dish. Serve with cream. Can be eaten hot or cold.

CELESTIAL PEACHES (Chinese)

large peaches, skinned, halved and stoned • thick ginger syrup
(from jar of Chinese preserved ginger) • ice cream, finely chopped
nuts and preserved ginger to serve

Arrange peaches cut side uppermost on baking dish. Fill centres
with a little ginger syrup. Bake lightly in a moderate oven (180°C)
and let get cold. Fill centres with ice cream, sprinkle with chopped
nuts and preserved ginger on top.

CHARLOTTE RUSSE (Norwegian)

1 cup cream • 4 egg yolks • 115g sugar • 1 dessertspoon gelatine
dissolved in a little water • 1 teacup rum • water • red currant jelly
or strawberry jam • cornflour

Whip cream. Beat egg yolks and sugar together, and mix with
cream. Add gelatine and rum. Pour into a mould and leave to set.
When turned out, serve with red sauce made with red currant jelly
or strawberry jam heated with a little water, strained, and thickened
with cornflour.

CHOCOLATE SPONGE JELLY

1 packet jelly crystals • 1 cup hot water • 2 egg yolks, beaten until
creamy • 1 cup milk • 1 dessertspoon cocoa • 2 egg whites, stiffly
beaten • cream and custard to serve

Dissolve jelly crystals in water (hot but not boiling). Mix egg yolks
well with milk and cocoa. Heat slowly until slightly thickened. It
must not boil. Allow both dissolved jelly and milk and egg mixture
to cool. Add egg whites to milk mixture. Whip all together and set in
a mould. Serve with cream and custard.

CHOCOLATE PEACHES (Or Apricots)

1 packet jelly crystals • 1 tin peach halves in syrup • hot water • chocolate custard • cream, whipped until stiff with sugar and essence of choice

Dissolve jelly as per instructions on packet, using syrup from peaches and hot water to make up quantity. Arrange peaches in a dish, cut side downwards, leaving 2 or 3 for the top. Pour jelly over and leave to set. Make chocolate custard and let it get almost cold. Then stir it up and pour over jelly. When thoroughly cold, cut remaining peaches into quarters and arrange in a ring on top. Pile cream in centre of dish.

CUSTARD FOR SPECIAL OCCASIONS

2 cups milk • 2 level tablespoons sugar • 1 egg • pinch of salt • 1 dessertspoon cornflour or arrowroot • 1 small tin cream

Bring milk slowly to the boil. Add sugar. Beat egg with salt. Mix with cornflour or arrowroot with a little milk. When milk is nearly boiling, pour on to egg and cornflour mixture and pour back into saucepan to thicken. When quite cold, beat in cream until quite smooth.

DATE AND BANANA SHORTCAKE

115g butter • 60g sugar • 1 egg • 115g wholemeal flour, sifted • 85g white flour, sifted • 30g cornflour, sifted • 1 level teaspoon baking powder • 1 banana, cut up • ½ cup dates • 2 tablespoons water • vanilla or other essence • whipped cream to serve

Cream butter and sugar, add egg, flours and baking powder. Roll out and, with half, line a sandwich tin. Spread with a banana. Boil dates with water and essence for 1 minute or two. Spread the dates and essence. Put on rest of pastry and bake at 180°C for about 30 minutes. Serve cold with whipped cream.

EGG BLANCMANGE

60g cornflour • 2 cups cold milk • 45g sugar • pinch of salt •
strip of lemon rind • knob of butter • 1 egg yolk, beaten •
1 egg white, beaten

Moisten cornflour with a little milk. Heat the rest with sugar, salt, lemon and butter. When hot, pour on to cornflour, pour back and let thicken. Remove lemon rind. When cool, add egg yolk and fold in egg white.

FLUMMERY

1 packet jelly • 1 tin unsweetened condensed milk • fruit or fruit pulp

Make up a good jelly and let it become cool, but not set. Whip up condensed milk, add to whipped jelly and whip again. Pour over fruit or fruit pulp and let set.

FRUIT BAVARIAN CREAM

fresh strawberries, raspberries or very ripe peaches (or plums) •
¼ cup boiling water • 30g gelatine soaked in ½ cup cold water •
2 cups whipped cream

Press sufficient fruit through a sieve to make 2 breakfast cups of pulp. Pour boiling water on to gelatine to dissolve it, and pour into the fruit. When the jelly begins to set, fold in whipped cream and stir until well mixed. Set in a glass or porcelain mould, rinsed with cold water. A tin mould will discolour the cream. Half quantities may be used.

GOOSEBERRY DELIGHT

450g gooseberries • 1 packet red jelly crystals • 2 tablespoons sugar • water • powdered cinnamon • whipped cream to decorate

Top and tail gooseberries and stew with sugar, a little water and cinnamon. When tender, rub through a sieve and allow to cool. Place purée in a glass dish. Make jelly according to instructions, and before it is quite cold pour over the gooseberries. When set, decorate the top with blobs of whipped cream.

GOOSEBERRY FOOL

450g green gooseberries • water • 1½ cups sugar • just over 1 cup milk, boiled • 1 dessertspoon condensed milk

Stew gooseberries with a little water and the sugar until perfectly tender. Rub through a sieve, and add boiled milk with condensed milk dissolved in it. Mix well, and put aside to cool.

HIDDEN TREASURE

2 packets jelly crystals • fruit, finely chopped • a little custard made with custard powder

Make up 2 jellies. Pour about 50mm of jelly into a mould and let it set. When set, stand straight jar or tin on the centre, and pour jelly all around to within 13mm of top. Let stand, then remove jar. If filled with hot water, it will come away quite cleanly. Fill the space with chopped fruit, and a little custard made with custard powder. Pour the remainder of the jelly over the top. The fruit is completely hidden in the centre of this jelly mould.

HONEYCOMB

30g gelatine • 4 cups milk • 3 egg yolks, beaten • 2 tablespoons
sugar • 1 teaspoon vanilla • 3 egg whites, beaten to a stiff froth

Soak gelatine in milk for 1 hour. Mix egg yolks with sugar and vanilla.
Bring milk to boiling point, and add egg yolk mix. Stir beaten egg
whites into the mixture and pour into a mould to set.

ICE CREAM

1 egg, beaten a little • 2 cups fresh cream • ⅓ cup sugar •
1½ teaspoons vanilla essence

Beat together like whipped cream, then put in freezer.

ICE CREAM (Bunty's)

3 tablespoons sugar • 8 heaped tablespoons full-cream milk powder •
3 cups milk • 1½ teaspoons gelatine dissolved in 2 tablespoons
hot water • ½ teaspoon caramel essence

Mix sugar and milk powder with 1½ cups milk. Beat until thick like
whipped cream or, better still, like creamed butter. Add remaining
1½ cups of milk, a little at a time. Add gelatine and beat well. Freeze
for 45 minutes, turn into a bowl and whip until nearly half more ice
cream than when you started. Add essence, beat well, and return to
trays and freeze. If using an electric beater, you may use 2 cups milk
which makes 2 trays of ice cream.

ICE CREAM (Delicious)

Blancmange will taste just like ice cream if, after making and cooling,
a tin of condensed milk is beaten into it. Chill in a cool place or
refrigerator. Serve with stewed fruit, etc., this ice cream is delicious.

ICE CREAM (Junket)

rennet • 2 cups fresh milk • 1 cup sugar • 1 large cup cream •
1 teaspoon vanilla essence

Add rennet to milk to make a junket. When at setting stage, add sugar, and beat well with an egg beater. Stir in cream. Add vanilla essence, pour into a tray, and place in freezer. It sets firmly and is not as sickly as other ice cream.

ICE CREAM (Quick)

1 tin sweetened condensed milk • 1 tinful of milk (use condensed milk tin to measure) • 1 tinful of cream (use condensed milk tin to measure)

Mix together and freeze, stirring twice during the freezing process. This is delicious.

WEE WYN'S ICE CREAM

The secret is to have both bowl and milk thoroughly chilled.

450g unsweetened evaporated milk • pinch of salt • ¾ cup sifted icing sugar • essence of choice • grated chocolate, passionfruit pulp or crushed pineapple (optional)

Empty evaporated milk into a bowl with salt and whip until thick. Add icing sugar and essence (and chocolate, passionfruit or pineapple). Whip again, then put in trays and freeze (this makes 2 trays). There is no further beating. Allow 2 hours to freeze.

ICES (Water)

675g sugar • 4 cups water • juice of 1 lemon • grated rind
3 lemons (or 1 dessertspoon lemon essence will do if lemons
not available) • strawberries, currants etc. (optional)

Make a syrup with sugar and water and add lemon juice and rind.
Mix well, strain through muslin and freeze. Fresh fruits may be used,
allowing 1 cup juice to each 2 cups syrup.

IVORY CREAM

5 bananas, peeled and mashed • 5 teaspoons icing sugar •
1 cup cream • 1 packet orange jelly • 1½ cups boiling water •
whipped cream to serve

Beat bananas with icing sugar until free of lumps. Whip cream stiff
and mix with banana pulp. Dissolve jelly in the water and leave
until cold. Stir in cream mixture and pour into a wet jelly mould, and
leave until set. Serve with whipped cream.

JELLY

1 packet jelly crystals • 1 cup plus of hot water • 2 egg yolks,
beaten • 1 tablespoon sugar • 1 cup milk • 2 egg whites, beaten
stiffly

Dissolve jelly crystals in the water. While cooking, mix egg yolks
with sugar and add to jelly. Add the milk. Add egg whites, folding
in. This sets very quickly.

JELLY EGGS (For Easter)

1 egg • 1 packet jelly crystals

Make a small hole in one end of egg, and get white and yolk out. With a small funnel, fill egg shells with jelly. Put in egg cup to set. When set, break shells carefully and remove. Can be served in pretty ways (chopped green lettuce all round, or in a nest with yellow chickens on edge).

LEMON CHIFFON PIE

1 tablespoon gelatine • ¼ cup cold water • 4 egg yolks, beaten until light • 1 cup sugar • ½ cup lemon juice • 1 teaspoon grated lemon rind • 4 egg whites • ½ teaspoon salt • pastry shell, baked

Soak gelatine in the water. In a separate bowl, beat together egg yolks, half a cup of the sugar, and the lemon juice and rind. When very light, place on a low heat, and cook, stirring until it is like custard. Add the gelatine and dissolve it. Leave to cool. Add the rest of the sugar to the egg whites and beat until stiff. Fold egg white into egg yolk mixture. Pour into baked pastry shell. Leave to cool, and to set. Serve with a thin layer of whipped cream. If making Orange Chiffon Pie, substitute ½ cup orange juice, 1 tablespoon lemon rind, 1 tablespoon orange rind.

LEMON CHIFFON PIE (No Oven)

Crust:

1 cup crushed wheatflakes • ¼ cup sugar • ½ teaspoon cinnamon • ¼ cup melted butter

Mix all together and press into a pie plate.

Filling:

4 egg yolks • ½ cup lemon juice • 1 teaspoon grated lemon rind •
1 cup sugar • 1½ teaspoons gelatine soaked in ¼ cup water •
4 egg whites, beaten

Cook egg yolks with lemon juice and rind, and half the sugar, in a double boiler. Cook until custard consistency. Stir in gelatine and water, let cool, stirring. Fold in egg whites and remaining sugar, and pour into pie shell. Leave 3 hours to set.

LEMON CUSTARD (Uncooked)

2 dessertspoons gelatine mixed with ¼ cup cold water in a cup •
2 eggs • 1 cup sugar • 2 cups milk • boiling water • juice of
1 lemon • a little grated lemon rind

Leave gelatine and water to stand while mixing other ingredients. Beat eggs and sugar well, add milk and beat again. Fill up cup containing gelatine with the boiling water, and stir until thoroughly dissolved. Add milk mixture and stir well. Add lemon juice and rind. Leave overnight to set.

LEMON MERINGUE TART

puff pastry • 2 cups water • 1 cup sugar • 1 tablespoon butter •
grated rind and juice of 2 lemons • 2 tablespoons cornflour •
pinch salt • 2 egg yolks, beaten • 2 egg whites, whipped until stiff •
3 tablespoons sugar

Line a deep pie plate with puff pastry and cook quickly to a light brown. Put water, 1 cup sugar, butter, lemon rind and juice in a saucepan. Let it come to the boil, thicken with cornflour, add salt and egg yolks. Boil about 5 minutes, then allow to cool before filling pastry case. Mix whipped egg whites with 3 tablespoons sugar. Place the meringue in the filled tart, and return to oven to brown slightly.

MILANESE SOUFFLE (Uncooked)

2 dessertspoons powdered gelatine • 1 breakfast cup cold water •
1 breakfast cup boiling water • 2 egg yolks • 3 tablespoons sugar •
essence of choice • 2 egg whites

Soak gelatine for 15 minutes in cold water, then add boiling water. Mix well. Let it cool but not set. While getting cold, beat egg yolks with half the sugar, the essence, and put aside. Beat egg whites with other half of sugar. When gelatine is cold, beat until stiff, then fold in egg yolks and then egg whites. Put aside to set. Can be used with fruit or raspberry jam and cream.

MOONSHINE

1 tin pineapple chunks, juice reserved • 1 packet strawberry jelly •
2 cups custard, cooled • whipped cream, a little desiccated
coconut to serve • cherries for decoration

Put pineapple in a dish. Make up the jelly using pineapple juice and water to make right amount. Pour over pineapple and let to set. Pour over custard and leave to cool properly. Before serving, arrange cream on top, sprinkle with coconut and decorate with cherries.

MOTHER'S DELIGHT (No Cooking)

Excellent for children.

3 egg yolks • 225g sugar • 2 or 3 oranges • 1 lemon • 30g
gelatine • ½ cup hot water • 3 egg whites • pinch of salt •
cream or custard to serve

Beat egg yolks and sugar together. Add juice of fruit. Melt gelatine in hot water. Beat egg whites to a stiff froth with salt, mix together and pour into a mould to set. Serve with cream or custard.

NGAURUHOE SNOW

1 round sponge cake • 6 egg whites • pinch of salt • blocks of ice cream • hulled strawberries • 180g sugar

Put sponge cake on a board. Beat egg whites to stiff peaks. Add salt while beating. Build up blocks of ice cream on sponge cake to represent a mountain. Stick this thickly all over with strawberries. Fold sugar into egg whites. Put meringue thickly all over ice cream and sponge cake. Put into oven for a few minutes, until meringue is pretty brown.

Chocolate sauce:

water • icing sugar • cocoa • rum (optional)

Mix ingredients together. Remove mountain from oven and pour over sauce to look like molten lava coming out the crater. For special occasions, heat some rum in the oven, pour rum over, set a match to it, put out the lights in the room and bring in the dish.

ORANGE TRIFLE

1 plain sponge cake • 1 or 2 tablespoons wine or sherry • 3 egg yolks, well beaten • 3 tablespoons sugar • juice and rind 3 oranges • juice and rind 1 lemon • 3 egg whites, whipped to a stiff froth

Line a glass dish with pieces of sponge. Pour over wine or sherry. Put egg yolks in a saucepan and beat with sugar and orange and lemon juice and rind. Heat slowly until thick, stirring continually. Do not let it boil. Fold egg whites into mixture in saucepan after removing from heat. Pour over sponge in dish, and serve cold.

PEACH CARDINAL

1 square sponge cake • peach halves, canned, cooked or fresh • sauce from: raspberries in thick syrup or thinned raspberry jam

Put sponge cake on a plate. Add peach halves, rounded side up. Pour raspberry sauce all over and serve.

PEACH CHIFFON PIE

1 cup puréed peaches • 1½ tablespoons powdered gelatine • ½ cup sugar • ¼ teaspoon salt • 4 egg yolks, well beaten • 4 egg whites, stiffly beaten • 2 tablespoons sugar • 1 cup cream • ¼ teaspoon almond essence • ½ teaspoon vanilla essence • baked pie shell

To one quarter cup peach purée, add gelatine and let it soak. To remaining three-quarter cup purée, add ½ cup sugar and the salt, and bring to the boil. Stir in softened gelatine and, carefully, the egg yolks. Cool. Fold in egg whites. Whip half the cream with 2 tablespoons sugar, add essences, and fold into mixture. Pour into baked pie shell and chill until firm. To serve, cover with rest of cream.

PEACH CUSTARD (For Children)

peach halves, canned, cooked or fresh ripe fruit • 4 eggs • 1½ cups milk • ⅓ cup sugar • ½ teaspoon salt • 1 teaspoon vanilla essence

Meringue:
¼ cup sugar • ½ teaspoon vanilla essence

Arrange enough peach halves to cover a shallow baking dish. Separate yolks and whites of 2 eggs. Beat yolks with 2 remaining whole eggs. Add other ingredients and beat well. Pour over peaches in dish. Set in dish of hot water, and bake for 30 minutes at 150°C until set.

Make meringue: beat remaining egg whites stiff. Fold in sugar and vanilla and heap on custard. Brown in oven. Serve cold.

PEACH FLAN

1 packet of jelly crystals (strawberry, pineapple or peach) • 1 tin sliced peaches, juice reserved • water • 1 pastry flan (see page 132)

Make up jelly using juice from peaches and water. Soak peaches in this jelly. Cook a pastry flan. When cold, put the slices of peaches on this shell, and pour over as much jelly as required. Very nice with almond custard.

PEACH SHORTCAKE

2 level breakfast cups flour • 2 level teaspoons baking powder • pinch of salt • 2 large tablespoons sugar • 3 full tablespoons butter, softened • 1 egg, beaten • about ½ cup milk • sliced peaches (fresh or stewed) • whipped cream

Mix together flour, baking powder, salt and sugar. Rub in butter, and mix with egg and milk to a soft dough. Place half the dough on a greased sandwich tin, smooth over, and spread with butter. Cover with other half of dough, which has been smoothed out to fit tin. Bake in hot oven until cooked. Split open while hot, and spread with peaches and cream. Replace top and cover similarly.

PEACH SUNDAE

vanilla or strawberry ice cream • 1 canned peach (or 1 lightly cooked fresh peach) • whipped cream and sponge lady's fingers to garnish

Arrange a portion of ice cream in the hollow of a peach. Pour a little peach syrup over ice cream. Garnish with cream and lady's fingers. Chopped nuts may be sprinkled over.

PEACH WHIP

peaches, cooked and mashed to a pulp (can use canned) • 2 egg whites, beaten stiffly • 4 tablespoons sugar • whipped cream and ginger wafers to serve

Put peaches through a sieve. Beat egg whites with 2 tablespoons sugar. Add 2 more tablespoons sugar and 1 cup peach pulp. Beat with an egg whisk until smooth and fluffy. Serve in individual glasses (long stemmed ones look nice). Put cream on top. Serve with ginger wafers.

PEAR SUNDAE

1 tin pears • 1 packet lemon jelly crystals • water • whipped cream or custard to serve

With juice from tin of pears, make up the jelly, adding water to make right quantity. When beginning to 'jell', whip until frothy. Place pears in individual dishes, pour on the jelly, and serve with cream or custard.

PEPPERMINT MARSHMALLOW

2 tablespoons sugar • ½ cup cold water • 1 teaspoon gelatine dissolved in ½ cup boiling water • 2 egg whites, unbeaten • peppermint essence • custard • 2 egg yolks • coconut

Dissolve sugar in cold water for 2 to 3 minutes. Add gelatine. When cool, add egg whites and gently stir. Set aside, and when just beginning to set, whip up until thick and foamy. Add peppermint and mix well. Set in wet greaseproof paper. Make a custard with egg yolks, top with coconut, and bake. Join together. Delicious served with ice cream.

PINEAPPLE PIE

2 tablespoons flour • 1 cup sugar • 1 cup pineapple juice, heated •
2 egg yolks • 1 tin crushed pineapple • 1 baked pie shell
(see page 132) • 2 egg whites, well beaten • 4 tablespoons sugar

Mix flour and sugar. Pour over a little juice, put in saucepan and cook until thick and clear. Stir until smooth. Add egg yolks and crushed pineapple. Put into pie shell. Cover with meringue made from egg whites well beaten with sugar. Brown in a slow oven (120°C).

PRUNE WHIP

¼ cup cold water • 1 tablespoon gelatine • ½ cup sugar •
pinch of salt • ¾ cup hot prune juice • ½ cup cool prune pulp •
2 tablespoons lemon juice • ¼ cup chopped nuts • 2 egg whites,
stiffly beaten • whipped cream to serve

Pour cold water on gelatine, sugar and salt. Add hot prune juice and stir until dissolved. Add prune pulp, lemon juice and nuts, then put aside to cool. When mixture starts to thicken, add egg whites and stir in. Put all into a wetted mould and let cool. When set, turn out and serve with whipped cream.

RHUBARB MOULD

2 dessertspoons gelatine (1½ dessertspoons if a refrigerator is
used) • ½ cup hot water • 2 egg yolks • 2 dessertspoons sugar •
pinch of salt • 2 egg whites, stiffly beaten • 1 large cup cold
stewed rhubarb • ½ teaspoon lemon essence

Dissolve gelatine in hot water. Beat egg yolks and add sugar and salt. Beat in egg whites, add gelatine, rhubarb and essence. Stir well and pour into a wetted mould to set.

SPANISH CREAM

15g gelatine • 2 cups milk • 3 egg yolks, well beaten • 1 cup sugar • juice of 1 lemon • 3 egg whites, well beaten • cream or custard to serve

Dissolve gelatine in milk, add egg yolks, sugar and lemon juice. Put on cooktop and bring to the boil. Take off, and when nearly cold, add egg whites. Put in a mould and serve with cream or custard. When turned out, there should be clear jelly on top and sponge underneath.

SPANISH CREAM (Three Minute)

2 packets jelly crystals • 2 cups boiling water • 2 cups milk • 2 eggs, beaten • a little sugar

Dissolve jelly in boiling water. Heat milk, and add eggs and sugar. Blend both together and set overnight.

SPONGE CAKE SURPRISE (San Francisco)

1 small sponge cake, cut into squares • ice cream • hot chocolate sauce • whipped cream (if desired)

Cut sponge squares horizontally and put ice cream between. Replace upper half and pour chocolate sauce over just before serving. A spoonful of whipped cream may be added.

STRAWBERRY BAVARIAN CREAM

2 tablespoons gelatine • ¼ cup cold water • ½ cup fruit juice, boiled • 1½ cups crushed strawberries • ½ cup sugar (if fresh strawberries used) • 1½ cups cream, whipped until thick • whole strawberries and cream, whipped until thick, to garnish

Soak gelatine in water and dissolve in boiling fruit juice. Cool. If fresh strawberries are used, add the ½ cup sugar. Add fruit and chill, stirring occasionally. When mixture begins to thicken, fold in cream. Turn into a mould dipped in cold water and leave to set. Garnish with whole strawberries and more cream.

STRAWBERRY SHORTCAKE
(Old Fashioned)

2 cups flour • 3 teaspoons baking powder • ½ teaspoon salt •
1 tablespoon sugar • 5 tablespoons butter • 1 egg • about ¾ cup
milk • a little softened butter • crushed strawberries

Sift dry ingredients. Cut butter into flour. Break egg into a cup, add milk to make ¾ cup. Mix, and add to dry ingredients. Sit until well mixed. It should be soft but not sticky. Add more milk if necessary. Divide into two. Pat out each half into round flat discs. Brush tops with softened butter. Put one on top of other and bake in 180°C oven until well baked through. Put strawberries between and on top. Or, stretch berries by mixing half and half with cooked rhubarb.

STRAWBERRY SPONGE

1 cup cooked strawberry pulp and juice • 1 cup sugar •
1 tablespoon gelatine softened in ¼ cup cold water • ¼ teaspoon
salt • ½ cup hot water • 1 tablespoon lemon juice • 2 egg whites,
stiffly beaten • ½ cup whipped cream (this makes it beautiful but
may be omitted)

Crush berries, add sugar and leave 30 minutes. To gelatine, add salt and hot water, and stir until dissolved. Add berry mixture and lemon juice. Cool, and when thickening fold in egg whites and, if using, whipped cream. Serve in either one bowl or individual glasses. About 6 servings. Sets in fairly quick time. Any fresh or canned fruit may be used, but use less sugar with canned fruit.

SWISS JELLY (No Cooking)

2 dessertspoons gelatine • ½ cup boiling water • 2 egg yolks •
½ cup sugar • 1 breakfast cup milk • juice of 1 lemon • finely
grated lemon rind (if liked) • 2 egg whites, stiffly beaten

Dissolve gelatine in boiling water. Beat egg yolks in a bowl with sugar. Add milk, gelatine mixture, lemon juice, and rind (if using). Add beaten egg whites and fold in. Set in wetted mould.

ZABAGLIONE (Yolks and Whites)

3 eggs yolks • juice of 1 lemon • ½ cup sugar • 1 glass (small tumbler) sherry, madeira or other sweet wine (or pure fruit juice if preferred) • 3 egg whites, stiffly beaten

Beat yolks, lemon juice, sugar and wine or fruit juice. Fold in egg whites. Cook in a double boiler but leave plenty of room. Put on a very low heat and beat continuously and vigorously with egg beater while cooking. After a few minutes the mixture will rise in the vessel until roughly double the size, then thicken to consistency of shaving lather. Eat at once.

ZABAGLIONE (Yolks Only)

3 egg yolks • ¾ cup sugar • 2 teaspoons grated lemon rind •
3 teaspoons lemon juice • ¼ cup sherry or marsala

Partly fill base of double boiler with water and bring to the boil. Beat egg yolks slightly in top of double boiler; add other ingredients. Cook over boiling water, beating constantly with egg beater until thick and fluffy like whipped cream. Remove at once. Serve hot or chilled in parfait or champagne glasses as dessert. Or use to top sponge cake or fruit.

HOT SWEETS

ADAM'S CUSTARD

3 cups milk • 115g breadcrumbs • 1 tablespoon butter • pinch of
salt • 170g sugar • 1 cup peeled and finely chopped apples •
½ teaspoon vanilla • 3 egg yolks, beaten • 3 egg whites •
1 tablespoon caster sugar

Boil milk and pour over breadcrumbs. Stir in butter, salt and sugar.
Leave for 30 minutes. Mix in apples, vanilla and egg yolks. Butter a pie
dish, pour in mixture and bake for 45 minutes. Beat egg whites stiffly
with caster sugar, heap over pudding and return to oven to brown.

APPLE AMBER

900g apples • 115g sugar • 60g butter • rind and juice of 1 lemon •
2 or 3 eggs • 1 tablespoon sugar to each egg white • extra sugar
for sprinkling

Cook apples with sugar, butter, lemon juice and rind. When cooked,
beat with a fork and rub through sieve. Add egg yolks and pour
mixture into a pie dish. Whip egg whites, add sugar and pile on top
of pudding. Sprinkle with sugar and place in a cool oven (120°C) for
about 50 minutes.

APPLE BROWN BETTY

2 cups fine breadcrumbs • 2 tablespoons melted butter or fat •
2 cups sliced apples or other fruit • ½ cup sugar or honey •
cinnamon or other spices • grated rind of 1 lemon or orange •
½ cup fruit juice or water

Mix breadcrumbs with butter. Arrange layers of buttered crumbs and apple slices in pudding dish. Sprinkle each layer of fruit with sugar, cinnamon and lemon rind. Finish with a layer of crumbs. Pour juice or water over top. Bake at 180°C for 45 minutes approximately.

APPLE CRISP

4 apples, peeled and sliced • ¾ cup cold water • cinnamon •
2½ tablespoons butter • ¾ cup flour • ½ cup sugar

Arrange apples in pie dish and pour over cold water and sprinkle with cinnamon. Rub butter into flour and sugar until crumbly, and sprinkle on top of apples. Bake for 30 minutes. No sugar is added to the apple as it soaks through from the top.

APPLE CURRANTY (Devonshire)

4 large sour cooking apples • 340g flour • 1 small teaspoon baking powder • 225g finely shredded suet • 2 tablespoons sugar •
pinch of salt • a few sultanas or currants • 1 egg • a little milk •
Devonshire cream to serve

Dice apples (1–2cm cubes). Put all ingredients except egg and milk in a basin. Mix with the egg and a little milk, not more moist than a cake. Bake at 160°C for about 1 hour, or boil in a basin 2½ to 3 hours. Serve with Devonshire cream.

APPLE DUMPLINGS

900g sour apples, peeled and quartered • 3 cups sugar •
1 cup hot water

Add apples to a syrup made with sugar and hot water. Simmer until soft but unbroken.

Batter:

⅓ cup butter • ⅓ cup sugar • 1 egg, beaten • 2¼ cups flour •
2¼ teaspoons baking powder • ¾ teaspoon salt • 1⅛ cups milk •
cinnamon

Cream butter, add sugar gradually, then add egg. Sift flour, baking powder and salt, adding alternately with the milk. Butter a good pie dish and drop in spoonfuls of batter, alternately with spoonfuls of hot apples and syrup. Pour remaining hot syrup over. Sprinkle with cinnamon and bake in a hot oven (220°C) for 30 minutes. Delicious with crisp brown bits of paste risen through little rivers of syrup.

APPLE DUMPLINGS BAKED IN SYRUP

2 cups flour • 2 teaspoons baking powder • 1 teaspoon salt •
¾ cup butter • ½ cup milk • apples, peeled and cored • sugar •
cinnamon • nutmeg • dates for stuffing (if liked) • custard to serve

Sift flour, baking powder and salt. Cut in the butter. Add milk and mix. Roll out to 6mm thick and cut into squares. Place an apple in centre of each, sprinkle with sugar, cinnamon and nutmeg. If liked, stuff with dates. Gather corners of the pastry, pinch together and put in a baking dish.

Syrup:

1 cup sugar • 1 cup water • 2 tablespoons butter • ¼ teaspoon
ground cinnamon • ¼ teaspoon ground nutmeg

Boil 5 minutes. Pour boiling water over dumplings and bake for 30 to 40 minutes in a moderate oven (180°C). Serve with custard.

APPLE GINGER UPSIDE-DOWN-CAKE

This is a dessert.

> 3 or 4 apples, thickly sliced • 2 teaspoons cinnamon • ⅓ cup sugar •
> ½ cup butter • ½ cup boiling water • 1 cup golden syrup •
> 2½ cups flour • 2 teaspoons ground ginger • 1 teaspoon
> baking soda • ½ teaspoon salt • cream or custard to serve

Put apples in a buttered dish. Sprinkle with cinnamon and sugar.
Melt butter in the boiling water. Add golden syrup. Sift in the flour,
ginger, baking soda and salt. Pour on top of apples. Bake for about
45 minutes in a moderate oven (180°C). Turn out upside down. Serve
with cream or custard.

APRICOT SPONGE (Steamed)

> 1½ cups white breadcrumbs • 1 cup flour, sifted • 1 teaspoon
> baking powder • ½ teaspoon salt • 2 tablespoons sugar •
> 2 tablespoons melted butter • ¾ cup hot milk • 1 egg yolk, well
> beaten • 1 cup apricot (stewed and drained), juice retained

Place breadcrumbs, flour, baking powder, salt and sugar in a basin.
Melt butter in milk and add egg yolk. Add apricots to flour mixture
and mix thoroughly. Pack into a greased mould and steam for 1 hour.
Serve hot with sauce.

Hot sauce:

> juice of 1 lemon • ½ cup sugar • 1 cup juice from apricots

Boil all together until thick.

BAKED ROLYPOLY

225g flour • 115g butter • 2 teaspoons baking powder • pinch of
salt • apricot jam

Make first 4 ingredients into a paste. Roll out and spread with apricot
jam. Roll up. Put in a baking dish and pour over syrup.

Syrup:
½ cup sugar • 60g butter • 1½ cups water

Bring to the boil, pour over the pudding, and bake for 1½ hours in a
moderate oven (180°C).

BLACKBERRY COBBLER

3 cups blackberries • 1 cup water • juice of 1 lemon • sugar to
taste • 2 tablespoons sugar • 2 tablespoons flour • dab of butter •
1 sheet short pastry (or crushed biscuits or sponge cake crumbs)

Cook blackberries in the water with lemon juice and sugar. When
cold, put into a pie dish. Sprinkle with sugar and flour and dab of
butter. Cover with a good sheet of pastry or crushed biscuits or sponge
cake crumbs, and dab with butter. Cook in a good oven (180°C) for
20 to 30 minutes.

BLACKBERRY SURPRISE

enough blackberries to almost fill a pie dish • 60g butter •
60g sugar • 115g flour • ½ teaspoon baking powder • cream or
custard to serve

If blackberries are seedy, it is nicer to pour through a sieve after they
are cooked. Mix dry ingredients well and sprinkle evenly over top
of hot fruit. Bake at 190°C for 30 minutes until a nice light brown.
Serve with cream or custard.

BREAD PUDDING

2 cups stale bread • 4 cups milk • 2 eggs, beaten until light • ½ cup
sugar • ¼ teaspoon salt • 1 teaspoon vanilla • ½ cup raisins (if liked)

Soak bread in milk until soft, and mash fine. Heat together with
raisins until nearly boiling. Mix eggs with sugar, salt and vanilla. Stir
into bread and milk. Pour into a baking dish. Set in a pan of water
and bake for 1 to 1½ hours at 170°C. To make a spice pudding, add
1 teaspoon cinnamon, ½ teaspoon cloves and ¼ teaspoon nutmeg to
bread while soaking.

BUTTERSCOTCH PIE (Beverley Hills)

2 heaped teaspoons butter • 1 cup brown sugar • 2 tablespoons
flour • 2 egg yolks • 1 cup milk • 1 baked pie shell • 2 egg whites •
4 tablespoons sugar

Cream butter, 1 cup of sugar and flour together. Mix egg yolks with
milk, and bring to boiling point. Remove from heat, pour over first
mixture, and cook until thick. Pour into pie crust. Beat egg whites to
meringues with 4 tablespoons sugar. Put on top and brown in oven.

CABINET PUDDING

1 stale sponge cake • currants or sultanas • 600ml hot milk •
3 eggs, beaten

Cut up or crumble sponge cake. Put in a buttered pie dish or pudding
basin (depending on whether you are going to bake it or steam it).
Sprinkle with currants or sultanas. Make a custard with hot milk
and beaten egg. Pour this over the cake. Leave to stand a little, then
either steam for 1 hour or bake at 180°C for 30 minutes. You can use
stale fruit cake if you wish.

CARAMEL CUSTARD

2 tablespoons sugar • 3 tablespoons water • 3 eggs, beaten •
1 tablespoon sugar • 2 cups milk

Put sugar and water in a small enamel bowl. Place on range and allow to boil until brown. Tilt bowl until lined with the brown liquid. Beat eggs with sugar and add milk. Pour this custard into the bowl and steam for 30 minutes.

CHOCOLATE NUT PUDDING

60g breadcrumbs • good 60g flour • 1 dessertspoon cocoa (or more) •
1 level teaspoon baking powder • 85g sugar • 60g sultanas •
85g chopped walnuts • 60g shredded suet• 1 egg, beaten

Put all dry ingredients together. Stir in suet, egg and milk to mix if necessary. Steam in a buttered basin for 1½ to 2 hours.

CHOCOLATE PUDDING — BAKED (Boston)

This sounds queer but works out beautifully.

1 cup flour • ¼ cup sugar • ¼ teaspoon salt • 2 teaspoons baking
powder • ½ cup milk • 2 tablespoons melted butter • 1 teaspoon vanilla
essence • 2 tablespoons melted chocolate • ½ cup chopped nuts

Sift flour, sugar, salt and baking powder. Add milk, butter, vanilla, chocolate and nuts. Put into a pie dish.

Topping:
½ cup white sugar • ½ cup brown sugar • 2 rounded
tablespoons cocoa • 1 cup cold water

Mix sugar and cocoa together, and spread over the mixture in the pan. Pour the cold water all over and bake for 40 minutes, at about 170°C. Serve hot or cold. Serves 8.

COFFEE SPICE PUDDING

115g butter • 1 cup flour • 1 teaspoon baking powder • 1 teaspoon spice • 1 teacup breadcrumbs • 1 cup sugar • ½ cup strong coffee • 2 tablespoons golden syrup • 1 cup mixed dates and walnuts

Rub butter into flour, baking powder and spice sifted together. Add breadcrumbs, sugar and coffee. Mix to a soft dough and add water if necessary. Put golden syrup at the bottom of a basin, put in dates and walnuts. Add mixture, cover with greaseproof paper, and steam for about 2 hours.

CRÊPE SUZETTES

4 eggs • 3 tablespoons milk • 1 tablespoon water • 3 tablespoons flour • pinch of salt • 1 teaspoon ground almonds • pinch of ground nutmeg • 1 tablespoon butter • strawberry jam • ½ glass pony (or shot glass) Curacao • ½ glass pony (or shot glass) brandy

Stir first seven ingredients smoothly to the consistency of thick olive oil, or until will pour back silently and smoothly from 30mm or more above the bowl. Heat a small frying pan and add butter. When it bubbles, pour in enough batter to cover bottom of pan. Move pan to spread batter thinly and keep it moving. After 1 minute, turn the pancake upside down, then turn again and again until nicely browned. Spread with jam. Fold the circle in half, and again, to form a triangle. Repeat until batter is used. Pour Curacao and brandy over pancakes.

CUSTARD TART

60g butter • 115g flour • 60g cornflour • 60g sugar • ½ teaspoon
bicarbonate of soda • ¾ teaspoon cream of tartar or 1 teaspoon
baking powder • 1 egg, well beaten

Rub butter and flour, and add cornflour, sugar, bicarbonate of soda
and cream of tartar (or baking powder). Mix to a stiff dough with
egg and roll out. Line sandwich or oblong tins with the crust.

Custard:

2 breakfast cups hot milk • 2 eggs, beaten • 2 tablespoons sugar

Mix hot milk with eggs beaten with sugar. Pour on to crust
immediately before baking. Quick oven at first (220°C), then slow
down (180°C). Cook on hot scone tray or shelf. An alternative
custard is made with 2 eggs, sugar to taste, and ½ cup cream, with
nutmeg sprinkled on top.

DUTCH APPLE TART

¼ cup butter • ½ cup honey • ½ teaspoon nutmeg • 1 teaspoon
cinnamon • 2 cups flour • 1 teaspoon baking powder •
pinch of salt • ⅓ cup butter or fat • milk • 3 large cooking apples,
peeled, cored, and sliced • cream to serve

Cream first 4 ingredients together and set aside. Make a pastry by
sifting flour, baking powder and salt. Rub in ⅓ cup butter and mix
with milk to a dough. Line a well-greased tin about 20cm square.
Arrange apple on top of pastry and bake in a hot oven (220°C) for
about 30 minutes. Spread creamed mixture on top of apples. Reduce
heat and continue baking for 15 minutes. Serve with cream.

EASY PUDDING

½ cup chopped dates • ½ cup chopped sultanas or peel (or anything liked) • 1 tablespoon butter • 1 tablespoon sugar • ½ cup boiling water • 1 cup flour • 1 teaspoon baking powder • 1 teaspoon baking soda

Put fruit in a basin, add butter, sugar and boiling water. Sift in flour, baking powder and baking soda. Mix all together. Cover with buttered paper and do not tie down. Steam in the same basin for 1½ hours.

FIG PUDDING

340g figs • 1 large apple • 115g flour • 115g shredded suet • 115g breadcrumbs • 115g sugar • 1 teaspoon baking powder • milk to mix

Chop up figs and apple small. Mix with other ingredients and moisten with milk. Steam for 2½ hours.

FOUNDATION STEAMED PUDDING

60g butter • 2 tablespoons sugar • 170g flour • 1 good teaspoon baking powder • pinch of salt • 1 egg • about 2 tablespoons milk • sweet sauce to serve

Cream butter and sugar. Add flour, baking powder and salt. Mix in egg and milk. Steam for 1½ to 2 hours in a buttered basin. Serve with sweet sauce.

VARIATIONS

Raspberry Pudding:
Add 1 teaspoon raspberry essence to creamed butter and sugar. Put 1 tablespoon raspberry jam on bottom of basin. Or use strawberry essence and jam.

Chocolate Pudding:
Sift 1 tablespoon cocoa with the flour and add 1 teaspoon vanilla to creamed butter and sugar. Use an extra 1 dessertspoon milk.

Coffee Pudding:
Add 1 tablespoon coffee essence to butter and sugar, and add only 1½ tablespoons milk.

Spice Pudding:
Add 1 dessertspoon mixed spice to sifted flour and sprinkle 1 tablespoon chopped walnuts over the bottom of the basin.

GINGER PUDDING (Bella's)

84g butter • 1 cup flour • 1 dessertspoon ground ginger •
1 teaspoon spice (optional) • pinch of salt • ½ cup sultanas •
½ cup golden syrup, warmed • ½ teaspoon baking soda •
½ cup milk • custard sauce to serve

Rub butter into flour, ginger, spice and salt which have been sifted together. Add sultanas and golden syrup. Add baking soda dissolved in milk. Beat well for 2 minutes, then steam in a covered basin for 2 hours. Serve with custard sauce. You may use ½ cup shredded suet instead of butter.

GOATHLAND TREACLE TART (Yorkshire)

short pastry • 1 breakfast cup dry breadcrumbs • 1 breakfast cup
mixed fruit (sultanas, currant and peel) • 1 apple, peeled, cored
and grated • juice and grated rind of 1 lemon • 1 salt spoon spice
• 1 salt spoon ground ginger • 2 tablespoons treacle •
1 tablespoon sugar • 2 tablespoons milk • brown sugar for sprinkling

Line a pie dish with pastry. Mix all other ingredients (except milk and brown sugar) together and put over pastry. Cover with top layer of pastry. Brush over top with milk, sprinkle with brown sugar, and bake at 180°C for about 40 minutes.

GOLDEN APPLE ROLL (Baked)

170g flour • pinch of salt • ½ teaspoon baking powder •
85g shredded suet • cold water to mix • apple purée, sweetened •
clove or lemon essence

Sift flour, salt and baking powder. Add suet and mix well. Bind to a firm dough with water and roll out fairly thinly. Spread with apple purée and essence. Leave a margin of pastry all round. Roll as for jam roll and press edges firmly together. Place in a shallow greased tin, pour over golden sauce and bake in a fairly quick oven (200°C) for about 40 minutes. Baste several times.

Golden Sauce:

¼ cup golden syrup • ¾ cup boiling water • 1 tablespoon butter •
squeeze of lemon

Dissolve golden syrup in boiling water. Add butter and lemon.

GOLDEN HONEY PUDDING (Boiled)

115g chopped dates • 115g shredded suet • 115g flour •
170g breadcrumbs • 1 egg • 1 cup chopped nuts • 2 tablespoons
honey • 1 teaspoon baking soda dissolved in 1 cup milk

Grease basin and line with dates. Mix suet, flour and breadcrumbs. Mix in egg, nuts and honey. Add baking soda and milk. Boil pudding in a saucepan, with paper on top of basin and water three-quarters of the way up.

GOOSEBERRY AMBER

60g butter • 900g gooseberries • 115g caster sugar • 30g cake or
breadcrumbs • 3 egg yolks • 3 egg whites, beaten to a stiff froth •
3 tablespoons caster sugar • a few drops of vanilla essence

Melt butter in a pan. Add fruit with sugar, and let cook gently until fruit is a thick pulp. Stir in crumbs. Beat egg yolks well into mixture. Slightly butter a pie dish. Pour in mixture and put in a moderate oven (180°C). Bake until mixture is well set. Mix lightly egg whites, caster sugar and vanilla. Heap this meringue roughly all over top of the pudding and sprinkle a little caster sugar over. Put into cool part of oven until meringue is pale brown. Serve at once.

GOOSEBERRY TART

short pastry • 1 cup stewed whole gooseberries • ½ cup milk •
1 teaspoon custard powder • sugar to taste • 1 egg

Half cook pastry shell on a pie plate. Drain berries. Take half a cup of the liquid, add milk, and bring to the boil. Dissolve custard powder in the milk and stir in. Cook and stir until smooth, adding sugar to taste. Cool slightly then beat in egg. Place berries in the half-cooked shell, sprinkle with sugar and pour over the custard. Bake in a moderate oven (180°C) for 20 minutes. Serve hot or cold.

HARLEQUIN PUDDING

60g butter or shortening • 60g sugar • 1 egg • 85g flour • 1 small teaspoon baking powder • 30g custard powder • a few raisins or sultanas • 2 tablespoons milk • 2 teaspoons cocoa

Cream butter and sugar. Beat in egg, and sift in flour, baking powder and custard powder. Mix with milk to right consistency. Place raisins in bottom of a well-greased pudding basin. Add half the mixture. Mix cocoa with rest of mixture, adding a little more milk if too stiff. Put on top of first half. Steam 1½ to 2 hours.

JAM LAYER PUDDING

jam • 285g flour • 1½ teaspoons baking powder • ¼ teaspoon salt • 85g shredded suet • cold water to mix

Grease a pudding basin and put 1 tablespoon jam on bottom. Sift flour, baking powder and salt in a basin. Add suet and mix to a light dough with water. Roll out a small round of pastry and put over the jam. Add more jam, and continue with layers of jam and pastry, finishing with pastry. Cover with greased paper and steam 2 hours.

Alternative Fillings:
1. Golden syrup, grated lemon rind and breadcrumbs.
2. Chopped dates, lemon juice and golden syrup.
3. Mincemeat.
4. Any surplus tinned or stewed fruit.

LEMON MERINGUE PIE

3 egg yolks, lightly beaten • ½ cup honey • 1 tablespoon flour • juice, flesh and grated rind of ½ lemon • 1 teaspoon melted butter • 1¼ cups milk • pie crust • 3 egg whites • 3 tablespoons honey • a few drops lemon juice

Mix thoroughly egg yolks, ½ cup of honey, flour, lemon juice, flesh and rind, and butter. Add milk. Pour into a pie dish lined with a good crust pricked to prevent air bubbles. Bake until set. Cover with meringue made from egg whites beaten with honey and a few drops of lemon juice. Bake until a nice brown.

LEMON PUDDING

½ cup sugar • 1 tablespoon butter • 2 tablespoons flour • pinch of salt • rind and juice of 1 lemon • 1 cup milk • 2 eggs, separated

Beat together the sugar and butter. Add in this order: flour, salt, lemon rind and juice, milk and egg yolks. Beat egg whites until thick then fold in to lemon mixture. Bake at 190°C in a buttered pie dish standing in a dish of hot water for about 1 hour. Seems a strange mixture, but comes out with a crust on top, and like lemon cheese underneath. Very delicious. Orange can be used instead of lemon.

MARMALADE PUDDING

115g flour • 160g cornflour • 1 teaspoon baking powder • 85g butter • 2 tablespoons marmalade • 1 egg • a little milk • 60g sugar • 115g cake crumbs • marmalade sauce to serve

Sift flour, cornflour and baking powder. Rub in butter and add marmalade. Add egg, milk, sugar and cake crumbs. Bake in a greased dish in a moderate oven (180°C) for approximately 40 minutes. Serve with marmalade sauce.

NOTHING PUDDING

1 cup boiling water • 1 teaspoon baking soda •
1 dessertspoon butter • 1 cup flour • 1 cup mixed nuts •
¼ cup sugar • 1 teaspoon spice

Mix water with baking soda and butter. Mix with other ingredients and tie up in a cloth. Boil for 2 hours. This appears to be sloppy but turns out a lovely pudding.

ORANGE HOT CAKE

1 cup raisins • ½ cup walnuts • thinly peeled rind of 1 orange •
115g butter or other shortening • 2 cups sugar • 1 small teaspoon
baking soda • 1 cup sour milk • 2 eggs, beaten • pinch of salt •
115g flour • 115g wholemeal flour • 1 small teaspoon vanilla essence
• orange juice

Put raisins, walnuts and orange peel through a mincer. Set aside. Cream butter and 1 cup sugar. Dissolve baking soda in milk. Add eggs, nut mixture, baking soda and milk, alternately with salt, flour, wholemeal flour and essence. Turn into an oblong oven dish and bake in a moderate oven (180°C) for about 45 minutes. While very hot, spread with remaining 1 cup sugar mixed with a little orange juice. Serve hot.

OVERNIGHT PUDDING

1 tablespoon butter • 1 large cup boiling water • 1 heaped cup
flour • 1 heaped cup currants, raisins or sultanas, or some of each •
2 tablespoons sugar • 1 egg • pinch of salt • 1 teaspoon baking
soda • 1 teaspoon mixed spice

Melt butter in boiling water. Mix all ingredients together and leave all night. Steam next day for 3 hours. Egg may be omitted.

PANCAKES

85g flour • ½ teaspoon salt • 1 cup milk • 3 eggs, well beaten •
a little butter • sugar • lemon juice

Put flour in a basin with salt. Mix gradually with milk, working to a smooth paste. Add eggs. Have a frying pan hot, put in enough butter to grease the pan. Pour in batter to well over bottom of pan. Turn with a knife, or toss when done underneath, and brown other side. Turn out on to a hot dish, sprinkle with sugar and squeeze over a little lemon juice. Roll up and serve at once or will be tough. The batter is better if it is stood several hours and, just before cooking, add about 1 teaspoon baking powder.

PEACH CAKE (A Sweet)

1 egg, well beaten • 3 tablespoons melted butter • ½ cup milk •
1½ cups flour • ½ cup sugar • ¾ teaspoon salt • 1½ teaspoons
baking powder • ¼ teaspoon almond essence • 1 teaspoon vanilla
essence • 1 tin sliced peaches • 3 teaspoons sugar • ½ teaspoon
cinnamon • cream or sauce to serve

Mix egg with butter. Add milk. Combine flour, ½ cup sugar, salt, baking powder. Stir in gently until batter is smooth. Add essences and stir. Spread in a sandwich tin. Arrange peaches on top, pressing slightly into the batter. Sprinkle with 3 teaspoons sugar mixed with cinnamon. Bake in a moderate oven (180°C), and serve with cream or sauce.

PEACH RICE PUDDING

peaches, peeled, stoned and halved • chopped nuts • sprinkle of cinnamon or nutmeg • 1 cup cooked rice • ½ cup sugar • 2 eggs • 1 large cup milk • cream to serve

Place peaches in a baking dish, cavities uppermost. Fill cavities with nuts and spice. Make a rice custard with remaining ingredients, and pour over peaches. Bake for 30 minutes. Serve with cream.

PENNSYLVANIA PUMPKIN PIE

2 cups cooked mashed pumpkin • ½ teaspoon nutmeg • 1 teaspoon ginger • ⅛ teaspoon cloves • ⅛ teaspoon allspice • 1 teaspoon cinnamon • ½ teaspoon salt • 3 egg yolks • 1 cup dark brown sugar • 3 cups scalded milk • 3 egg whites, stiffly beaten • pastry

Mix pumpkin, spices, salt, egg yolks and sugar. Add milk. Fold in egg whites. Pour mixture into a pie dish lined with pastry brushed with egg white. Bake at 230°C for 15 minutes, then 180°C until baked. For flavouring, marmalade can be added in place of spices, and the rind and juice of 2 lemons.

PRUNE PIE WITH ORANGE CUSTARD

1½ cups prunes • 2 cups cold weak tea • grated rind and juice of 1 orange • 2 dessertspoons sugar • pastry • custard

Soak prunes overnight in tea, grated orange rind and sugar. Put prunes in a pie dish (they should come just above the level of the dish), with just enough juice to come halfway up. Cover with pastry. Prick holes for steam to escape. Make a good custard and when cooked add juice of the orange. Serve together.

RAISIN APPLE COBBLER (California)

4 tart apples, peeled, cored and sliced • 1 cup raisins • 1 cup
sugar • several knobs of butter • 1 egg • 1 cup flour, sifted • 1
teaspoon baking powder • ½ cup milk • 2 tablespoons melted
butter • vanilla essence to taste

Put apples in a buttered dish with raisins, ½ cup sugar and knobs
of butter. Beat egg until very light and add the rest of the sugar.
Mix the rest of sugar, sifted flour and baking powder and add to
mixture alternately with milk. Beat until smooth. Add melted butter
and vanilla. Pour over fruit and bake in a moderate oven (180°C) for
about 35 minutes.

RHUBARB AND BANANA BETTY

2 cups stale bread cut into small cubes • 4 tablespoons butter
• 3 cups cut up rhubarb • 1 cup brown sugar • good pinch of
cinnamon • 2 bananas, sliced • 1 tablespoon orange juice •
1 tablespoon lemon juice • 2 tablespoons water

Lightly fry bread cubes in butter until light brown. Layer rhubarb,
a sprinkle of sugar and cinnamon, bananas and bread cubes in a
buttered dish. Repeat, finishing with bread. Sprinkle top with two
juices mixed with water. Bake in a moderate oven (180°C) for 45
minutes. Eat hot or cold.

RHUBARB SWEET

450g rhubarb • water • sugar • grated rind of 1 lemon •
3 egg yolks, beaten well • 1 cup breadcrumbs • 30g butter •
pastry • 3 egg whites • 1 tablespoon sugar

Stew rhubarb with water to a pulp, sweeten and add lemon rind, eggs,
breadcrumbs and butter. Grease and line a pie dish with pastry, pour
mixture in, and bake in a hot oven (220°C). Whisk egg whites to a stiff
froth with sugar. Spread on top of pie and return to oven to set.

SAGO CREAM

3 level tablespoons sago • 2 level tablespoons sugar • 2 cups milk
• 2 egg yolks, beaten • 3 egg whites, stiffly beaten

Boil sago, sugar and milk in a double saucepan, stirring occasionally. Add egg yolks to a little hot sago and stir. Pour back into cooked sago. Pour into a buttered pie dish and stir in egg whites. Bake in medium oven (180°C) until set, and brown.

SAGO PUDDING

1 cup sago • 1¼ cups milk • 1 cup sugar • 1 cup breadcrumbs • 1 cup raisins • an egg-sized piece of butter, melted • ½ teaspoon baking soda

Soak sago in milk and leave overnight. Mix in other ingredients and steam for 3 hours.

STRAWBERRY PIE

short crust pastry, rolled thin • melted butter • 2 cups strawberries, washed and hulled • ½ cup sugar • 2 tablespoons flour • 2 teaspoons lemon juice

Line a pie dish with pastry and brush with butter. Mix strawberries with sugar and flour. Add lemon juice. Place in the prepared plate. Cover with pastry top. Slash for steam to escape. Bake in a hot oven (220°C) for 10 minutes, then turn down to moderate (180°C) for 20 minutes longer.

SPICED PRUNE PUFF

2 cups prunes, washed • 2 cups water • ¾ cup sugar • a little
cinnamon • a few cloves • rind of ½ lemon • ½ teaspoon sugar •
½ teaspoon butter • ½ teaspoon cinnamon • ½ teaspoon flour

Soak prunes overnight in the water. Stew prunes with sugar,
cinnamon, cloves and lemon rind. When tender, about 30 minutes
to one hour, pour into a dish. Spread Puff Top mixture over prunes
and bake in a moderate oven (180°C) for 30 minutes. While pie is
still hot, spread with a mixture of sugar, butter, cinnamon and flour.
Serve hot or cold.

Puff Top:

⅓ cup butter or dripping • ½ cup sugar • 1 egg, beaten •
1 cup flour • 1 dessertspoon cinnamon • ½ teaspoon baking
powder • ½ cup milk

Cream butter and sugar, and add egg. Sift in lightly the flour, baking
powder and cinnamon. Lastly add the milk to make a mixture that
will drop from a spoon.

SPONGE CRUST

1 egg • 1 teacup sugar (or less) • 30g butter • 3 tablespoons milk
(or more) • 1 breakfast cup flour • vanilla (if liked) • pinch of salt •
hot fruit

Beat egg and sugar. Melt butter with milk and add. Stir in flour,
vanilla and salt. Pour over hot fruit. Cook in a hot oven (220°C) for
about 20 minutes.

SUET DUMPS

2 cups flour • 2 small teaspoons baking powder • pinch of salt •
1 cup finely shredded suet • 1 cup golden syrup • ½ cup sugar •
2 cups boiling water • rind and juice of 2 or 3 lemons

Mix flour, baking powder, salt and suet to a paste with water, and make into little balls. Boil golden syrup, sugar, water, and lemon juice and rind. Pop in the little balls. Keep boiling for 30 minutes. Serve with the liquid.

TENTERDEN APPLE PIE

1.35kg cooking apples • 115g sugar • cloves • ½ teacup water •
115g cheese, cut into thin slices • pepper • nutmeg • ½ teaspoon
caster sugar • short pastry, rolled out

Peel, core and cut apples into thick slices. Place a layer of apples in a pie dish. Sprinkle with 1 tablespoon sugar. Add another layer of apples and sugar, and the cloves. Pour in the water. Cover the apples with cheese. Sprinkle with the merest suggestion of pepper, a little nutmeg and the caster sugar. Line edge of the pie dish with pastry and put on pastry cover. Press edges together and raise them slightly with a knife. Sprinkle with caster sugar and bake in a good oven (180°C) for 40 to 50 minutes.

TOFFEE APPLE PUDDING

225g flour • 140g shredded suet • 1 teaspoon baking powder •
pinch of salt • water to mix • apples, cored, peeled, sliced and
cooked • 6 teaspoons brown sugar

Mix flour, suet, baking powder, salt and water, and roll out thin.
Carefully cover sides of a pie dish with Toffee. Line the dish with
half the suet crust. Pile in plenty of apples. Sprinkle with brown
sugar. Cover with remaining crust. Bake in a hot oven (220°C) for
1¼ hours, or until done. This pudding may be served from the pie
dish. Or turn out on to a separate dish and the rich toffee sauce will
be seen to cover it.

Toffee:

60g butter • 60g brown sugar

Mix together.

YORKSHIRE PUDDING

1 cup flour • salt to taste • milk • 2 eggs •
2 tablespoons cold water

Put flour and salt in a basin, make a hole in the middle, and pour in
a little milk. Break eggs into mixture and beat to a smooth batter.
Add cold water. Beat again for a minute or two. Grease a meat tin
and pour in mixture (or pour into small saucers or tiny dishes). Bake
at 200°C for 20 to 30 minutes. Have greased dishes very hot which
makes pudding light.

SWEET SAUCES

BANANA SAUCE

1 cup icing sugar • ⅓ cup butter, creamed • 1 banana, mashed •
1 egg white, well beaten • a little lemon juice

Add icing sugar to creamed butter gradually. Mix in other ingredients and beat together.

BUTTERSCOTCH SAUCE

½ cup white sugar • ½ cup brown sugar • 2 tablespoons golden syrup • ½ cup cold water • 1½ tablespoons butter • ¼ cup hot water • ½ teaspoon vanilla

Cook white sugar, brown sugar, golden syrup and cold water together until a little dropped into cold water becomes quite brittle. Take from stove, and beat in butter, hot water and vanilla. Serve hot.

CHOCOLATE SAUCE (Hot)

4 tablespoons unsweetened chocolate • 1½ cups sugar • ¼ cup cold water • ½ teaspoon vanilla essence • ¼ cup boiling water

Dissolve chocolate in a basin over a pan of hot water. Boil sugar and cold water together for 5 minutes. Let cool. When cool, stir in chocolate and vanilla. Keep hot in a double boiler or basin over hot water until ready to serve. At the last minute, add the boiling water.

CUSTARD (Thin)

1 cup milk • 1 egg • 1½ tablespoons sugar • pinch of salt •
¼ teaspoon essence of choice

Scald milk. Beat egg and sugar. Pour the milk over, and return to double boiler, stirring until it coats the base of a spoon. Cool, add salt and essence, and strain if necessary. Half a teaspoon of cornflour beaten with the egg and sugar keeps it extra smooth.

FOAMY SAUCE

6 tablespoons butter • 1 cup icing sugar • 3 egg yolks, beaten until thick • 3 egg whites, stiffly beaten • 1 teaspoon vanilla essence • 2 tablespoons boiling water

Cream butter and sugar slowly, beating continually. Add egg yolks and beat well. Add egg whites, essence and water. Before serving, heat over boiling water for 5 minutes, stirring constantly.

FOUNDATION DESSERT SAUCE

1 tablespoon cornflour • ½ cup sugar • pinch of salt • 1 cup hot water • 1 egg yolk, beaten • 2 tablespoons butter • 2 teaspoons vanilla • 1 egg white, beaten

Mix cornflour, sugar and salt. Gradually add the hot water and cook until thick, stirring constantly. Add egg yolk and cook a minute or two. Add butter and vanilla. Cool a little then fold in egg white.

Lemon Sauce:
Omit vanilla. Add 2 tablespoons lemon juice and 1 teaspoon grated rind.

Nutmeg Sauce:
Add 1 teaspoon ground nutmeg.

Chocolate Sauce:

Add 1 tablespoon unsweetened chocolate, or 1 dessertspoon cocoa, blended with the cornflour and sugar.

FUDGE SAUCE

½ cup cocoa • 1 cup water • 2 cups sugar • a little salt •
2 tablespoons butter • 2 teaspoons vanilla

Mix cocoa and water, and cook until smooth. Add sugar and salt, and stir until dissolved. Cook for 5 minutes. Add butter and vanilla, and serve at once.

FRUIT SAUCE

1 cup fruit juice and pulp • ½ teaspoon lemon juice •
½ tablespoon cornflour • ¼ to ½ cup sugar, as needed
sprinkle of nutmeg

Mix fruit juices and bring to boiling point. Mix cornflour with a little cold water, and add to mixture. Sweeten to taste. Add nutmeg and bring to the boil, stirring all the time. Serve hot.

HARD SAUCE (Foundation Recipe)

½ cup butter • 2 cups caster sugar • 1 teaspoon vanilla essence •
½ teaspoon lemon juice or essence • 1 tablespoon hot water

Cream the butter. Add sugar gradually, beating until fluffy. Add essences and hot water and pile in sauce dish.

Molasses Hard Sauce:

Add 2 or 3 tablespoons molasses to Hard Sauce, and work in smoothly. Black treacle could be used.

Spiced Hard Sauce:
Add half a teaspoon of cinnamon, nutmeg, ginger and cloves to the Foundation Hard Sauce.

Marmalade Hard Sauce:
Add 3 tablespoons marmalade to the Hard Sauce while beating.

Ginger Hard Sauce:
Add 4 tablespoons finely crushed Ginger Snaps to Hard Sauce.

MAPLE SYRUP (Mock)

¼ cup honey • ¼ cup golden syrup • ¼ cup boiling water • a squeeze of lemon juice

Blend together.

Alternative: golden syrup warmed in a little water and a little lemon juice.

MARMALADE SAUCE

15g cornflour • grated rind and juice of 1 lemon • 1½ cups water • 1 tablespoon marmalade • 1 tablespoon sugar

Dissolve cornflour in a basin with lemon juice. Bring the water to the boil in a saucepan and add lemon rind. Pour this boiling water over cornflour and re-boil it. Add marmalade and sugar.

MELBA SAUCE

1 cup fresh or tinned raspberries • ¼ cup sugar

Put raspberries through a sieve. Add sugar, and cook gently for 5 minutes. Let cool. Keep in a cool place until needed.

ORANGE SAUCE

¼ cup sugar • 1 tablespoon cornflour • 1 cup boiling water •
1 tablespoon butter • ¼ cup orange juice • 1 teaspoon lemon
essence • ½ cup orange sections (or 1 medium orange cut into
sections) • gingerbread or stale cake to serve

Mix sugar and cornflour on top of a double boiler. Add water and
cook, stirring, until thick and smooth. Remove, add butter and
stir until melted. Add orange juice and lemon essence. Add orange
sections. Serve over gingerbread or stale cake.

PINEAPPLE SAUCE

1 dessertspoon butter • 1½ tablespoons sugar •
1 good dessertspoon cornflour • pinch of salt • ½ cup crushed
pineapple • ½ cup hot water • 1 dessertspoon lemon juice

Mix together butter, sugar, cornflour and salt. Add mix of crushed
pineapple and water and boil for 5 minutes, stirring constantly. Then
add lemon juice. Serve hot.

Raisin Nut Sauce:
Omit pineapple and add ½ cup chopped raisins and nuts, and
1 teaspoon grated orange rind, mixed together.

SAVOURY SAUCES

INTRODUCTION
Sauces give extra flavour and a luxury touch to any dish. They can also make a small serving go further — a little minced ham in a white sauce helps out with potato cakes; an egg sauce with fish cakes, and so on.

A LA KING SAUCE
(Makes Leftovers Into Luxuries)

3 tablespoons butter or margarine • ½ large green pepper cut in squares • ½ red pepper, cut in squares • ½ cup shredded mushrooms • 3 tablespoons flour • ½ teaspoon salt • a shake of pepper • 1½ cups milk • 1 egg yolk, beaten • dash of dry sherry • bits of chicken, veal, slices hard-boiled eggs, flaked cooked fish or tinned fish, chopped crayfish

Melt butter in a small frying pan. Add peppers and mushrooms, and cook slowly. Stir in flour and seasonings. Add milk gradually, stirring all the time. When sauce boils, turn heat low. Pour sauce into beaten egg yolk. Put all in a double boiler. Add sherry and whatever meat or fish you are going to serve it in. This is often served on hot buttered toast.

APPLE SAUCE (For Duck, Roast Pork, etc.)

apples, sliced • water • sugar (if liked)

Put apples with hardly any water in a saucepan and cook on a low heat until soft. Then mash and beat with fork. Very little sugar may be added.

BARBECUE SAUCE (American)

115g butter • 1¼ cups water • 3 tablespoons Worcestershire sauce • 2 tablespoons tomato sauce • 2 tablespoons lemon juice • 1 teaspoon sugar • salt and pepper to taste

Mix all together and simmer about 8 minutes. Good on roast or grilled meat, or used to baste veal or pork chops while grilling.

BECHAMEL SAUCE

Make a white sauce (see page 123) using half chicken broth and half milk.

BREAD SAUCE (With Fowl, Turkey, etc.)

7 cloves • ~~1 medium white onion~~ • 2 cups milk • 1 cup fresh white bread (no crusts), finely broken into small pieces • 2 tablespoons butter • ¾ teaspoon salt • ¼ teaspoon white pepper (or pinch of cayenne pepper)

Stick cloves into ~~the onion and~~ place in milk. Put on stove and simmer for at least 30 minutes (double boiler is best). Pour boiling milk through strainer on to bread. Let soak at least 1 hour. Add butter, salt and pepper, and reheat, beating well.

CHEESE SAUCE (For Cabbage or Sprouts)

30g butter • 30g wholemeal or white flour • 1 cup milk • 85g grated cheese • sprouts or cabbage • a little more grated cheese

Melt butter, stir in flour, and cook. Gradually add milk, cook and let thicken nicely. Add cheese and melt. Put over sprouts or cabbage, with a little more grated cheese on top. Pop in oven, or put under griller to melt cheese and brown the whole.

CHILLI SAUCE (Quick)

▓▓▓▓▓▓▓▓▓▓▓ • 1 tablespoon vegetable oil • 1 teaspoon pickle spices • 4 hot peppers, minced • 4 cups canned tomatoes • ½ teaspoon salt • 2 teaspoons sugar

▓▓▓▓▓▓▓▓▓▓▓▓▓▓. Tie spices in cheesecloth, add remaining ingredients and simmer until smooth and thick. Remove spices. Chill and use.

CLARET GRAVY (For Meatballs or Ham or Reheated Sliced Veal or Beef)

½ cup rich brown soup • 1 cup red wine • 1 tablespoon lemon juice • 1 teaspoon sugar • ½ tablespoon grated horseradish (optional) • dash of paprika or other pepper • salt to taste

Combine ingredients. Heat, gradually, to boiling point. Serve at once.

CRANBERRY SAUCE (For Turkey)

450g cranberries • 450g sugar • ½ cup cold water

Place ingredients in a saucepan and boil slowly for 20 minutes. As cranberries boil, a foam will form on top. Skim this off from time to time. After boiling 20 minutes, remove from stove and chill. Do not mash. Serve them just as they are; the berries will be whole and transparent, and the juice a heavy jelly when cold.

CREAM SAUCE
(For Creamed Leftover Meats or Vegetables)

2 tablespoons butter • 2 tablespoons flour • 1 cup milk •
¼ teaspoon salt (or season to taste) • ⅛ teaspoon pepper

Melt butter in upper part of a double boiler, or over low flame. Add flour and stir until well blended. Pour milk in, stirring constantly, until sauce thickens. Add salt and pepper, stirring thoroughly. Cook until raw starch taste has left the sauce — about 3 minutes.

CURRY SAUCE
(For Reheating Minced or Chopped Cold Meat)

dripping or butter • onion, chopped • curry powder • sugar •
hot water • a few sultanas • vinegar • chutney • best cornflour •
chopped meat • dry boiled rice or mashed potatoes, and a green
vegetable, to serve

Melt dripping or butter in a saucepan. When very hot add onion. Fry until brown, stirring often. Add curry powder to taste and continue frying and stirring for a minute or two. Sprinkle with sugar and stir again. Add hot water, according to how much sauce you require. Stir well, add sultanas and cook over a low heat until onion is soft. Taste, and add sugar to taste, a little vinegar and chutney. Thicken with cornflour mixed with a little water, stirring all the time. This sauce can be made beforehand (but not thickened), if desired. When mealtime comes, just warm the sauce, stirring, and add chopped meat, just until all is very hot, but not to boil or re-cook the meat. Serve with rice or mashed potatoes and a green vegetable.

EGG SAUCE (For Boiled Fish)

Make a white sauce (see page 123) and add finely chopped hard-boiled eggs.

GOOSEBERRY SAUCE
(With Pork, Fish or Poultry)

2 large cups gooseberries • 1 large cup water • 1 tablespoon butter • 1 tablespoon sugar • salt and pepper • nutmeg

Cook gooseberries and water until soft. Put though a sieve and return to pan. Stir in butter, sugar and seasoning, and make hot without boiling. Serve hot with pork, fish, duck, etc.

GRAVY

meat drippings • 2 tablespoons flour • salt and pepper to taste • 1 cup hot water

Make gravy in the pan the meat was roasted in. Pour off fat very carefully leaving about 2 tablespoons good brown part and meat juice in bottom of pan. Sift in flour, salt and pepper, stirring and mixing so no lumps are left, over a low heat. Stir in hot water, raise heat a little and stir constantly so meat juices are all mixed in. Any commercial gravy mixes are very suitable for adding, instead of plain water. Follow the directions.

HOLLANDAISE SAUCE (For Hot Asparagus, Broccoli, Corn, Cabbage, etc.)

2 egg yolks • ½ teaspoon salt • dash of cayenne pepper • ½ cup melted butter or margarine • 1 tablespoon lemon juice

Beat egg yolks until thick and lemon coloured. Add salt and cayenne. Add 3 tablespoons melted butter, a little at a time, beating constantly. Slowly beat in rest of butter alternately with lemon juice.

HORSERADISH SAUCE

2 tablespoons grated horseradish • 1 dessertspoon mustard •
3 dessertspoons sugar • 3 dessertspoons malt vinegar •
4 tablespoons whipped cream • a little salt and pepper

Mix all well together.

MAITRE D'HOTEL BUTTER (For Grilled Steak or Fish or Cooked Vegetables)

¼ cup butter or margarine • 1 tablespoon minced parsley •
4 tablespoons lemon juice • ½ teaspoon salt • dash of cayenne
pepper • ▓▓▓▓▓▓▓▓▓▓▓▓ or 2 teaspoons minced red or
green pepper (if desired)

Work butter with a spoon in a bowl until creamy. Stirring constantly, add very slowly parsley, salt, pepper and lemon juice. You may add ▓▓▓▓▓▓▓▓ minced red or green pepper.

MINT SAUCE

mint, washed, leaves pulled off and stalks discarded • a little sugar
• boiling water • vinegar

Put mint on a chopping board, sprinkle with sugar and chop very finely. Put in a sauce boat and barely cover with boiling water. Leave to stand a few minutes to draw out flavour. Add vinegar and sugar to taste. Stir well.

MUSHROOM CREAM SAUCE

450g mushrooms, peeled and cut up • 2 tablespoons butter •
½ teaspoon salt • 1 teaspoon paprika • 1 cup cream

Fry mushrooms, turning often, in butter for about 10 minutes. Stir in salt and paprika, then cream. Simmer slowly to a thick sauce. Serve with cutlets or steak.

MUSTARD SAUCE (American)

1 tablespoon melted butter or margarine • 2 tablespoons flour • 1 cup boiling water • 2 beef bouillon cubes • 3 tablespoons prepared mustard • 1 tablespoon Worcestershire sauce

Blend butter and flour in a saucepan. Stir in the boiling water and bouillon cubes. Cook until thickened. Add prepared mustard and Worcestershire sauce. Serve hot or cold with sliced ham or other meats.

ONION SAUCE

onions, peeled and sliced • salt • milk • best cornflour • salt and pepper • a good knob of butter • chopped parsley (if desired)

Boil sliced onions in water with salt until very soft. Strain and chop finely. Cover with milk and bring to the boil. Thicken with cornflour first moistened with milk. Add salt and pepper to taste, finally, butter. A little chopped parsley may be added.

ORANGE SAUCE (For Duck)

3 tablespoons fat from pan in which duck has been roasted • 3 tablespoons flour • 2 tablespoons finely shredded orange rind • 2 tablespoons currant jelly • ¾ cup orange juice • ¾ cup water • salt and pepper (if needed)

Leave fat in roasting pan, add the flour, and stir until smooth. Simmer orange rind in a little water until tender. Add to pan with currant jelly, orange juice and water. Stir and cook until smooth and thickened. Add salt and pepper if needed.

PORTUGUESE RAW GRAVY
(For Roast Lamb or Fish)

~~...~~ • 2 tablespoons finely minced parsley • ½ tablespoon fresh mint • ¼ cup vinegar • ¼ cup water • pinch of salt • pinch of sugar (optional)

Combine all carefully.

TARTARE SAUCE (For Fish)

1 cup mayonnaise dressing (see pages 127–128) • 1 tablespoon finely chopped olives • 1 tablespoon finely chopped pickles • 1 tablespoon finely chopped parsley • 1 tablespoon finely chopped chives (if desired)

Mix together and serve.

TOMATO SAUCE (Fresh)

3 tablespoons butter • 3 tablespoons flour • a little salt • tomato purée • ¼ teaspoon ground cloves • 1 tablespoon sugar • ½ teaspoon allspice • pepper to taste

Melt butter. Add flour and salt. Blend very well. Then, as if making a white sauce, pour in the tomato purée instead of milk. Add cloves, sugar, allspice and pepper. Very nice with cold meats, etc.

VINAIGRETTE SAUCE

3 tablespoons sweet pickle relish • 2 tablespoons minced parsley • ¾ teaspoon sugar • 1 teaspoon salt • 6 tablespoons vinegar • ¾ cup salad or olive oil

Combine all ingredients. Beat thoroughly to blend. Serve on asparagus (hot or cold), broccoli, Brussels sprouts.

WHITE SAUCE (Foundation)

2 tablespoons butter • 2 tablespoons flour (wholemeal if liked) • pinch of salt and pepper • 1¾ cups milk

Melt butter. Stir in flour and seasoning, removing pan from heat as you do so. Gradually stir in milk, and continue stirring. Bring to the boil and cook until thick.

Thick White Sauce:
Use more butter and flour, but the same quantity of milk.

Piquant Sauce:
Make white sauce, but when cooked add 1 egg yolk beaten with 1 tablespoon vinegar.

Parsley Sauce:
Add 2 or 3 tablespoons of finely chopped parsley just before serving.

Cheese Sauce:
Add ½ cup or more of grated cheese, ¼ teaspoon dry mustard, a few drops Worcestershire sauce, and a few drops of lemon juice.

Crayfish Sauce:
Add chopped crayfish, or tinned shrimps, or lobster.

SALAD DRESSINGS

BOILED DRESSING

¾ teaspoon salt • 1 teaspoon dry mustard • 1½ teaspoons sugar • pinch of cayenne pepper • 1½ teaspoons cornflour • 1 egg or 2 egg yolks, slightly beaten • 1½ teaspoons melted butter • ¾ cup milk • ¼ cup vinegar

Mix dry ingredients. Add eggs, butter, milk and vinegar. Cook over hot water until mixture thickens. Pour into a glass jar. Store, and use as needed. [Note: the 'cooking over hot water' can be done using a double boiler, or in a bowl placed over a saucepan of simmering water.]

COTTAGE CHEESE DRESSING

½ cup cottage cheese • ½ cup evaporated milk • ½ cup lemon juice • 1 tablespoon honey or sugar • ½ teaspoon salt • dash of paprika • 1 tablespoon chopped chives

Beat all ingredients together until smooth. Makes 1⅓ cups.

CUCUMBER CREAM DRESSING

2 tablespoons lemon juice • 1 cup heavy whipped cream • dash of cayenne pepper • ¼ teaspoon salt • dash of white pepper • ¾ cup grated cucumber, drained

Stir lemon juice gradually into whipped cream, add seasonings and cucumber. Serve with fish or aspic.

EVERYDAY SALAD DRESSING

1 salt spoon salt • 1 teaspoon mustard • 1 dessertspoon sugar •
1 tablespoon full milk (or cream) • 2 tablespoons vinegar •
4 tablespoons milk

Mix salt, mustard and sugar with cream. Drop in vinegar, stirring all
the time. Add milk very slowly.

FRENCH DRESSING

1 cup olive oil • 1 teaspoon salt • ⅓ teaspoon pepper • 1 teaspoon
sugar • ¼ teaspoon paprika • ⅓ cup vinegar or ¼ cup lemon juice

Combine oil and seasonings. Gradually beat in vinegar. Keep in a
cool place. Shake before using.

GOLDEN SYRUP DRESSING

Any boiled salad dressing may be made by adding golden syrup
instead of sugar. Some people prefer it to sugar.

HONOLULU SALAD DRESSING

1 tin tomato soup • ¼ cup sugar • ½ cup vinegar • ½ cup salad oil •
1 teaspoon Worcestershire sauce • 1 teaspoon mustard •
~~1 tablespoon grated onion~~

Put all in a jar and shake well.

ITALIAN DRESSING

3 parts salad oil to 1 part vinegar • salt and pepper • ~~a few drops onion juice (if desired)~~

Drop oil slowly into vinegar. Add salt and pepper to taste. ~~Add onion juice (if using).~~

LEMON FRENCH DRESSING

½ cup olive or salad oil • ½ cup lemon juice • ½ teaspoon salt •
a few grains of cayenne pepper • 2 tablespoons sugar or honey

Combine all ingredients and shake well before using. Makes 1 cup. Variations using 1 cup Lemon French Dressing:

Cream Cheese Ginger:
Beat 2 tablespoons each of cream cheese and chopped ginger.

Fruit:
2 tablespoons each of lemon, lime, pineapple and orange juice instead of ½ cup lemon juice.

Maraschino:
Add 1 tablespoon chopped toasted almonds and 1 tablespoon minced maraschino cherries.

Mint:
Add 2 tablespoons chopped mint.

Orange:
Use ¼ cup orange juice or ¼ cup lemon juice and reduce sugar to 1 teaspoon.

Pineapple:
Use ¼ cup pineapple juice instead of ¼ cup lemon juice and reduce sugar to 1 teaspoon.

LYALL BAY DRESSING

yolk of 1 hard-boiled egg • salt, pepper and mustard to taste •
1 small tin cream • vinegar

Mash hard-boiled egg yolk with salt, pepper and mustard to taste.
Mix with cream. Break down with vinegar to correct consistency.

MAGIC MAYONNAISE

¼ cup vinegar or lemon juice • ½ cup salad oil or melted butter •
⅔ cup sweetened condensed milk • 1 teaspoon dry mustard •
1 egg yolk, unbeaten • ½ teaspoon salt • few grains of cayenne
pepper

Place ingredients in a 500ml jar. Fasten top and shake vigorously for
2 minutes. Chill before serving. May be made by stirring ingredients
in a bowl.

MAYONNAISE

395g tin sweetened condensed milk • ¾ of condensed milk tin
of vinegar, then filled to brim with water • 1 teaspoon salt •
1 teaspoon pepper • 1 teaspoon mustard • 1 or 2 eggs (if liked)

Add vinegar and water to milk and seasonings and beat all together
with rotary beater. Beat in eggs (if using), but it is just as nice without.
This recipe fills a 1 litre preserving jar.

MAYONNAISE (Five Minute)

1 egg yolk • pinch of salt • ½ teaspoon sugar • 1 teaspoon
mustard • 4 tablespoons olive oil • lemon juice

Beat the first 4 ingredients well. Add olive oil gradually, whipping
constantly. Add lemon juice to taste.

PINEAPPLE CREAM DRESSING

3 egg yolks • ½ cup sugar • 5 tablespoons lemon juice • ½ cup
pineapple juice • dash of salt • ½ cup whipped cream

Beat egg yolks and sugar together. Add fruit juices and salt. Cook
on top of a double boiler until mixture thickens. Cool and fold in
cream.

Orange:
Use orange juice instead of pineapple.

QUICK MAYONNAISE

1 egg • 1 teaspoon salt • 1 teaspoon sugar • ½ teaspoon mustard •
⅛ teaspoon paprika • 1 tablespoon vinegar • 1 cup salad oil •
1 tablespoon lemon juice

Beat egg, salt, sugar and seasonings together until thick. Add vinegar
and beat well. Add oil slowly, 1 teaspoon at a time, beating well
between each addition. When half the oil is added, the remainder
may be added alternately with lemon juice. For a thicker mayonnaise,
use 1 or 2 egg yolks in place of the whole egg.

SALAD DRESSING (1)

1 small cup sugar • 2 eggs • 1 dessertspoon salt • 1 small cup
malt vinegar • 1 tablespoon butter • 1 teaspoon mustard • cream
or top milk

Blend well together, and cook slowly until it thickens. Do not let it
boil. This keeps indefinitely and is sufficient for several salads. Add
cream to taste each time, or top milk.

SALAD DRESSING (2)

1 egg • 1 salt spoon salt • 1 mustard spoon of made mustard •
4 dessertspoons water • 1 teaspoon sugar • 2 dessertspoons
vinegar • butter the size of a walnut

Beat egg well and put with other ingredients in a saucepan. Stir over
heat until thick, but do not boil.

SOUR CREAM DRESSING

2 hard-boiled egg yolks • 1 cup sour cream • 1 teaspoon lemon
juice • ½ teaspoon sugar • dash of salt and pepper

Press egg yolks through a sieve and beat into sour cream. Beat in
lemon juice, sugar and seasonings. Makes 1¼ cups.

SOUR CREAM SALAD DRESSING
(Uncooked)

1 tablespoon sugar • ¼ teaspoon salt • a little pepper • 1 teaspoon
lemon juice • 2 tablespoons vinegar • ½ cup sour cream, whipped

Mix sugar, salt and pepper in a bowl. Add lemon juice and vinegar.
Stir this mixture gradually into cream. Serve on cabbage, cucumbers
or lettuce.

THOUSAND ISLAND DRESSING (1)

½ cup mayonnaise (see pages 127–128) • 2 teaspoons chopped
chives • 2 tablespoons ketchup • 2 tablespoons chilli sauce •
2 hard-boiled eggs, chopped • ½ cup cream • 2 tablespoons
chopped red peppers

Combine and chill well.

THOUSAND ISLAND DRESSING (2)

1 cup mayonnaise (see pages 127–128) • ½ tablespoon minced chives • 5 tablespoons chilli sauce • 1 red pepper, chopped

Combine and chill well.

THOUSAND ISLAND DRESSING (3)

1 cup mayonnaise (see pages 127–128) • 2 tablespoons chopped sweet pickle • 2 tablespoons chopped green olives • 2 tablespoons chopped capers • 2 tablespoons chopped parsley

Easiest, but not quite correct. Mix all ingredients together.

WHIPPED CREAM DRESSING

⅔ cup sugar • 2 tablespoons flour • 2 eggs, beaten • 2 tablespoons salad oil • 3 tablespoons lemon juice • 4 tablespoons orange juice • 1 cup pineapple juice • ½ cup heavy cream, whipped

Combine sugar and flour in top of a double boiler. Add remaining ingredients except cream, and cook until thickened, stirring constantly. When cool, fold in cream. Makes 2 cups.

Ginger:
Add 3 teaspoons chopped crystallised ginger.

PASTRY

BISCUIT PASTRY

115g butter • 60g sugar • 1 egg yolk • 1 tablespoon water • 225g flour, sifted • ¼ teaspoon baking powder • 1 teaspoon lemon juice • salt

Soften together butter and sugar, adding egg yolk and water, followed by flour, baking powder and lemon juice.

CHEESE PASTRY

60 to 85g cheese • short pastry

Add together. Use for apple pies or savoury tart shells.

CHOUX PASTRY (For Cream Puffs)

½ cup boiling water • 60g butter • 85g flour • 2 whole eggs • 1 egg yolk • pinch of salt

Put water and butter in a pan and place over medium heat. When butter has dissolved, add flour at once, remove from heat, and beat free of lumps. Return to heat until mixture leaves side of the pan clean. Remove from heat and let cool a little. Break in 1 egg and beat well using a wooden spoon. Add other egg and extra yolk, and beat again until pastry has a shiny appearance.

To cook:

Have hot oven, about 220°C. Drop spoonfuls on hot floured tray and bake until well puffed up and browned (about 20 to 30 minutes according to size). Remove from tray, split open and remove any soft part. When quite cold fill with cream or savoury mixture. Do not open oven door for first 20 minutes. A pinch of alum added when beating in the eggs keeps them dry. Some people prefer a cold greased oven tray to a hot floured one. If making the Choux pastry into éclairs, use a forcer and put them in finger lengths on a cold greased oven tray. For savouries, make them small. For éclairs, ice when cool with a little chocolate icing.

FLAKY PASTRY

450g butter or margarine • 450g flour • salt • ¼ teaspoon cream of tartar • water to mix

Cut butter to size of walnuts and mix in flour, salt, cream of tartar. Roll out and fold like a sponge roll. Let stand a little while and roll out twice more — is ready for use. This makes a nice flaky pastry.

FLEUR PASTRY

170g flour • 100g butter • ¼ teaspoon baking powder • pinch of salt • 30g caster sugar • 1 egg yolk

Sift all dry ingredients into a bowl. Rub butter lightly into flour. Add egg yolk. Work into a pliable dough. Suitable for cases, and open tarts.

GOOD PASTRY FOR HOUSEWIVES

450g flour • 115g fat, preferably butter • ½ teaspoon salt • 1 level tablespoon lemon juice

Work in the ordinary way with enough cold water to requisite consistency. Roll out once. Wrap up in one piece greased paper and put away on shelf. This is to be done in the cool of the evening. Next day roll it twice and there is your pastry ready to be put on the pie.

PASTRY (With Dripping)

1 cup good clean dripping • 1 cup milk • 2 cups flour • 1 teaspoon baking powder • salt

Cream dripping, add milk slowly — the more creamed the better. Then sift flour and baking powder and salt, and roll.

PASTRY (With Vinegar)

115g cup good dripping • 2 teaspoons vinegar • 1 large cup flour • 1 teaspoon baking powder • milk to mix

Cream dripping and add vinegar. Whip well. Add flour and baking powder, and enough milk to mix.

PUFF PASTRY (Rough)

395g flour • 1 good teaspoon baking powder • ½ teaspoon salt •
225g butter • ¾ breakfast cup cold water • 1 dessertspoon
lemon juice

Sift dry ingredients. Chop in butter coarsely with a knife. Mix with
lemon juice and water to a fairly stiff dough. Roll out, and fold in
twice to resemble an envelope. Turn rough edges to the right. Repeat
this 4 times. This pastry is good for fruit and meat pies.

SHORT PIE CRUST

115g dripping • 225g flour • 1 teaspoon cream of tartar •
½ teaspoon baking soda • small ½ cup water

Cream dripping. Rub into flour sifted with cream of tartar. Dissolve
soda in the water and add. Roll out and put on either meat or fruit
pie, or use for tarts.

BISCUITS AND SMALL CAKES

AFGHANS

Ordinary Recipe: • 170g butter • 85g sugar • 170g flour •
pinch of salt • 1 tablespoon cocoa • 60g cornflakes

Cream butter and sugar. Add dry ingredients. Roll into balls and cook on a cold tray in a moderate oven (180°C).

Variation:
Substitute 60g cornflour for cornflakes, or 30g cornflour and 2 tablespoons cornflakes. Add about 2 tablespoons boiling water when creaming butter and sugar. When cold, ice with chocolate icing, and put a piece of walnut on top.

ALMOND SHORTBREAD

285g butter • 115g icing sugar • 30g cornflour • 30g ground
almonds • 285g flour • salt

Cream butter and sugar together, gradually adding dry ingredients. Work into a firm smooth paste. Roll out evenly on a baking sheet, or cut into shapes as required. Cook in a moderate oven (180°C).

ALMOND FINGERS

115g flour • ¼ teaspoon baking powder • good pinch of salt •
60g butter • 115g sugar • 38g ground almonds •
1 egg yolk, beaten • 1 egg white, beaten • 60g icing sugar •
30g chopped almonds

Sift flour, baking powder and salt. Rub in butter, add sugar and ground almonds and mix with egg yolk to a stiff paste. Roll out oblong on a floured board. Mix egg white and icing sugar. Spread over paste and sprinkle chopped almonds over. Cut into fingers. Bake on a greased tray in a moderate oven (180°C) for 10 to 15 minutes.

ANZAC BISCUITS

115g butter • 1 tablespoon golden syrup • 1 teaspoon baking powder dissolved in 2 tablespoons boiling water • 1 cup sugar •
1 cup coconut • 1 cup wheatmeal • 1 cup chopped walnuts •
¾ cup flour

Melt butter with golden syrup. Add baking powder. Add all other ingredients. Take small teaspoonfuls and roll into balls. Place on a cold oven sheet, leaving space between each. Cook for 30 minutes in a slow oven (120°C).

AOTEA DATE KISSES

450g butter • 340g sugar • 4 egg yolks • 45g cocoa • 790g flour •
1 teaspoon baking powder • 4 egg whites, beaten • dates

Cream butter and sugar. Add egg yolks then cocoa. Add sifted flour and baking powder. Mix well and roll into little balls. Press a date in centre. Brush with egg white. Cook in a moderate oven (180°C) for 15 to 20 minutes. Makes about 84 kisses.

BIFFS

85g butter • ½ breakfast cup brown sugar • 1 egg • 1 breakfast cup cornflakes • ½ teaspoon baking powder • ¼ teaspoon vanilla essence • ½ cup walnuts • 1 salt spoon of salt • 1 teacup flour

Mix into a firm dough and shape into rounds. Place on greased trays and bake in a moderate oven (180°C) for 15 to 20 minutes.

BRANDY SNAPS (Old Fashioned)

170g butter • 170g golden syrup • 170g sugar • 2 teaspoons ground ginger • ½ teaspoon lemon essence • ½ teaspoon vanilla • 170g flour

Put all ingredients except flour into a saucepan and allow to warm slightly until butter is melted. Mix in flour. Drop in small teaspoonfuls on a greased oven tray, leaving plenty of room to spread. Bake at 180°C for about 10 minutes.

BRIAN O'BRIEN'S BRAN BISCUITS

115g butter • 1 cup sugar • 1 cup flour • 1 heaped cup bran • 1 teaspoon baking powder • 1 egg

Cream butter and sugar. Mix in other ingredients. Roll out and cut into rounds. Bake on a greased oven tray at 180°C for 15 minutes.

BUMBLE BEES

1 cup chopped dates • ½ cup walnuts • ½ cup preserved ginger • ½ cup figs • 1 cup sultanas or raisins • 1 cup coconut • 1 small tin condensed milk

Mix all together and squeeze into oval shapes. Put on a greased tray and bake in a moderate oven (180°C) until golden.

CHEESE BISCUITS

115g butter • 170g flour • 60g finely grated cheese • ½ small teaspoon baking powder • salt and pepper • a little cold milk to mix

Rub butter into flour. Add cheese, baking powder, and salt and pepper. Mix to a stiff paste with milk and roll to 3mm thick. Cut into shapes. Bake in a hot oven (220°C) for 7 to 10 minutes until golden brown.

CHEESE CAKES

115g butter • 115g sugar • 2 eggs, beaten • 140g flour • 1 teaspoon baking powder • 115g flaky pastry • a little raspberry jam

Cream butter and sugar. Add eggs and add alternately with sifted flour and baking powder. Roll out pastry and line about 21 patty tins. Put 1 teaspoon raspberry jam on bottom of each, then 1 large spoonful of cake mixture on top. Place a small strip of pastry on top. Bake about 20 minutes at 200°C.

CHOCOLATE CHINESE CHEWS

¼ cup melted butter • 1 cup sugar • 2 eggs • 2 tablespoons milk •
1 cup flour • 1 teaspoon baking powder • 2 tablespoons cocoa •
1 teaspoon vanilla essence • 1 cup chopped walnuts •
1 cup chopped dates

Beat butter and sugar. Add eggs one by one then milk. Sift in flour, baking powder, cocoa and essence. Add nuts and dates. Spread in pan 6mm thick. Put in oven at 190°C for about 20 minutes. When cooked, cut into squares.

CHOCOLATE FINGERS

225g flour • 85g butter • 85g sugar • 1 egg yolk • 1 dessertspoon
cocoa • 1 teaspoon baking powder • icing made with white of egg
and icing sugar • chopped walnuts

Mix all together (except last 2 ingredients) like shortbread. Roll out
and cut into fingers. Bake in a steady oven (about 180°C). Spread
with icing. Sprinkle with walnuts.

CHOCOLATE ROUGHS

1 egg • pinch of salt • ¾ cup brown sugar • 1 tablespoon butter •
1 tablespoon cocoa • 1 tablespoon boiling water • 1 teaspoon
vanilla essence • 1 cup coconut • 1 large cup rolled oats

Beat egg with salt and sugar until thick. Melt butter and cocoa
in boiling water and add. Stir in vanilla, coconut and rolled oats.
Place small heaps on a greased tray and cook about 30 minutes in a
moderate oven (180°C).

COCONUT FUDGE BISCUITS

1 cup flour • 115g coconut • 115g sugar • 1 tablespoon cocoa •
vanilla essence • 115g butter, melted

Put all dry ingredients into a basin and pour over melted butter.
Mix until like breadcrumbs. Press into a sponge roll or sandwich tin.
Bake at 180°C until set. Cut while warm. This is good for cooking in
oven after cooking dinner.

CORNFLAKE MERINGUES

2 egg whites • ½ cup sugar • ¼ teaspoon vanilla essence •
½ teaspoon vinegar • pinch of salt • 2 cups cornflakes •
½ cup chopped walnuts

Beat egg whites until stiff. Add other ingredients and mix. Place teaspoonfuls on a cold greased tray and bake at 120°C for 1½ hours.

CREAM PUFFS

You will find the recipe for Cream Puffs and Chocolate Eclairs in the Pastry section — Choux Pastry (see page 131).

DOG BISCUITS

450g wholemeal flour • 115g white flour • 1 dessertspoon salt •
115g mince • cold water

Put flours and salt in a basin and rub mince in like butter. Then mix to a stiff dough with water. Roll out and put on a slide, marked into squares. Prick with a fork. Bake in a slow oven (120°C) until brown. Sometimes 1 tablespoon of cod liver oil is added, as it is good for building puppies' bones.

FRUIT NUT MARSHMALLOWS

½ cup cornflour • 1 breakfast cup fine wholemeal flour • 2 level teaspoons baking powder • ½ teaspoon salt • ½ cup brown sugar • 115g melted butter • 1 egg, beaten • milk to mix • minced sultanas • walnuts • honey

Sift flours, baking powder and salt and mix with sugar. Add butter, egg and enough milk to make a stiff mixture. Roll out thin and put on cold greased trays. Mark into squares. Cook about 15 minutes at 230°C. When cold, stick two together with a layer of sultanas and walnuts, blended with honey.

Marshmallow:

2 teaspoons gelatine • ½ cup hot water • 1 egg white, beaten • lemon essence • 1 cup icing sugar • walnut halves

Dissolve gelatine in hot water. Let it cool. Add egg white, lemon essence and icing sugar. Beat and beat until white and thick and creamy. Spread on top of biscuits and finish with half a walnut.

GEMS

2 eggs • ½ cup sugar • 30g butter, melted • 1 cup milk • 2 cups flour • 3 teaspoons baking powder

Beat eggs and sugar very well. Add butter. Add milk then other ingredients. Have gem irons very hot and grease with butter or lard. Half fill with mixture and cook in a hot oven (220°C). Makes 24 gems.

GINGER NUTS

72g butter • ½ cup golden syrup • 225g flour • 1 dessertspoon ground ginger • ¼ teaspoon bicarbonate of soda • pinch of salt

Melt butter and syrup. Add other ingredients. Mix to a stiff paste. Roll out on a floured board. Cut into rounds. Put on a greased baking slide. Bake in a moderate oven (180°C) for about 15 minutes.

GINGER NUTS (Eltham)

1.15kg flour • 450g light brown sugar • 30g ground ginger • 225g butter • 900g golden syrup, warmed

Rub dry ingredients together well. Beat in the butter. Mix with sufficient syrup to make a stiff dough. Make into little marbles by rolling pieces of dough into thin strips, chopping bits off (as though chopping rhubarb). Roll each one into a little marble. Flatten slightly. Bake for 15 minutes or less at 190°C. No rising.

HOKEY POKEY BISCUITS

1 dessertspoon golden syrup • 1 dessertspoon milk • 1 teaspoon baking soda • 115g butter or good fat • ½ to ¾ cup sugar • 1 large cup flour

Melt syrup and milk together. When nearly cold, add baking soda and beat until frothy. Cream butter and sugar. Add frothy mixture, then the flour. Roll into balls and press with a fork. Cook in a slow oven (120°C) for about 30 minutes.

HONEY RAISIN CAKES

60g butter • 30g caster sugar • 30g honey • 1 egg • 85g flour • ½ teaspoon baking powder • 1 dessertspoon milk • 60g chopped raisins

Cream butter, sugar and honey. Add egg and beat very well. Stir in other ingredients. Cook in greased patty tins for about 20 minutes in a medium oven (180°C). 60g honey may replace the honey and caster sugar.

JELLY CAKES

½ cup butter • ½ cup sugar • 2 eggs, well beaten • 1 cup flour •
1 small teaspoon cream of tartar • ½ teaspoon baking soda • a little
milk • essence of choice • 1 packet red jelly crystals • coconut

Cream butter and sugar. Add eggs then flour sifted with cream of tartar and baking soda. Add milk and essence. Place in patty tins or paper cases and cook. Make up the jelly, and when nearly set, dip cakes in, then roll in coconut. One teaspoon of baking powder may replace the cream of tartar and soda.

KIWI BISCUITS

115g shortening (butter is best) • ¼ cup sugar • 2 tablespoons
sweetened condensed milk • 1 cup flour • 1 teaspoon baking
powder • pinch of salt • 1 cake of dairy chocolate, chopped into
pieces the size of a pea

Cream butter and sugar. Add condensed milk. Sift in flour, baking powder and salt. Stir in chocolate. Roll into little balls and place on a cold tray. Press down with a fork dipped in boiling water. Cook in a very moderate oven (160°C).

MAORI KISSES (Eggless)

2 heaped tablespoons butter • 4 tablespoons sugar • very little milk •
1 cup flour, sieved • 1 tablespoon cocoa • 1 teaspoon baking
powder • ½ cup chopped walnuts • ¾ cup chopped dates •
¼ cup preserved ginger • a few drops of vanilla essence

Melt butter and add sugar, milk, flour, cocoa, baking powder, nuts, fruits and essence. Make into small teaspoon-sized balls. Cook on a cold tray neither greased nor floured. Cook at 190°C for 10 to 15 minutes. Join when cold with vanilla butter icing, or make bigger and ice separately with Caramel Icing.

Caramel Icing:

2 tablespoons milk • 5 tablespoons brown sugar • 3 tablespoons butter

Bring to the boil for 3 or 4 minutes. Beat until thick. Takes 10 to 20 minutes to beat.

MELTING MOMENTS

115g butter • 30g icing sugar • 60g flour • 60g cornflour • ½ teaspoon baking powder

Cream butter and sugar and work in other ingredients. Bake in small lots in a moderate oven (180°C). Stick together with icing filling:

Icing:

115g icing sugar • vanilla essence • a walnut-sized piece of butter

Mix well with a little cold water.

MERINGUES

2 egg whites • 115g caster sugar • 1 level teaspoon baking powder • pinch of salt • a little extra caster sugar

Whip egg whites until they won't fall out of a basin when inverted. Gently whip in half the sugar with a pinch of salt, a little at a time. When stiff again, gently fold in the rest of the sugar and the baking powder. Put dessertspoonfuls on greaseproof paper laid on greased oven tray. Sprinkle with extra sugar. Takes 1½ to 2 hours in a very cool oven (120°C).

NOUGATINES (French)

Pastry:

115g flour, sifted • 72g butter • cold water

Rub flour with butter until it resembles fine breadcrumbs. Add sufficient cold water until mixed to a stiff paste. Grease some fluted patty tins. Roll out pastry to rather less than 6mm, cut into rounds, and line bottom and sides of pans with pastry. Trim around top edge to make even.

Filling:

60g butter • 60g caster sugar • 1 egg • 30g ground almonds • 30g sponge cake crumbs • a few drops almond essence • jam • 2 tablespoons whole almonds, blanched and chopped finely

Cream butter and sugar. Quickly stir in egg, and beat well for a few minutes. Add ground almonds and sponge cake crumbs. Mix thoroughly then mix in essence. Put enough jam into bottom of each patty tin to cover. Fill pans three-quarters full with mixture. Sprinkle top with chopped almonds and bake in a moderate oven (180°C) for about 20 minutes. Place on a sieve to cool.

NOVELTY BISCUITS

Use breakfast cups for all measures

2 cups coconut • 1 cup chopped raisins and sultanas mixed • 1 cup chopped dates • 1 cup chopped walnuts • 1 tin sweetened condensed milk

Mix all together and make small balls about the size of a walnut. Bake on greased oven shelf very slowly for 15 minutes (120°C). Pack in a tin — will keep a long time. Can halve or double this quantity. No flour, butter, sugar or eggs.

OVERNIGHT BISCUITS

115g butter • ¾ cup sugar • 1 egg • 1 tablespoon treacle •
1½ cups flour • 1 teaspoon baking soda • ½ cup walnuts •
½ cup cherries • ½ cup preserved ginger

Cream butter and sugar. Add egg and all other ingredients. Form into 2 pats like butter and leave all night. Cut very thin next day, and cook in a slow oven (120°C).

PEANUT BUTTER LUNCH COOKIES

1½ cups sweetened condensed milk • ½ cup peanut butter •
3 cups shredded coconut

Mix and drop in spoonfuls on a greased baking sheet. Bake for 15 minutes at 190°C, or until brown, about 30 minutes.

PEANUT COOKIES

115g butter • 1 teacup brown sugar • 1 egg • 1 dessertspoon
cocoa • 1 salt spoon of salt • 1 teacup wheat flakes • 1 teaspoon
baking powder • 1 level cup flour • 225g roasted peanuts

Cream butter and sugar. Break in egg. Add cocoa, then other dry ingredients, then peanuts. Place in rocky pieces on greased scone trays and bake in a moderate oven (180°C).

RICHMOND MAIDS OF HONOUR

170g butter • 1 teacup cream • 1 boiled potato • 4 egg yolks •
30g finely ground almonds • 1 tablespoon lemon juice •
170g sugar • 30g minced nuts • grated rind of 2 lemons •
a little nutmeg • 2 tablespoons brandy (or hot water flavoured with
brandy essence) • puff pastry (see page 134)

Mix butter and cream. Rub potato to a smooth flour. Mix all other ingredients together. Line patty tins with puff pastry and fill with mixture. Bake as usual.

SPIDERS (No Cooking)

225g vegetable shortening • 4 cups corn or wheat flakes • 1 cup icing sugar • ½ teaspoon vanilla essence • 1 cup coconut • 4 tablespoons cocoa • 1 cup raisins (if desired)

Melt shortening, and pour over dry ingredients. Mix well. Press into a flat tin and set aside to cool. Cut when cold or put in teaspoon lots on greaseproof paper to set. Leave overnight to set.

SPONGE CAKES (Gem Iron)

3 small or 2 large eggs • 1 cup sugar • 1 cup flour • 1 teaspoon baking powder • 1 dessertspoon butter dissolved in ½ cup boiling water • pinch of salt • vanilla or lemon essence

Beat eggs, and add sugar until creamy as for sponge. Sift flour and baking powder and fold in very lightly. Add butter and water, salt and essence. Stir slightly. Have gem irons very hot (as for gems) and butter them well. Fill about three-quarters full. They only take 5 or 6 minutes to cook. This quantity makes about 36 little sponges. (If a good pinch of salt is added to eggs and they are beaten well before adding sugar, it will not take as long to beat the eggs and sugar creamy.)

STUFFED MONKEYS

340g butter • 225g sugar • 450g flour • 15g cinnamon • 1 egg

Mix and roll out thin. Cut in rounds. Put following mixture between 2 rounds and pinch together. Bake in a moderate oven (180°C).

Mixture:

115g sultanas or raisins • 115g lemon peel, cut small •
30g chopped walnuts • ½ cup dates • cinnamon or spice to taste

TANGO CAKES

60g butter • 1 small cup sugar • 1 egg, beaten • 1 large cup flour •
2 tablespoons cornflour • 1 teaspoon baking powder •
1 tablespoon cocoa • vanilla essence • 115g chopped dates •
115g chopped walnuts • walnut halves

Cream butter and sugar. Add egg. Sift flour, cornflour, baking powder and cocoa. Stir into butter and sugar with vanilla. Add dates and walnuts. Bake in paper cases for 10 minutes in a hot oven (220°C). Ice with icing made from icing sugar and cocoa dissolved in a little boiling water. Place walnut half on top of each. These are nice economical little cakes. Makes about 20 to 24.

TEDDIES

1 small tin condensed milk • 1 cup chopped walnuts •
1 cup chopped dates • 1 cup coconut

Mix together milk, walnuts and dates. Roll in coconut. Bake on a greased tray in a moderate oven (180°C) for 10 to 15 minutes.

TRIFLE CAKES

85g wholemeal flour• 85g flour • 85g butter • 60g brown sugar •
½ teaspoon spice • ½ teaspoon baking powder • 1 egg yolk •
raspberry jam • whipped cream to serve

Make biscuit pastry with wholemeal flour, flour, butter, brown sugar, spice, baking powder and egg yolk. Line patty tins and bake at 190°C for 15 minutes. When cooked put a layer of jam in the bottom and fill with Filling.

Filling:

3 tablespoons cake crumbs • 2 tablespoons sultanas • a little
brandy or brandy essence • 2 dessertspoons raspberry jam

Mix together and top with a little whipped cream.

WALNUT CRISPS

115g butter • 115g sugar • 1 egg • 60g flour • 4 teaspoons cocoa •
1 teaspoon baking powder • ½ cup chopped walnuts • 170g fine
wholemeal flour • vanilla essence

Cream butter and sugar. Add egg and other ingredients. Spread 3mm thick on bottom of a shallow tin. Bake in a slow oven (120°C) for 30 to 45 minutes. Cut into squares while hot.

WALNUT WAFERS

2 eggs • 1 cup brown sugar • ¼ teaspoon salt •
1 cup chopped almonds and walnuts mixed •
vanilla essence • 3½ tablespoons flour

Beat eggs and sugar well. Add salt, nuts and essence, and mix well. Add flour, beat well again and flavour. Cut out and bake in a moderate oven (180°C) until a nice golden colour.

WIENCO TORTE

4 tablespoons finely minced nuts • 1 teaspoon bicarbonate
of soda • 2 teaspoons cream of tartar • 2¼ tablespoons butter •
4 tablespoons icing sugar • 3 egg yolks, well beaten •
4 tablespoons flour • 3 egg whites, stiffly beaten • raspberry or
strawberry jam • chocolate icing

Mix all dry ingredients except icing sugar. Cream butter and sugar with egg yolks. Add flour and then egg whites. (A little hot water or milk may be necessary to make the cake the usual sponge-sandwich consistency.) Bake in sandwich tins for about 15 minutes. Put together with jam and ice with chocolate icing.

YO YO BISCUITS

170g plain flour • 60g custard powder • pinch of salt • 170g butter •
60g icing sugar • butter icing (see page 180)

Sift flour, custard powder and salt. Cream butter and icing sugar. Blend both mixtures. Make into 2 balls, put on a greased oven slide, and press with a fork. Bake until pale golden brown in biscuit oven. Put together in pairs with butter icing (see page 180).

LARGE CAKES

ALMOND CAKE

60g butter • 85g sugar • 60g ground almonds • 60g cake crumbs •
60g plain flour • 30g cornflour • 2 eggs, beaten • ½ teaspoon
almond essence • ½ teaspoon baking powder

Cream butter and sugar thoroughly. Add almonds and cake crumbs. Sift flour and cornflour together, and add alternately with eggs, beating all well. Add almond essence and baking powder. Turn into a greased sandwich tin. Bake at about 200°C for 20 to 30 minutes.

ALMOND MADEIRA

225g butter • 225g sugar • 4 eggs • 170g flour •
170g ground almonds • 1 teaspoon baking powder •
1 teaspoon salt

Cream butter and sugar. Add eggs, then sifted dry ingredients. Bake in a deep tin at 180°C for about 1½ hours.

To make this into Sand Cake, use half cornflour and half ordinary flour. Just ice with plain icing mixed with almond essence. Then decorate with a small piece of maidenhair fern in one corner, and little knobs of yellow icing to imitate wattle blossom.

ANGEL CAKE

⅔ cup milk • ¾ cup sugar • ⅛ teaspoon salt • 2 egg whites •
1 cup flour • 1 teaspoon baking powder • ½ teaspoon cream
of tartar • ½ teaspoon almond extract • ½ teaspoon vanilla extract •
icing (if desired)

Heat milk and sugar just to boil. Add salt to egg whites and beat stiff. Add milk and sugar slowly to egg whites, beating continually. Let cool. Sift together 5 times: flour, baking powder and cream of tartar. Fold into egg mixture. Add flavouring. Pour into a small ungreased angel cake tin. Bake at 180°C for about 30 minutes. Remove from oven. Invert pan and allow to stand until cold. Cover top and sides with icing if desired.

Note: Excellent to make with the Gold Cake (see page 163). Only 3 eggs are required for both.

APPLE CAKE

½ cup butter • 1 breakfast cup brown sugar • 2 eggs, well beaten •
1½ cups flour • 1 teaspoon baking soda • 1 teaspoon
mixed spice • ½ cup raisins • ½ cup walnuts • 1 cup thinly
sliced apples • 1 tablespoon sugar • pinch of cinnamon •
1 tablespoon brown sugar • a little cinnamon and nutmeg

Cream butter and sugar. Add eggs. Add flour sifted with baking soda and spices. Stir in raisins and nuts. Place half mixture into a prepared tin. Add apples sprinkled with the 1 tablespoon sugar and cinnamon. Add remaining mixture. Put in a good oven (180°C) for about 1 hour. When nearly cooked, sprinkle top of cake with 1 tablespoon brown sugar. Put greased paper on top so sugar won't burn. Take off just before taking cake from oven. Keep 2 or 3 days before cutting. If preferred, raisins and nuts may be omitted.

APPLE FRUIT CAKE

Do not cut this cake for a fortnight.

1 tablespoon butter • 1½ cups stewed apple sweetened with ½ cup sugar • 1 cup brown sugar • 1 tablespoon cocoa • 1 dessertspoon spice • ½ teaspoon baking soda • 2 large cups flour • about 1½ cups lemon peel and dried fruits to taste • a little milk (if necessary)

Melt butter into apple and sugar. Mix together all other ingredients. Add apple mixture and a little milk if needed. Line a tin with greased paper. Bake in a moderate oven (180°C) for about 1½ hours.

APPLE MERINGUE CAKE

½ cup shortening • 1 cup brown sugar • 2 egg yolks, unbeaten • 2 cups sifted flour • 1 teaspoon baking soda • ¼ teaspoon salt • 1 teaspoon cinnamon • ½ teaspoon cloves • ½ teaspoon nutmeg • 1 cup thick, unsweetened apple sauce • finely chopped nuts to sprinkle

Cream shortening and sugar. Add egg yolks and blend well. Sift flour, baking soda, salt and spices well together. Add to creamed mixture alternately with the apple sauce. Pour into a greased pan (20 x 30cm), lined with wax paper. Top with meringue.

Meringue:

2 egg whites • ½ cup brown sugar • ½ cup nuts, chopped fine

Beat egg whites until stiff. Gradually add sugar and beat until mixture peaks. Spread over raw batter. Sprinkle with chopped nuts. Bake in a moderate oven (180°C) until done.

BANANA SPONGE

115g butter • 1 teacup sugar • 1 egg, well beaten • 1½ cups flour •
1 teaspoon baking powder • 3 firm bananas, mashed • 1 small
teaspoon baking soda dissolved in 2 tablespoons milk • mock cream
or real cream to serve

Cream butter and sugar. Add egg, then flour, baking powder and bananas. Add soda in milk. Bake in a moderate oven (180°C) for 30 minutes. This sponge can be baked either in sandwich tins and mock cream filling put between, or in a flat baking tin with whipped cream on top.

BATTENBURG CAKE

4 tablespoons butter • ¾ cup sugar • 2 cups flour • 2 teaspoons
baking powder • ½ teaspoon salt • ½ cup milk • ½ teaspoon vanilla •
2 egg whites, beaten stiff • pink colouring • strawberry filling

Cream the butter. Add sugar gradually and beat until light and fluffy. Sift flour with baking powder and salt. Add alternately with milk. Add vanilla. Fold in egg whites. Divide batter and colour one half pink. Bake in 2 greased square sandwich tins in a moderate oven (180°C) for about 20 minutes. Cool. Cut each into 6 even strips. Join layers like a chequerboard, with Strawberry Filling.

Strawberry Filling:

2 tablespoons strawberry jam • 1 cup sifted icing sugar •
1 teaspoon melted butter • hot water

Beat jam into icing sugar. Add butter and sufficient hot water to make a smooth spreading paste.

Coconut Paste:

1 tablespoon butter • 1½ cups sifted icing sugar • ⅛ teaspoon
salt • 2 tablespoons lemon juice • ¼ teaspoon almond essence •
green colouring • ½ cup desiccated coconut

Cream butter, icing sugar, salt and lemon juice. Add sufficient hot water to make a smooth paste. Add almond essence and green colouring. Add coconut and beat well. Should be as thick as possible. Spread evenly on cake.

BLOCK CAKE

225g butter • 2 heaped cups flour • 1 cup sugar • 2 eggs, well beaten • 1 cup boiling milk • 85g almonds • 450g raisins • 115g cherries • 85g peel • 450g sultanas • 1½ teaspoons vanilla essence • 1 teaspoon baking soda dissolved in a little milk

Rub butter well into flour until it resembles crumbs. Add sugar and mix. Mix eggs and milk. Put in a saucepan and let get very hot until like a custard. Do not let boil or you will have a curdled mixture — just very hot. Take off heat and let cool, but not too cold. Add nuts, fruit and essence to mixture. Pour custard into mix. Stir well until blended. Add soda. Bake in a square tin in a moderate oven (180°C) for about 2 hours. If a dark cake is required, put in 1 tablespoon blackcurrant jam, but very nice as it is.

CANADIAN DATE CAKE

Use breakfast cup for measuring.

1 cup sugar • 225g butter • 2 eggs, beaten • 1 teaspoon bicarbonate of soda dissolved in ¾ cup cold water • 1 cup dates • 1 cup walnuts • 1 tablespoon maple or golden syrup • 2 cups flour

Cream butter and sugar. Add eggs. Dissolve soda in water and pour over dates. Let it stand 1 hour. Add to creamed sugar. Add nuts. Mix in syrup and flour. Bake 1½ hours in a moderate oven (180°C) in a tin lined with buttered paper.

CANADIAN ORANGE CAKE

½ cup butter • 1 cup sugar • 2 eggs, beaten well • 1 teaspoon
vanilla essence • 1 teaspoon baking soda dissolved in ¾ cup warm
water • ½ teaspoon salt sifted with 2 cups flour • 1 whole seedless
orange (skin and all) • 1 cup raisins • ½ cup walnuts

Cream butter. Add sugar, eggs, vanilla, baking soda, salt and flour.
Beat well. Mince orange, raisins and walnuts in a mincer. Add
to mixture and beat well. Bake at 180°C for approximately 50
minutes.

CHOCOLATE CAKE

1 tablespoon butter • ½ cup brown sugar • 1 tablespoon golden
syrup • 1 egg • ½ teaspoon baking soda dissolved in ½ cup milk •
1 cup flour • 1 teaspoon baking powder • 1 tablespoon cocoa •
icing and chopped nuts to serve

Cream butter and sugar. Add syrup and egg, then milk with baking
soda dissolved in it. Add flour, baking powder and cocoa. Bake in
one tin at 190°C for about 30 minutes. Ice and sprinkle with chopped
nuts.

For Coffee Cake:
Substitute 1 tablespoon coffee essence for cocoa, and add 2 extra
tablespoons flour.

CHOCOLATE CAKE (Foolproof)

115g butter • 1 small teacup sugar • 1 egg • 2 tablespoons golden
syrup, melted • 2 cups flour • 2 tablespoons cocoa • 1 teaspoon
baking soda dissolved in 1 cup milk • 1 teaspoon baking powder

Beat butter, sugar and egg. Add syrup. Sift flour and cocoa together. Add soda in milk and beat well until smooth and light. Add baking powder. Bake in a moderate oven (180°C) for about 45 minutes in a tin about 30cm x 20cm. Keeps well.

CHOCOLATE CAKE (Special)

4 tablespoons butter • 4 tablespoons sugar • 2 eggs • 6 tablespoons milk • 6 tablespoons flour • 2 tablespoons ground rice • 2 small teaspoons baking powder • 2 tablespoons cocoa

Beat butter and sugar to a cream. Add eggs and beat well. Add milk. Sift dry ingredients together and add. Bake in 2 flat tins for about 20 minutes at 180°C.

Filling:

1½ tablespoons butter • icing sugar • ½ cup strong cocoa made with milk • a little vanilla essence • chopped walnuts

Beat butter to a cream with icing sugar. Beat in cocoa. Add vanilla essence. Put filling between cake, and on top. Top with chopped walnuts.

CHOCOLATE ROLL

3 egg yolks • 1 small teacup caster sugar • 2 tablespoons warm water • 1 teacup flour • ½ teaspoon baking powder • 3 teaspoons cocoa • 3 egg whites, stiffly beaten

Line a Swiss roll tin with greased paper. Beat egg yolks and sugar in a basin over a pan of water until thick and creamy. Add water. Stir sifted flour, baking powder and cocoa in lightly. Fold in egg whites. Pour into a prepared tin. Bake about 12 to 15 minutes at about 180°C. Turn on to sugared paper, roll up and hold 1 minute. Unroll. Spread with warm raspberry or apricot jam. Roll up again.

COFFEE CAKE

85g butter • 170g sugar • 3 eggs • 1 tablespoon coffee essence • ½ teaspoon vanilla essence • 125g flour • 1 teaspoon baking powder • 3 tablespoons cornflour • 3 tablespoons milk

Cream butter and sugar. Beat in eggs and essences. Sift together dry ingredients. Add to butter mixture alternately with milk. Place in cake tin and bake for about 40 minutes at 180°C.

CRUMBLY TOP CAKE, SPICED

2 cups flour • 2 teaspoons baking powder • ½ teaspoon salt • ½ teaspoon nutmeg • ¼ teaspoon cinnamon • ¾ cup sugar • 60g butter • 2 eggs, unbeaten • ⅔ cup milk

Sift flour, baking powder, salt, nutmeg and cinnamon. Add sugar. Rub in butter. Add eggs. Mix well. Add milk and stir until smooth. Pour into a square tin. Cover with the following mixture.

Mixture:

60g butter • 1 cup brown sugar • 4 tablespoons flour • ½ teaspoon cinnamon • ⅛ teaspoon salt

Blend with a fork. This makes a crumbly mixture which is sprinkled on top of the uncooked cake. Half a cup of chopped walnuts is very nice too. Bake in a moderate oven (180°C) for 30 to 45 minutes.

CRUSTY CAKE

1 cup butter • 2 cups flour • 1 teaspoon baking powder • 2 eggs, beaten • 1 tablespoon milk • ½ cup sugar

Rub butter into flour and baking powder with tips of fingers. Add eggs, milk and sugar. Mix to a stiff dough. Roll out very thin and bake in a moderate oven (180°C) until nicely brown. Cover with marshmallow.

Marshmallow:

½ cup sugar • 1 cup water • 2 tablespoons gelatine, melted •
melted chocolate • walnut halves to decorate

Boil sugar and water for 15 minutes. Must not be brown. Whip gelatine into boiled sugar and water. When cool, spread marshmallow on top of cake, then chocolate. Cut into dainty squares. Place ½ walnut on each. (Very good.)

DATE SANDWICH CAKE

1 cup dates, cut up • vanilla essence • 115g butter • 115g sugar •
1 tablespoon golden syrup • pinch of salt • 1 egg, beaten • ½ cup
flour • 1 breakfast cup wholemeal flour • 1 teaspoon baking powder

Simmer dates with 2 dessertspoons water until soft, then beat with a fork. Add vanilla to taste. Set aside to cool. Cream butter and sugar. Add syrup and salt. Add egg, flour and baking powder as usual. Put half the mixture in a cake tin, and spread over date mixture. Put on rest of cake mixture. Bake about 30 minutes in a moderate oven (180°C). Nice moist cake.

DOLLY VARDEN CAKE

115g butter • ½ cup sugar • 4 eggs, beaten • 1 teaspoon baking
powder • 1½ cups flour • 1 cup mixed fruit

Cream butter and sugar. Add eggs, baking powder and flour. Divide mixture into three and add fruit to one. Bake in three cake tins at 190°C for about 25 minutes. When baked, place the three together (with fruit cake in middle) with the following mixture:

Mixture:

1 good tablespoon butter • 225g icing sugar • juice of a good-
sized lemon

Mix together. Cake can also be iced on top if desired.

EGGLESS FRUIT CAKE

1 breakfast cup sugar • 1 breakfast cup cold water • 2 breakfast cups mixed fruit (raisins, currants and sultanas) • 115g butter • 2 cups flour • 1 teaspoon baking soda

Put sugar, water, fruit and butter in a saucepan, and slowly bring to the boil. Simmer gently for 3 minutes. Leave to get cold. Sift flour and baking soda and add to mixture. Stir well. Line a tin with greased paper and add mixture. Cook in a moderate oven (180°C) for 1½ to 2 hours. Moist, and should keep for weeks.

FOUNDATION CAKE

85g butter • 140g sugar • 2 eggs • 140g flour • 1 teaspoon baking powder

Cream butter and sugar. Add eggs, flour and baking powder.

Plain Sponge:
Add 3 tablespoons cold milk.

Chocolate Sponge:
Add 2 dessertspoons cocoa mixed with 3 tablespoons boiling water.

Orange Cake:
Add only rind of orange. Use juice for icing. Sultanas, etc., may also be added.

FRUIT CAKE (Ship's — One Egg)

225g butter • ½ cup sugar • 1 egg • 1 tablespoon golden syrup • 1 tablespoon raspberry jam • 1 teaspoon vinegar • 2 large cups flour • 450 to 675g mixed fruit • 1 teaspoon baking soda dissolved in 1 cup milk

Cream butter and sugar. Add egg and beat. Add golden syrup, jam and vinegar. Add flour and fruit. Add soda and milk. Bake slowly for 2½ hours in a moderate oven (180°C).

FRUIT CAKE (The Best in the World)

2 cups butter • 2 cups light brown sugar • 7 egg yolks •
7 egg whites, beaten until stiff and dry • 2 tablespoons milk •
2 tablespoons fruit juice • 450g nuts • 900g currants • 900g raisins •
225g dates • 225g peel • 4 cups flour • 2 teaspoons mace •
2 teaspoons cinnamon • 2 teaspoons baking powder • a few
grains of salt

Cream butter. Add sugar gently and beat for 5 minutes. Beat egg yolks until light and lemon coloured. Add egg whites. Add to butter and sugar mixture. Add milk, fruit juice and nuts. Roll fruit in flour and add. Add well-sifted dry ingredients. Beat mixture thoroughly. Place in a deep, round cake tin lined with several thicknesses of baking paper. Bake for 4 hours or longer at 170°C.

FUDGE CAKE

450g crushed wine biscuits or any stale crushed-up cake •
225g butter • about 1 cup sugar • 2 eggs, beaten •
chocolate icing and nuts to decorate

Melt butter with sugar. Add eggs. Heat up until like honey. Add crumbs. Press into a cake tin and leave until next day. Ice with chocolate icing, and put some nuts on top. Walnuts or sultanas may be added.

GENOA CAKE

225g butter • 225g sugar • 4 eggs • drop of lemon essence • 285g flour • 450g currants • 225g candied peel

Cream butter and sugar. Beat in eggs and essence. Mix together flour and fruit, then add to butter mixture. Mix well. Bake at 160°C for 2 hours.

GINGERBREAD WITH SOUR MILK

115g butter or shortening • 6 tablespoons sugar • 1 large egg • ½ cup black treacle • ½ teaspoon baking soda • ½ cup sour milk • 2 cups flour • 1 teaspoon ground ginger • 1 good teaspoon baking powder • ½ teaspoon salt • 1 cup seedless raisins

Cream butter and sugar. Beat in egg, then treacle, and mix well. Beat soda into sour milk and add. Stir in flour, ginger, baking powder, salt. Add raisins. Spread on a well greased and floured shallow tin. Bake for about 35 minutes in an oven not too hot (about 180°C). Moist, light and fruity — sour milk keeps cake moist without heaviness.

GINGER CAKE

115g butter • 115g sugar • 2 eggs • ½ cup golden syrup, warmed a little • ½ cup milk • 2 teaspoons cinnamon • 2 teaspoons ground ginger • 1 teaspoon baking powder • ¼ teaspoon salt • 2 teaspoons spice • ½ teaspoon nutmeg (or to taste) • 2 good cups flour • 1 teaspoon baking soda in ½ cup boiling water • coffee icing to decorate • pieces of preserved ginger cut small, to decorate

Cream butter and sugar. Add eggs, then syrup. Add milk and all dry ingredients. Lastly, add baking soda in water. Makes a nice ginger cake. Ice with coffee icing and top with preserved ginger.

GINGER SPONGE WITH ARROWROOT

3 eggs • ½ cup sugar • ½ cup arrowroot • 1 teaspoon plain flour •
1 teaspoon cream of tartar • ½ teaspoon bicarbonate of soda •
1 teaspoon cinnamon • 1 teaspoon ground ginger • 1 teaspoon
cocoa • 1 dessertspoon golden syrup • cream to serve

Beat eggs for 5 minutes. Add sugar gradually, and continue beating until light. Sift all other ingredients in and then add the golden syrup. Bake in a sandwich tin in a moderate oven (180°C) for 15 to 20 minutes. Put together with cream.

GOLD CAKE (Economical — Egg Yolks)

2 cups flour • 2 teaspoons baking powder • ¼ teaspoon salt •
½ cup butter or shortening • 1 cup sugar • 2 egg yolks, beaten
until light • ¾ cup milk • 1 teaspoon vanilla essence

Sift flour. Add baking powder and salt. Sift twice more. Cream butter, add sugar gradually, and cream until light. Add egg yolks to butter mixture. Add flour and milk alternately. Beat after each addition until smooth. Add essence and beat. Bake in a greased pan at about 120°C to 150°C for 50 to 60 minutes. Use egg whites in Angel Cake (see page 152), or Meringues (see page 144) or Silver Cake (see page 171).

Frosting:

1 tablespoon grated orange rind • 3 tablespoons butter • 3 cups
sifted sugar • 2 tablespoons lemon juice mixed with 1 tablespoon
water • pinch of salt

Add orange rind to butter and cream well. Add 1 cup sugar gradually. Add lemon and water alternately with 2 cups sugar. Beat until smooth. Add salt. Cover top and sides as well.

HONEY DATE CAKE

450g dates, stoned • 1 teacup boiling water • 1 teaspoon baking soda • 225g butter • 225g honey • 3 eggs • 255g flour, sifted • 1 teaspoon grated nutmeg • ½ small teaspoon salt • 1 breakfast cup chopped walnuts

Pour boiling water on to dates with baking soda. Allow to stand until nearly cold and mix with a wooden spoon. Beat together butter, honey and eggs. Add flour, nutmeg, salt, dates and walnuts. Bake in a greased tin for about 1½ hours in a moderate oven (180°C).

HONEY ROLL (No Butter)

3 eggs • 60g sugar • 1 large tablespoon honey • 115g flour, sifted • 1 teaspoon baking powder • 1 teaspoon cinnamon • 2 tablespoons hot water • whipped cream to fill (optional)

Beat eggs and sugar well. Add honey. Add flour, baking powder and cinnamon. Add hot water. Bake about 10 minutes in a quick oven (220°C). Turn out quickly on a damp cloth. Trim off edges. Roll up in cloth and allow to stand 2 minutes. Unroll, and roll up without cloth. When cold, fill with the following (or whipped cream):

Filling:

115g icing sugar • 1 dessertspoon butter • 1 dessertspoon honey • 1 teaspoon lemon juice

Beat all together. A few chopped nuts may be added.

LINDY LOU'S FRUIT CAKE

115g sugar • about 1 teacup milk • 450g flour • ¼ teaspoon baking soda • 225g butter • 60g lemon peel • 225g currants • 225g sultanas • 2 eggs • 115g golden syrup, melted • almonds (if liked)

Dissolve sugar in milk. Sift flour with soda. Rub in butter until it resembles breadcrumbs. Add peel and fruit. Beat eggs and add melted syrup. Add sugar and milk to this. Combine, and beat well. Bake in a moderate oven (180°C) for 2 hours.

LOG CAKE

icing sugar, sifted and free of lumps • 115g butter • 1 egg, beaten • essence • 1 tablespoon cocoa • 24 malt biscuits • chopped nuts (optional)

Have sifted icing sugar ready. Melt butter to a liquid. Add egg. Add essence, cocoa and enough icing sugar to make a nice spreadable consistency. Beat well together. It is nice done in a double saucepan. Place 4 biscuits end to end. Cover with a thin layer of icing. Lay 4 more biscuits on top and cover again with icing, just like bricks and mortar. Ice all over, and if liked, sprinkle with chopped nuts. If icing begins to harden in the bowl before it is all spread, place the bowl in hot water for a few minutes. Leave 2 or 3 days before cutting, and cut in thin slices.

LOUISE CAKE

115g butter • 45g sugar • 3 egg yolks, well beaten • 225g flour • 1 level teaspoon baking powder • raspberry jam • 3 egg whites, very stiffly beaten • 170g sugar • 85g desiccated coconut

Cream butter and 45g sugar. Add egg yolks. Add flour and baking powder. Spread in a flat tin about 26cm square. Spread with jam. Add egg whites to 170g sugar and coconut. Spread on top of cake and bake for 30 minutes in a moderate oven (180°C). Cut into squares while hot.

MACAROON CAKE

115g butter • 115g sugar • 3 egg yolks, beaten well • ½ cup milk •
1 teaspoon vanilla essence • 170g flour, sifted • 2 teaspoons
baking powder • pinch of salt

Cream butter and sugar. Add egg yolks to milk and essence, mixing well. Add to creamed mixture. Fold in flour, baking powder and salt. Spread in a flat greased tin and cover top with the macaroon mixture. Bake at 200°C for approximately 40 minutes.

Macaroon mixture:

3 egg whites, beaten • 115g sugar • 1 cup coconut

Mix together.

MADEIRA

170g butter • 170g sugar • 3 eggs • 225g flour • 1½ teaspoons
baking powder • lemon essence

Cream butter and sugar well. Add eggs one by one, beating well. Sift in flour, baking powder and essence. Bake in a moderate oven (180°C).

MARZIPAN CAKE

170g butter • 170g caster sugar • 225g flour • 1 teaspoon baking
powder • pinch of salt • 3 eggs, beaten • ½ teaspoon almond
essence • strawberry jam • almond paste

In a warm basin, cream butter and sugar. Sift flour, baking powder and salt — all slightly warmed, alternately with eggs and essence. Bake at 180°C in 2 sandwich tins for about 30 minutes. When cold, spread each half thinly with jam. Stick together with a thin layer of almond paste.

MERINGUE CAKE

85g butter • 115g caster sugar • 4 egg yolks • 1 tablespoon milk •
1 breakfast cup flour • 1 small teaspoon baking powder •
¼ teaspoon vanilla essence • a few grains of salt

Cream together butter, sugar and egg yolks. Add other ingredients and mix. Line a 20cm square baking tin with buttered paper. Place mixture evenly in tin. Spread meringue mixture on top. Bake for 1¼ hours at 180°C.

Meringue Mixture:

4 egg whites • ¾ cup sugar • 115g ground almonds

Mix together.

NAPOLEON CREAM CAKE

2 cups cream • 1 egg white, stiffly beaten with 1 teaspoon vanilla •
2 tablespoons icing sugar • 2 dessertspoons gelatine dissolved in
2 tablespoons cold water • puff pastry to serve • vanilla icing
to serve

Beat half the cream, not too stiffly. Add egg white. Do not beat again but just leave on one side. Pour other half of cream into a saucepan with icing sugar and gelatine. Keep warm until gelatine is fully dissolved. If you boil this it will curdle. Leave to cool. Beat and when it starts to get thick, add the other cream and whip. Turn out into a wetted tin 18 x 18cm. When set, place between 2 layers of puff pastry and ice with vanilla icing.

ORANGE CAKE (No Butter)

3 eggs • nearly 1 breakfast cup sugar • grated rind and juice of
1 orange • 1 heaped breakfast cup flour • 1 teaspoon
baking powder • pinch of salt

Beat eggs with sugar for 10 minutes (all the beating need not be done at once). Add orange juice and rind, and beat again. Add flour, baking powder and salt. Bake in a greased tin at 200°C for about 30 minutes.

ORANGE COCONUT CAKE

115g butter • 115g sugar • 2 eggs, beaten • 115g flour •
1 teaspoon baking powder • 2 tablespoons desiccated coconut •
grated rind of 1 orange • 1 tablespoon orange juice • butter icing
to ice cake

Cream butter and sugar. Add eggs. Add dry ingredients and orange rind and juice. Bake at 190°C for about 20 minutes. A very light and soft cake. Ice with butter icing (see page 180).

ORANGE CREAM SPONGE

1 cup sugar • 1 cup flour • 2 teaspoons cream of tartar • ½ teaspoon
bicarbonate of soda • pinch of salt • 2 eggs • cream • 1 teaspoon
orange juice • a few drops of vanilla essence • a little orange peel

Sift together sugar, flour, cream of tartar, bicarbonate of soda and salt. Break eggs into a cup and fill to top with cream, orange juice and essence. Beat all well together. Grate orange peel into mixture. Bake in sandwich tins in a moderate oven (180°C). Make a filling of butter, icing sugar and orange juice.

ORANGE SPONGE CAKE (California)

3 eggs whites • pinch of cream of tartar • 3 egg yolks •
1 cup sugar • ½ cup orange juice • 2 teaspoons grated orange
rind • 1½ cups flour • 1½ teaspoons baking powder •
pinch of salt • white frosting to decorate • orange rind to decorate

Whip egg whites and cream of tartar until stiff. Beat in egg yolks, one at a time. Add sugar gradually, beating vigorously. Add orange juice and rind. Fold in lightly with sifted flour, baking powder and salt. Bake in 2 layer cake pans in a moderate oven for about 10 minutes.

Filling:

¼ cup sugar • 1 tablespoon flour • pinch of salt • 1 egg yolk •
1 dessertspoon butter • 1 teaspoon lemon juice

Mix all together and cook in a double boiler until smooth and thick. Remove from heat and add lemon juice.

Ice cake with white icing (see page 189) and sprinkle with grated orange rind.

PATCH CAKE

225 to 285g butter • 2 cups sugar • 4 eggs, well beaten • 3½ cups
flour • 3 teaspoons baking powder • 1 teaspoon salt • 1 cup milk •
½ teaspoon nutmeg • 1 tablespoon cocoa • ½ teaspoon vanilla
essence • 1 teaspoon spice • 2 tablespoons golden syrup •
¾ cup chopped seeded raisins • plain butter icing, slightly
flavoured with vanilla

Cream butter and sugar. Add eggs. Sift in flour, baking powder and salt. Mix. Add milk. Mix well and divide batter into two. Leave one plain; add spice, syrup, raisins, cocoa and essence into second half. Grease and line a square cake tin. Put batter in, in alternate spoonfuls of each mixture. Bake in a moderate oven for 1½ to 2 hours. Ice when cool.

PAVLOVA CAKE

4 egg whites • ¾ cup caster sugar • 1 teaspoon vinegar •
1 teaspoon cornflour • a few drops of vanilla essence • pinch of
salt • strawberries and cream to serve • chopped raisins soaked in
sherry or whisky to serve

Whisk eggs and sugar in a dry basin for 10 minutes with a very strong egg whisk. Add vinegar, then cornflour, vanilla and salt. Beat stiff enough to stand when cut. Line a tin with well-buttered paper (or bake in paper alone, formed into a high-sided container). Put into oven heated to 120°C, and turn off heat. Leave in the oven until cold. Cover with strawberries and cream, or raisins.

PRUNE CAKE (California)

2 eggs, beaten • 1 small cup sour milk • 1 cup sugar • 1½ cups
flour • 1 teaspoon cinnamon • 1 teaspoon baking soda • ⅓ cup
melted butter • 1 cup chopped, cooked prunes • 1 cup chopped
nuts • ½ teaspoon vanilla essence

Add eggs to milk and sifted dry ingredients. Add butter. Add prunes, nuts and vanilla. If more moisture is needed, add prune juice. Bake in a moderate oven (180°C).

RAINBOW CAKE

225g butter • 1 cup sugar • 4 eggs • vanilla essence •
2 cups flour • 2 teaspoons baking powder • 1 dessertspoon
cocoa or allspice • jam

Beat butter and sugar. Add eggs, one by one. Add vanilla, flour and baking powder. Divide into 3 lots. Make one pink, one plain, and add cocoa or allspice to the other. Cook in 3 tins and stick together with jam.

SEED CAKE

225g butter • 225g sugar • 3 eggs • 2 heaped cups flour •
½ teaspoon salt • 1 large teaspoon baking powder • 6 tablespoons
cold water • 4 teaspoons caraway seeds

Cream butter and sugar. Add eggs one by one. Add flour to salt and baking powder. Add half this mixture with the water.

Add rest of flour mixture and the seeds. Bake at 180°C for about 1 hour.

SELBY CAKE

115g butter • 115g sugar • 1 egg • 200g flour • 1 teaspoon baking
powder • raspberry jam

Beat butter and sugar to a cream. Add egg. Sift flour and baking powder, and add. Grease and flour a sandwich tin. Put in half the mixture and flatten out. Spread with a thin layer of jam. Cover with remaining mixture and spread evenly. Bake in a moderate oven (180°C) for about 30 minutes.

SILVER CAKE

4 egg whites • 115g butter • 115g sugar • ¾ cup cornflour •
lemon essence • ¾ cup flour • 1 teaspoon baking powder •
milk (if necessary)

Beat egg whites until stiff. Cream butter and sugar. Add egg whites and other ingredients. Use milk to make right consistency. Bake at 180°C for 30 minutes.

SIMNEL CAKE

225g butter • 225g sugar • 4 eggs • 285g flour • 1 teaspoon
baking powder • 60g ground rice • 115g chopped mixed peel •
450g currants • 60g cherries

Cream butter and sugar. Add eggs one at a time. Add flour, baking
powder and rice, alternately with fruit. Put half the mixture in a
tin. Cover with a layer of half the almond paste. Add other half
cake mixture. Bake cake in a moderate oven (180°C) for about 2½
hours. When cooked decorate with other half almond paste mixture.
(Almond paste may be bought ready made.)

Almond Paste:

225g ground almonds • 85g icing sugar • 1 teaspoon almond essence •
85g caster sugar • 1 tablespoon melted butter • 1 egg, beaten well

Mix wet and roll.

SNOW CAKE (Uncooked)

2 tablespoons sugar • ½ breakfast cup cold water • 1 tablespoon
best gelatine • ½ breakfast cup boiling water • 2 egg whites •
a little vanilla essence

Boil sugar and cold water for a minute or two. Dissolve gelatine in
the boiling water. Combine the two, and when a little cooler, stir in
unbeaten egg whites and vanilla. When cool, and just beginning to
set, whip up until foamy and thick. Line a sandwich tin with wet
greaseproof paper. Pour in mixture. Sets very quickly. Delicious
spread with whipped cream and passionfruit.

SPONGE (Cold Oven)

3 eggs • 1 teacup sugar • 1 breakfast cup flour • 1 teaspoon
cream of tartar • 1 tablespoon butter • 2 tablespoons milk •
½ teaspoon baking soda

Do not turn oven on until sponge is ready to be put in. Beat eggs and
sugar well. Mix in flour and cream of tartar. Dissolve butter and milk
in a saucepan. Add baking soda. Mix all well together. Put mixture in
sandwich tins and put in the oven. Bake at 190°C for 25 to 30 minutes.

SPONGE (Easy)

3 egg whites, beaten until stiff • 1 breakfast cup sugar • 3 egg
yolks, unbeaten • 1 level cupful sifted flour • 1 teaspoon baking
powder • a walnut-sized piece of butter • ¼ cup boiling water

Fold egg whites into sugar. Let stand for 10 minutes to dissolve.
Drop in unbeaten egg yolks and beat well. Fold in flour and baking
powder. Add butter dissolved in the boiling water. Bake in a slow
oven (120°C) for 30 minutes.

VIENNA CAKE (2 Eggs)

1½ tablespoons cocoa • about ¾ cup boiling water • 1½ small
tablespoons raspberry jam • 115g butter • 170g sugar • 2 eggs •
vanilla essence • 225g flour • 2 teaspoons baking powder • pinch
of salt • chocolate icing

Make cocoa to a thin paste with a little of the boiling water. Stir in the
jam. Make up to ¾ cup with boiling water. Let it cool. Cream butter and
sugar. Add eggs one by one, beating well. Add vanilla essence. Sift flour,
baking powder and salt very well. Add alternately with the liquid. Bake
in a flat tin in a moderate oven (180°C) for approximately 45 minutes. Ice
with chocolate icing. Mark with a fork.

WALNUT CAKE

115g butter • 170g sugar • 3 eggs • 2 tablespoons warm milk •
60g walnuts (crushed through a mincer) • 1 teaspoon spice •
1 teaspoon baking powder • 170g flour • icing • walnuts

Cream butter and sugar. Add eggs one by one. Add milk alternately
with dry ingredients and walnuts. Ice and put walnuts on icing.

WEDDING CAKE (Three-tiered)

565g butter • 565g sugar • 12 to 14 eggs, depending on size, well
whipped • 675g flour • 2 large teaspoons baking powder (or 1 good
teaspoon each cream of tartar and bicarbonate of soda) •
pinch of salt • 15g mixed spices • 450g raisins • 225g dates •
450g currants • 450g sultanas • 225g candied cherries •
115g mixed peel • 115g almonds • 1 teaspoon lemon essence •
a few drops of almond essence • 2 tablespoons brandy

Work butter and sugar until creamy. Add eggs, alternately with flour
sifted with baking powder, salt and spices. Clean and chop fruit, but
not too finely, and add with nuts and essences. Add brandy and mix
thoroughly. Place mixture in a 30cm diameter, 10 cm deep tin lined
with several layers of white paper. Bake 6 to 7 hours in a moderate
oven (180°C).

Prepare the same mixture again and put two-thirds in a 25cm
diameter tin. Put remaining mixture in a 20cm diameter tin. Bake
for 4 hours or longer. Make the large tier one day and the 2 smaller
ones the next day, as few home owners would have an oven to hold
3 tins at a time. Do not open oven until large cake has been cooking
for 2 hours. Ice with Almond Icing then Royal Icing.

Almond Icing:

1.8kg icing sugar • 4 egg whites, beaten stiff • 674g ground almonds • a little almond essence

If too stiff, add an egg yolk beaten in. If not stiff enough, add more icing sugar.

Royal Icing:

4 egg whites, beaten stiff • enough icing sugar to make icing stiff and to spread nicely and force through icing tubes • lemon essence

Mix and flavour with lemon essence.

WEDDING OR FESTIVAL CAKE

675g sultanas • 675g currants • 450g raisins • 225g mixed peel • 115g preserved ginger • 115g preserved cherries, if desired (for colour, not flavour) • 1 teaspoon grated mixed orange and lemon rind • 450g butter beaten with 1 teaspoon glycerine • 340g light brown sugar • 8 eggs • 570g flour • 1 small level teaspoon baking powder • light sprinkling of cayenne pepper (to bring out flavour — no spirits needed) • 1 teaspoon ground ginger • 1 teaspoon nutmeg • 1 teaspoon vanilla essence • 1 teaspoon almond essence

After mixing the fruit together, make it hot in the oven. Cream butter and sugar, then beat in eggs, adding one by one. Mix together the flour, baking powder and spices. Stir into the creamed mixture. Fold in the fruit and essences. Mix well.

Grease a 28cm tin and line with paper. Place cake batter in the tin. After scraping the bowl, mix that batter from sides of the bowl well into cake mixture in the tin. Make a fair-sized hole in the centre of the cake with your hand so it will rise evenly as it cooks. Cook at 150°C for 5 to 6 hours, according to depth of cake.

WHOLEMEAL CHOCOLATE SPONGE
(One Egg)

115g butter • 1 cup brown sugar • ½ teaspoon baking soda dissolved in ½ cup milk • 1 egg • ½ cup wholemeal flour • salt • 2 tablespoons cocoa • 1 teaspoon baking powder • 1 cup flour • vanilla • ¼ cup hot water

Cream butter and sugar. Add baking soda and milk, egg. Add remaining ingredients, with vanilla last. Add hot water. Bake in a moderate oven (180°C) for 30 minutes.

WHOLEMEAL FAMILY CAKE

1½ cups milk • 225g sugar • 115g butter • 3 tablespoons golden syrup • 1½ teaspoons baking soda • ½ cup white flour • 3 cups wholemeal flour • 1 tablespoon cocoa • 1½ teaspoons cinnamon • 2 cups nuts • 1 cup dates

Stir 1 cup milk in a saucepan with sugar, butter and golden syrup, until butter melts. Dissolve soda in the other ½ cup milk. Mix the dry ingredients, and add the warm mixture and nuts and dates. Add the soda last. Bake at 180°C for 30 minutes and allow to cool before turning out.

WONDER SPONGE CAKE

1 cup flour • 2 teaspoons baking powder • 1 small cup sugar •
2 level teaspoons butter • 2 eggs • a little milk

Sift flour with baking powder, and mix with sugar in a basin. Make a well in the centre. Melt butter in cup. Drop in eggs with butter in the cup, and fill cup up with milk. Pour into flour and beat for 5 minutes. Bake in a moderate oven (180°C) for 8 to 10 minutes.

YANKEE DOODLE CAKE

½ cup butter • 1 small cup sugar • 2 eggs, well beaten • 1½ cups flour • 1 cup minced raisins • ½ teaspoon baking soda dissolved in ½ cup milk • cream filling (or good knob of butter, icing sugar, vanilla and chopped walnuts) • icing and nuts to decorate • rum essence (or real rum) (optional)

Beat butter and sugar. Add eggs. Add flour, raisins and then baking soda and milk. Mix raisins in well. Cook in 2 sandwich tins in a moderate oven (180°C) for about 30 minutes.

Join with cream filling, or dissolve butter in a little boiling water and add icing sugar to make a rich filling. Add vanilla and chopped walnuts. Ice top and decorate with nuts. A little rum essence (or real rum) can be added to the raisins — they sink to the bottom when cooking.

ICINGS AND FILLINGS

ALMOND ICING (Plain)

450g icing sugar • 225g caster sugar • 115g ground almonds •
whole eggs or yolks to bind • almond essence

Sieve icing sugar, add caster sugar and ground almonds. Rub all
well together, bind to a nice consistency with the eggs. Add essence
and knead all together. Roll out, use as desired. The more ground
almonds used, the longer the icing will keep soft.

ALMOND PASTE (For Christmas Cake)

225g ground almonds • 450g icing sugar • 1 whole egg, beaten •
white of ½ an extra egg

Mix almonds and sugar well together. Add beaten egg and about
half the white of another. Mix over a low heat until a stiff paste but
it must be only warm. Dredge a board with icing sugar and roll paste
to required shape and thickness. Brush top of cake with egg white to
make paste stick, and press paste on to cake.

APPLE FILLING

4 large apples • juice of 1 orange • a little grated orange peel •
½ cup brown sugar • 2 tablespoons melted butter or cream •
2 tablespoons honey • pinch of cinnamon (optional)

Bake apples. Mix apple pulp with other ingredients. Beat, and keep in little jars. A pinch of cinnamon may also be added.

APPLE LEMON CURD

225g apples, peeled, cored and cut up • juice and rind of 1½ lemons • 2 eggs, beaten • 1 cup caster sugar • 60g butter

Cook apples until soft. Beat to a pulp. Add lemon juice and rind. Add eggs with sugar to mixture, and beat well. Melt butter in a basin and add the mixture to it. Cook over a double boiler and stir until mixture is thick, about 20 minutes. Put in jars, and cover tightly when cool.

BANANA BUTTER

4 bananas • 225g sugar • 2 eggs • juice of 2 lemons • grated rind of 1 lemon • 2 tablespoons butter

Mash bananas, and beat in sugar and eggs. Put into a saucepan with other ingredients and cook until like lemon honey with banana flavour.

BANANA BUTTER FROSTING

1 large banana mashed smooth • 1½ teaspoons lemon juice • ¼ cup butter or margarine • 3½ cups sifted icing sugar

Mix banana and lemon juice. Beat butter until creamy. Add sugar and banana alternately. Keep beating until frosting is light and fluffy.

BOSTON MOCHA FROSTING

¼ cup sweetened condensed milk • 1½ tablespoons strong black coffee • 1 teaspoon vanilla essence • 2¼ cups icing sugar • 2 teaspoons cocoa • ⅛ teaspoon salt

Blend condensed milk, coffee and vanilla. Sift sugar, cocoa and salt, and add. Blend and spread.

BUTTER FROSTING

2 tablespoons butter • ¼ cup sweetened condensed milk • 1½ cups finely sifted icing sugar • ½ teaspoon vanilla (or other essence)

Cream butter and condensed milk thoroughly. Gradually add icing sugar. Add essence. Beat until frosting is smooth, creamy and light in colour.

CHOCOLATE FOAM

1 teaspoon gelatine dissolved in ½ cup hot cocoa • a little vanilla essence • 1 egg white, beaten • 1 cup sifted icing sugar

Let cocoa and gelatine cool. Add vanilla. Beat egg white and gradually add cocoa mixture. Gradually stir in icing sugar. Spread on cake or use as filling.

COCONUT ORANGE FILLING

½ cup sugar • 4 tablespoons flour • dash of salt • ⅓ cup orange juice • 3 tablespoons lemon juice • 2 tablespoons water • 1 egg, well beaten • 2 tablespoons butter • 1½ teaspoons grated orange rind • ¼ cup desiccated coconut

Combine sugar, flour and salt on top of a double boiler. Add juices, water and egg. Cook over rapidly boiling water for 10 minutes, stirring constantly. Remove from heat and add butter and orange rind. Beat. Fold in coconut. Makes a filling to spread generously between two 23cm layers.

COFFEE ICING (Fluffy)

4 tablespoons butter • 1 egg white, unbeaten • about 2½ cups icing sugar • ¼ teaspoon cinnamon • 3 tablespoons strong cold coffee

Cream the butter. Add unbeaten egg white and 1 cup of the sugar. Stir in cinnamon. Add remainder of sugar alternately with cold coffee. Icing should have a fluffy texture, and be spread on cake roughly.

DATE FILLING

1 tablespoon sugar • 115g dates • 2 tablespoons water • juice of ½ lemon • grated rind of 1 lemon

Boil dates, sugar and water until soft. Add lemon juice and rind. Beat well.

DEVONSHIRE CREAM

Set a shallow pan full of fresh whole milk in a cool place for 12 to 24 hours. Carefully carry pan to stove and bring slowly to scalding point — until the thick, yellow cream begins to wrinkle. Put back in cool place until quite cold. Skim carefully with a perforated skimmer. The cream should come off in a thick blanket.

ENGLISH LEMON FILLING

3 tablespoons butter • juice of 2 lemons • grated rind of ½ lemon •
2 eggs, beaten until thick • 1 cup white sugar • pinch of salt

Put butter in top of double boiler. Add lemon juice and rind. Stir eggs into sugar. Add salt and stir all into first mixture. Cook and stir over hot water until thick. Cool. May be used as a cake, tart or sweet sandwich filling.

EVERYDAY FILLING

2 tablespoons butter • 4 tablespoons sugar • essence of choice •
2 tablespoons boiling water

Put butter, sugar and essence in a basin. Add boiling water. Beat thoroughly until like whipped cream. Leave for 15 minutes, then use.

FILLING WITH CONDENSED MILK

Cream together equal quantities of butter and sweetened condensed milk. Add either minced dates, sultanas or preserved ginger, or cherries, or a mixture.

FLUFFY MOCHA FROSTING

1 tablespoon butter • 2 cups sifted icing sugar • 1 tablespoon cocoa • ¼ teaspoon salt • ½ teaspoon vanilla essence •
2 tablespoons strong coffee

Beat butter to cream. Add all other ingredients and beat until smooth. Spread between layers of gingerbread, or on top.

GINGERBREAD FILLING

1 cup sweetened condensed milk • 3 tablespoons lemon juice •
6 tablespoons mashed cheese (use silver fork) • gingerbread

Mix condensed milk with lemon juice, and stir until thick. Add cheese. Beat until smooth. Spread between layers of gingerbread, or on top.

GRAPEFRUIT CHEESE

115g butter • 2 cups sugar • juice of 3 large grapefruit • grated rind of 1 grapefruit • 2 eggs, well beaten

Put butter, sugar, and grapefruit juice and rind into a large basin or double saucepan. Stand over pan of boiling water. When melted and blended together, add eggs, stirring constantly and thoroughly until mixture thickens. Pour into small pots, and cover when cold. This will keep a considerable time, and is a delightful change from lemon.

ICING (For Lamingtons)

60g butter • 3 teaspoons cocoa • ½ teaspoon vanilla •
4 tablespoons water • 1 cup icing sugar • coconut

Put all ingredients (except coconut) in a pan and stir until blended. Do not boil. Let cool, then dip in pieces of sponge (or stale Madeira cake). Roll in coconut.

LEMON CHEESE

85g butter • 225g sugar • 4 wine biscuits, finely crushed •
juice and grated rind of 3 lemons • 4 eggs, well beaten

Melt together first 4 ingredients. Add eggs. Cook until mixture
thickens, stirring all the time. Do not boil or it will spoil!

LEMON CHEESE (For Tartlets)

1 cup sugar • juice and grated rind of 4 lemons • 2 tablespoons
butter • 2 eggs

Cook until thick in a double boiler.

LEMON CHEESE (Good)

4 eggs, beaten just a little • juice and grated rind of 4 lemons •
225g butter • 450g sugar

Cook in a double boiler, or a basin in a saucepan of boiling water. See
that water boils all the time. Keep in airtight jars.

LEMON CHEESE (Without Butter)

1 cup water • 4 tablespoons sugar • juice of 2 large lemons •
1 heaped tablespoon cornflour • 1 egg, well beaten • a little milk
(if needed)

Boil together water, sugar and lemon juice. Mix cornflour with egg,
and milk if necessary. Pour boiling liquid over it. Mix and return to
pan. Boil for 5 minutes.

LEMON HONEY (Without Eggs)

60g butter • 1 breakfast cup sugar • juice and grated rind of 2 large
lemons • 1 tablespoon cornflour moistened with water

Melt butter and sugar very slowly with lemon juice and rind. When
sugar is dissolved, add cornflour. Remove from heat while stirring in
cornflour. Cook all very slowly until clear golden.

MARSHMALLOW (Simple)

2 dessertspoons gelatine soaked in 1 cup water • 1 breakfast cup
sugar • a few drops of vanilla or other essence • shortbread (or
other biscuit) • icing • nuts as topping

Mix gelatine with sugar and boil in a saucepan for 10 minutes. Add
essence. Let cool. Beat until white and thick. Spread on shortbread,
etc. Ice when cold and sprinkle with nuts.

MARSHMALLOW FILLING

30g powdered gelatine • 2 cups water • 450g sugar • pinch of salt •
1 teaspoon vanilla essence • biscuits • nuts and cherries to decorate

Put gelatine in 1 cup water and stand for 10 minutes. Add other
cup of water. Put on stove to melt. When melted, add sugar, salt
and vanilla, and boil gently for 30 minutes. Cool in a basin then
beat until like a snowball. Almost cover biscuits and decorate with
chopped nuts and cherries.

MERINGUE CAKE TOPPING

1 egg white • 1 tablespoon sugar

Beat egg white and sugar to a meringue. Spread about 3mm thick over top of cake mixture before cooking.

MOCHA ICING AND FILLING

1½ tablespoons butter • 2½ cups sugar • 2½ tablespoons cocoa • 4 tablespoons strong coffee • ¼ teaspoon salt

Cream butter and sugar. Add cocoa, coffee and salt. Stir until smooth. Spread between layers and on top of cake.

MOCK ALMOND ICING

equal amounts icing sugar and ground rice • 1 egg • about 2 teaspoons almond essence • a little lemon juice

Sift icing sugar, mix well with ground rice. Add egg, essence and lemon juice. Work well together. If well blended, this closely resembles real almond icing.

MOCK ALMOND PASTE

3 egg yolks, beaten • 900g icing sugar • 225g desiccated coconut • 2 teaspoons almond essence

Mix egg yolks with dry ingredients. Beat in the essence. Stand in a basin in a saucepan of boiling water. Knead well for a few minutes. If too dry, add a little water.

MOCK CREAM (1)

2 heaped tablespoons full cream milk powder • 2 teaspoons sugar •
½ cup fresh milk (or more if cream is required thinner) •
essence of choice

Mix milk powder with sugar. Stir in fresh milk. Add essence and beat with an egg beater for a minute or two. This can be used as a topping for trifle, or if made thinner, as a pudding sauce.

MOCK CREAM (2)

2 cups milk • 2 tablespoons full cream milk powder •
2 teaspoons gelatine dissolved in 1 dessertspoon boiling water •
1 teaspoon sugar • a little vanilla essence

Warm milk to blood heat. Mix milk powder to a paste with a little milk, then stir in the rest. Add gelatine and sugar. Stand aside to chill thoroughly, to let the gelatine set a little. Then beat again.

MOCK CREAM (3)

This is a rich mixture.

2 level tablespoons cornflour • 1 cup milk • 30g butter •
15g sugar • essence if desired

Mix cornflour with a little milk. Warm the remaining milk in a saucepan. Add cornflour and return to pan. Stir over heat until well cooked. Put aside to cool. Cream butter and sugar very well. Beat in thickened cornflour and essence, by the teaspoonful. Continue to beat until creamy. The above quantity makes about ½ cup of cream, very similar to whipped cream.

ORANGE FILLING

85g flour • 1 cup sugar • grated rind of 1 orange • ½ cup orange juice • 3 tablespoons lemon juice • ¼ cup water • 1 egg, slightly beaten • 1 dessertspoon butter

Combine ingredients in the order given. Cook in a double boiler for 10 minutes, stirring constantly. Cool. May also be used as a filling for éclairs, or with shredded coconut for pastry tarts.

ORANGE FILLING FOR SPONGE

1 tablespoon gelatine • juice of 1 large orange • 1 cup cream • a little sugar • 1 teaspoon brandy • grated rind of 1 orange

Soak gelatine in orange juice. Whip cream with a little sugar and brandy. Add orange rind. Stand gelatine and juice in a cup in a saucepan of boiling water. Stir until gelatine is dissolved. Let cool. Add to cream, and whip again.

PASSIONFRUIT HONEY

10 passionfruit • 1 tablespoon butter • 1 small cup sugar • 1 egg, beaten

Heat all in a saucepan over boiling water until thick, stirring with a wooden spoon. A delicious filling.

PINEAPPLE FILLING (Quick)

1 cup icing sugar • 1 tablespoon pineapple juice • 2 egg whites, whipped stiff • finely chopped pineapple

Beat icing sugar and pineapple juice into egg whites. Stir in as much chopped pineapple as the icing will hold. Add a little more sugar if necessary.

PLAIN WHITE ICING

2 tablespoons hot milk • 1 teaspoon essence (orange, pineapple or other) • about 1⅓ cups icing sugar

Put hot milk in a small bowl. Add essence. Cream in sugar until the right consistency.

WHIPPED CREAM (Mock)

1 teaspoon gelatine mixed with 3 tablespoons boiling water • 115g butter • pinch of salt • 1½ tablespoons sugar • vanilla or lemon essence • ½ teaspoon cream of tartar

Stir gelatine in the boiling water until dissolved. Put butter, sugar, salt and essence into a basin. Cream a little. Add cream of tartar. Add dissolved gelatine. Whip well (about 10 minutes) until it looks like whipped cream. An excellent filling for sponge or puffs.

WHITE ICING (Ordinary Sugar)

1 breakfast cup plain white sugar • 15g fresh butter • ½ breakfast cup milk • essence (of choice)

Put sugar in a saucepan. Add butter and milk. Boil for 8 minutes, stirring well. Flavour with essence and beat until thick as cream. Spread over cake with a knife and it will be white when cold. Double this quantity for a large cake.

BREADS, SCONES AND TEACAKES

BELGIAN BUN

115g butter • 115g sugar • 225g flour • 1 teaspoon baking powder •
1 egg, well beaten • a little milk • lemon cheese (see page 184) •
blanched almonds to decorate

Cream butter and sugar. Add flour and baking powder. Make into
a fairly stiff dough with egg and milk. Divide into two parts. Press
each with fingers into a round shape. Place one half in a pie plate or
dish, spread with lemon cheese. Put other round on top. Decorate
with blanched almonds. Bake in a moderate oven (180°C) for 15 to
20 minutes.

BRAN AND DATE MUFFINS
(Could use Raisins or Sultanas)

1 cup chopped dates, stoned and cut up coarsely • 1 cup white or
wholemeal flour • 1 cup bran • 3 level teaspoons baking powder •
½ teaspoon salt • 2 teaspoons sugar • 1 egg, beaten well • 1 cup
milk • 2 tablespoons melted butter

Add dates (or sultanas) to dry sifted ingredients. Mix egg, milk and
butter. Pour at once into dry ingredients, and mix just enough to
blend. Do not beat. Grease small muffin pans (or deep patty tins) and
fill to two-thirds full. Bake at 200°C for approximately 20 minutes.

BREAD

10 cups flour (3 wholemeal and 7 white is a good light loaf) •
1 level tablespoon salt • 2 teaspoons compressed yeast •
2 tablespoons sugar • 3½ to 4 cups warm water • melted butter

Sift flour and salt into a warmed bowl. In another basin, work yeast and sugar together until liquid. Add warm water. Pour yeast mixture into middle of flour and gradually work in flour from the sides until a light dough (slightly moister than scone dough). Cover with a clean cloth, then a rug or blanket — it must not cool too quickly. Put in a warm place overnight. Next day, turn out on a floured board and sprinkle with flour. Knead with back of fingers, folding in as much air as possible. Knead for at least 15 minutes. Shape into loaves and put in greased tins to half full. Stand in a warm place for 1 hour, or until it rises to double the size. Bake for about 1 hour at 200°C. Do not open oven for first 45 minutes. Brush over top with melted butter.

BROWN HEALTH LOAF

2 large cups wholemeal flour • 2 good teaspoons baking powder •
½ teaspoon salt • 1 good tablespoon butter • 1 cup chopped
dates, raisins and nuts • 1 dessertspoon golden syrup or plain malt
dissolved in 1 cup hot water • ½ cup cold milk

Mix wholemeal flour, baking powder and salt. Rub in butter. Add dates and nuts. Mix golden syrup and water with milk. Mix with dry ingredients. Bake in a greased tin for about 1¼ hours in a moderate oven (180°C).

CHEESE DROP SCONES (Australian)

2 cups sifted flour • 2 teaspoons baking powder • 1½ teaspoons salt • 60 to 85g butter • ¾ cup milk • 1 cup grated cheese

Sift together flour, baking powder and salt. Melt butter in a cup and fill cup with milk. Pour into flour. Add cheese. Mix lightly into a nice dough, until all liquid is used. Stir vigorously until dough is nice and soft. The bowl should now be clean. Drop from a teaspoon or dessertspoon onto an ungreased baking sheet. Bake in a hot oven (220°C) for 10 to 15 minutes. Makes about 18 to 20 scones. Nice for supper.

CHEESE MUFFINS

1 egg, beaten lightly • ¼ teaspoon salt • ¾ cup milk • 1½ cups flour • 2 teaspoons baking powder • ½ cup finely grated or finely sliced cheese • extra beaten egg to brush muffins

Mix egg with salt and milk. Sift flour and baking powder, and add cheese. Make into a dough with the liquid, mixing well. Roll out, cut into rounds. Brush with beaten egg. Bake for 10 minutes in a fairly hot oven (200°C), or cook in patty tins. Delicious split, spread with butter, and eaten hot.

CINNAMON TEA CAKE

1 teaspoon salt • 450g flour • 2 teaspoons baking powder • 3 tablespoons butter • 1 egg, beaten • 2 cups milk • vanilla or lemon essence • cinnamon • sugar • melted butter or cream

Mix first three ingredients. Rub in butter. Add beaten egg, milk and vanilla. Mix to a soft dough. Roll out to 20mm thick. Place in a shallow dish and cover with a mixture of cinnamon, sugar and melted butter or cream. Bake in a quick oven (200°C) for about 15 minutes. May be served hot or cold.

CRUMPETS (Berkshire)

15g compressed yeast • a little sugar • 450g flour • ½ teaspoon
salt • 1 egg, beaten • 1 cup milk and tepid water

Stir yeast to a cream with sugar. Sift flour and salt into a warm basin.
Stir egg into yeast with milk. Pour into flour. Beat well until smooth,
adding more milk or water until a smooth batter, slightly thicker
than pancake mix. Cover and leave in a warm place for 1½ hours.
Put muffin tins on a hot griddle. Half fill with batter and cook,
turning once only. Serve toasted and buttered. Condensed milk tins
or similar can be used cut down for muffin rings.

DATE BREAD

1 cup dates, stoned and cut into pieces • 1 level teaspoon baking
soda • ¾ cup boiling water • 1 egg, beaten • just under
½ breakfast cup sugar • pinch of salt • 1 teaspoon vanilla essence •
1½ breakfast cups flour • 1 large teaspoon baking powder

Put dates in a basin with the baking soda. Pour boiling water over
and stand to cool. Mix egg with sugar, salt and vanilla in a basin.
Add date mixture. Stir in flour and baking powder. Bake in a well-
greased tin for about 1¼ hours, or less, depending on size. To have
bread smooth and glossy, cover with paper while baking.

DATE AND RAISIN LOAF

1 cup dates • 1 cup raisins or sultanas • ½ cup sugar • ½ cup nuts
(optional) • 60g butter • 1½ cups hot water • 2 breakfast cups flour •
2 level teaspoons baking soda

Put dates, raisins, sugar, nuts, butter and hot water in a saucepan
and boil for 8 to 10 minutes. Allow to cool then add flour and baking
soda. Mix all together in a shallow tin and bake fairly slowly (160°C)
for 45 minutes. This is a moist loaf and keeps well. Improved by
using wholemeal flour.

GINGERBREAD (No Eggs)

½ cup sugar • 1 level tablespoon ginger • 2 cups flour • ¼ cup or
4 tablespoons butter, melted • ½ cup treacle • 1 teaspoon baking
soda dissolved in a little hot water • ½ cup milk

Put all dry ingredients into a basin. Melt butter and treacle together.
Mix baking soda, butter and treacle with dry ingredients. Beat in
milk. Bake at 180°C for 1½ hours. This keeps beautifully moist.

GINGERBREAD (2 Eggs)

2 tablespoons butter • 1 breakfast cup brown sugar • 2 teaspoons
ground ginger • 2 teaspoons cinnamon • 2 tablespoons golden
syrup • 2 eggs, beaten • 2 breakfast cups flour • 2 level teaspoons
baking soda dissolved in warm water • 1 breakfast cup milk

Cream butter and sugar. Add ginger, cinnamon, syrup and beaten eggs.
Add flour, baking soda and milk. Bake at 180°C for 30 minutes.

Icing:

225g brown sugar • 4 tablespoons cream • 30g butter • vanilla to taste

Boil together until it thickens.

GIRDLE SCONES

2 heaped teacups flour • ½ teaspoon salt • 3 teaspoons baking
powder • milk and water to mix

Mix all together into a soft dough. Do not have dough too stiff. Roll
out and cut into quarters. Take each section in right hand, turn over
on to left hand, and slip onto girdle. Thus the underneath floury side
is on top. Lightly brush off flour from what is now the top, and turn
when brown. This helps to stop toughness. Stand them on edge for a
few minutes when cooked.

HOT CROSS BUNS

450g flour • pinch of salt • 1 teaspoon mixed spice • 60g butter •
60g mixed candied peel • 60g sultanas • 60g currants • 1 level
teaspoon powdered cinnamon • 2 tablespoons caster sugar •
22g compressed yeast • 1 cup lukewarm milk • 1 egg

Sift flour with salt and spice. Rub in butter and add prepared fruit, cinnamon and sugar (keep back half the sugar to mix with yeast). Mix sugar and yeast until liquid. Stir in milk. Strain liquid into centre of dry ingredients. Make into a soft dough, adding the egg. Divide into small portions, shape into buns, and put on a greased slide. Mark with a cross. Leave to rise until twice the size. Bake in a hot oven (200°C) for 20 minutes. Brush over with sugar and milk. Return to oven for 2 minutes.

MARY'S BREAD

6 cups pure wholemeal flour • 2 teaspoons salt • 2 good
teaspoons dried yeast • 2½ to 3 cups milk at blood heat •
2 good teaspoons honey

Sift wholemeal flour and salt. Mix yeast with milk and honey. Make sure it is well dissolved. Add to flour and salt. Mix into a scone consistency and turn out. Knead a little and replace in basin. Leave in a warm place for 2 hours, or until it doubles in size. Turn out and knead well. Form into loaves and leave again for 45 minutes to 1 hour in a warm place. Bake in a moderate oven (180°C) for 45 minutes to 1 hour.

MUFFINS

2 tablespoons sugar • 30g yeast dissolved in a little lukewarm water • 900g flour • 15g salt • 2 cups milk, or milk and water • rice flour

Add sugar to yeast. Sift flour with salt. Put milk in a basin and add a little of the flour. Pour in yeast and sugar, and work together. Work in remainder of flour, and knead well. Leave to rise in a warm place for 1 hour. Then knead dough and divide as required. Round each piece carefully, and leave in a warm place to rise, about 1 hour or more. Dust each piece with rice flour if available. When double in size, roll out with a rolling pin to about 25mm thick, still keeping the round shape. Bake on an ungreased hot plate, but not too hot, or muffins will be doughy in centre. As they bake, turn each over with a broad knife. When brown on both sides, reduce heat until thoroughly cooked. Two tablespoons of butter may be added to the mixture if liked.

NUT AND RAISIN LOAF (Special)

3 cups plain flour (or 2 cups plain and 1 cup wholemeal) • 3 teaspoons baking powder • 1 cup sugar • 1 teaspoon salt • 1 teaspoon ground cinnamon • 1 egg, beaten • 1½ cups milk • 1 cup seeded raisins • 1 cup chopped walnuts

Sift dry ingredients. Add egg and milk, stir in and mix well. Add raisins and nuts. Pour into a greased tin. Let stand for 30 minutes. Bake in a moderate oven (180°C) for about 1½ hours.

PANCAKES (Griddle)

1¼ cups flour • 1 teaspoon baking powder • ½ teaspoon salt • 1 teaspoon sugar • 1 cup milk • 2 egg yolks, slightly beaten • 2 tablespoons melted butter • 2 egg whites, beaten • quince or other jelly, or bacon or sausage to serve

Sift flour, baking powder, salt and sugar twice. Mix milk and egg yolks. Add flour gradually and mix to a smooth batter. Add butter. Fold in egg whites. Bake on a hot greased griddle. Spread with jelly and roll, or roll around bacon or sausage.

PIKELETS

1 cup flour • 1 tablespoon sugar • ½ teaspoon salt • 1 teaspoon cream of tartar • ½ teaspoon baking soda • 1 egg • milk to mix to stiff paste • 1 teaspoon melted butter

Put all dry ingredients in a bowl. Break in egg and mix in milk. Add butter. Mix well and let stand for 30 minutes. Drop in spoonful lots on hot girdle.

PIKELETS WITHOUT BUTTER

1 breakfast cup flour • 2 level teaspoons cream of tartar • pinch of salt • 1 level teaspoon baking soda • 2 level tablespoons sugar • 1 egg • ¾ cup milk

Sift flour, cream of tartar, salt and baking soda into a basin. Add sugar. Make a well in centre of flour, and break in the egg. Add milk and mix well. Cook on hot greased girdle. Place on towel and keep covered to make them nice and soft.

POTATO AND CHEESE GEMS

2 dessertspoons butter • pinch of salt • 1 cup milk • 2 eggs, beaten • 3 cups mashed potatoes • ¾ cup grated cheese

Dissolve butter and salt in milk. Add eggs. Mix with potato and cheese, stirring slowly to mix. Drop in buttered, very hot gem irons, sprinkle with flour and cook until brown on top. Split and butter, and eat hot.

RAISIN CHEESE SCONES

2 cups flour • 2 teaspoons baking powder • ½ teaspoon salt •
½ cup good juicy seeded raisins • 8 tablespoons grated cheese •
3 tablespoons butter • 1 cup milk •

Sift flour, baking powder and salt together. Add raisins and cheese. Cut in the butter. Add milk and mix. Roll out lightly, shape into biscuits. Bake in a hot oven (220°C) until brown, about 15 minutes. These should be eaten hot.

RUSKS

Make usual scone mix (see page 199), using a beaten egg instead of part of the milk. Bake as usual. When taken from oven, split them apart into halves with fingers, or use 2 forks. Replace in oven turned down a little, and bake crisp and brown. Very nice if a little sugar is added to mixture.

SALLY LUNNS (With Baking Powder)

2 breakfast cups sifted flour • 2 teaspoons baking powder •
good pinch of salt • ½ cup soft sugar • 1 tablespoon butter •
¾ cup milk • 1 egg • ½ teaspoon lemon essence •
slices of candied peel

Mix all dry ingredients together. Rub butter in well. Add milk, beaten with egg and essence. Pat on a board until 12mm thick. Cut into diamond-shaped cakes. Glaze each with milk and sugar, or with egg. Place 1 piece candied peel on top of each cake. Bake until well browned in a hot oven (220°C).

SALLY LUNNS (Real)

30g compressed yeast • 2 cups milk, scalded and cooled to
lukewarm • 30g sugar • 2 eggs, beaten well • ½ teaspoon salt •
60g butter • 675g flour • white sugar for sprinkling

Dissolve yeast in a portion of the milk and add sugar. Add salt to
eggs. Cream butter well and just melt it. Mix all together well with
flour — add yeast last. Beat until smooth. Pour into well-greased
shallow pans, or muffin rings on a baking sheet. Half fill rings, then
cover and allow to rise in a warm place for about 1 hour, until nearly
full. Just before baking, sprinkle tops with granulated sugar. Bake in
a good oven (180°C) for about 20 minutes. Condensed milk tins, or
similar tins, may be cut down for muffin rings.

SCONES

Basic recipe:

225g flour • ½ teaspoon salt • 4 level teaspoons baking powder •
2 tablespoons butter • ⅔ cup milk

Sift flour, salt and baking powder together. Rub in butter until like
crumbs. Make a well, and pour in milk. Mix quickly with a knife
or spatula. Knead very lightly for about half a minute. Pat or roll
lightly to 12mm. Cut with floured knife or cutter. Place on ungreased,
unfloured oven tray. Bake in hot oven at 220°C for about 10 minutes,
until golden brown.

SCONES (Wholemeal, Never Fail)

Chief points for success: Quite a moist mixture; plenty of rising; quick working; and a hot oven.

2 heaped cups wholemeal flour • 2 large heaped teaspoons baking powder • ½ large teaspoon salt • 30 to 60g melted butter (quite liquid) • about 1 cup milk • 1 dessertspoon brown sugar (optional)

Mix dry ingredients. Fill the cup containing the butter with milk. Mix into dry ingredients very quickly, making a soft dough. Turn on to a board, press quickly with palm of hand to about 6mm thick. Cut in squares. Flour slightly and shake flour off. Cook in hot oven (220°C) for about 15 minutes. If liked, mix in 1 dessertspoon brown sugar with butter. Turn oven down a little if browning too fast.

SELKIRK BANNOCK

115g lard • 225g butter • 900g baker's dough • 225g sugar • 340g sultanas (or 225g currants) • 115g finely chopped peel

Work lard and butter into the dough. Add sugar, sultanas and peel. Knead well. Place dough in a buttered tin and put in a warm place to rise for about 30 minutes. Bake in a moderate oven (180°C).

SUGAR TOP BUNS

½ cup sugar • ½ cup butter • 1 cup water • 2 cups flour • 2 teaspoons baking powder • ½ cup sultanas • 1 egg, well beaten • few drops of lemon essence

Boil sugar, butter and water. Set aside to cool. Sift flour and baking powder in a basin. Add sultanas. Mix all to a soft dough with the liquid. Add egg and essence. Put dessertspoonfuls on to a greased oven tray. Sprinkle tops with sugar. Bake at 180°C for about 15 minutes. They should rise and crack, and be beautifully light. The secret is to have the dough very light.

VIENNA ROLLS

900g flour • 60g butter • 1 teaspoon salt • 1 tablespoon
compressed yeast • 15g sugar • 2 eggs, beaten • 2 cups
lukewarm milk

Put flour in a warm basin. Rub in butter and add salt. Put yeast in
a cup with sugar, and work until smooth and liquid. Add half the
milk and leave in a warm place for about 10 minutes. Mix eggs with
remainder of milk. Add to yeast mixture. Put into flour, mixing well.
Knead to a light dough. Leave in a warm place for 1 hour. Knead
and divide into 12 pieces. Knead each to form into a roll. Place on
baking tin in a warm place for about 1 hour. Bake in a quick oven
(220°C) for about 20 minutes. When baked, brush over with beaten
egg straight away.

VIRGINIAN SHORT'NIN' BREAD

2 cups flour • ½ cup light brown sugar • 225g butter

Mix flour and sugar. Rub in butter. Put on a floured board and pat to
12mm thickness. Cut into shapes. Bake in a moderate oven at 170°C
to 180°C for 20 to 25 minutes.

WAFFLES (1)

2 cups flour • ¼ cup cornflour • 4 teaspoons baking powder •
½ teaspoon salt • 2 eggs, beaten well • 2 cups milk •
4 tablespoons melted butter or vegetable fat • butter and
maple syrup to serve

Beat dry ingredients into eggs and milk. Add butter and beat well
with an egg beater. Bake in hot waffle irons. Recipe may be halved.
Serve hot with butter and maple syrup.

WAFFLES (2)

2 cups flour • 3 tablespoons baking powder • ½ teaspoon salt •
2 egg yolks, beaten slightly • 1¾ cups milk • 4 tablespoons melted
butter • 2 egg whites, beaten stiff

Sift flour, baking powder and salt. Mix egg yolks with milk. Add to
dry ingredients and beat thoroughly. Add butter and stir well. Fold
in egg whites. Bake in hot waffle irons.

WHITE BREAD

4 dessertspoons sweetened condensed milk • 2½ cups
tepid water • 40g dried yeast • 1 cup flour • 6 cups sifted flour •
1 slightly rounded dessertspoon salt

Pour condensed milk into a basin and add water. Stir until thoroughly
blended. Add yeast and beat until slightly frothy. Add 1 cup flour
and fold in. Lightly cover, and leave in a warm place to work for
about 15 minutes. Put 6 cups sifted flour and the salt in a large basin.
When yeast is frothy, and has a scum on top, combine with flour and
salt. Mix to a good stiff dough using a knife. Remove from basin and
knead well on a floured board. Dust inside basin with flour and place
kneaded dough back in and cover. Let rise again for 45 minutes. The
dough should be half its size again. Take out and knead again. Pat
out to a good 25mm thickness and cut into quarters. Shape up and
place 2 pieces in each of 2 bread tins. Cover and allow to rise until
dough is about 18mm from top of tins. Place in oven at 230°C for 3 to
4 minutes. Lower oven to 180°C and bake another 45 minutes. After
8 minutes' baking, look at it and lower oven temperature if necessary.

WHOLEMEAL BREAD (No Kneading)

8 breakfast cups wholemeal flour • 1 teaspoon salt • 40g dried
yeast • about 3½ cups warm water • 1 teaspoon raw or brown
sugar • 1 tablespoon malt (if liked)

Mix flour and salt. Dissolve yeast in water with sugar (and malt if
using). Pour into flour, and stir and knead for 5 minutes. If not the
right consistency, add flour or water accordingly. Mould into loaves
and put in greased tins. Cover and put in a warm place (oven slightly
heated) until double in size, about 1½ hours. Bake about 30 minutes
at 220°C to 230°C. When baked, take loaves from tins and return to
oven for a few minutes to crisp up.

WHOLEMEAL BREAD (No Yeast)

1 tablespoon syrup or treacle • 1 cup milk • 2 cups wholemeal flour •
¼ teaspoon salt • 4 teaspoons baking powder

Melt syrup in milk. Mix flour, salt and baking powder. Stir into syrup
and milk quickly. Let mixture stand for a short while to rise. Put in a
greased tin and bake about 45 minutes in a moderate oven (180°C).
A nice moist loaf.

WHOLEMEAL LOAF

1 tablespoon golden syrup • ½ cake compressed yeast •
3 breakfast cups wholemeal flour • 1 dessertspoon salt •
1½ breakfast cups milk (or milk and water), warmed to blood heat

Mix syrup and yeast on a saucer. Sift flour and salt. Make a well in
flour. Pour in yeast and syrup mixture. Add milk, beating all the time
and working in the yeast. Continue to beat when all milk is in for 3
or 4 minutes. A fairly moist mixture is needed for this bread, so that if
more milk is needed, heat to blood temperature as before. Let rise in a
greased tin for 1 hour. Bake for about 1 hour in a fairly hot oven. No
kneading required.

YEAST (Home Made) (1)

4 cups cold potato water from cooked potatoes • 1 tablespoon
flour • 1 tablespoon sugar • 1 teaspoon compressed yeast
(or old yeast)

Mix potato water with flour, sugar and yeast. Make during morning and by evening it should have a frothy top, ready for use. After taking some out each time, leave enough in the jar to start the next lot. Replenish cold potato water and above quantities of flour and sugar each day. Do not add any more compressed yeast.

YEAST (Home Made) (2)

6 breakfast cups cold water • handful of hops • 2 tablespoons
flour and 1 tablespoon sugar mixed together • 2 medium potatoes,
unpeeled

Slice potatoes into a pan and add water and hops. Boil for 30 minutes. Strain water from potato and hops through a colander into flour and sugar mix. Mix smooth. Strain again through a fine sieve. Bottle when nearly cold and put in a light warm place.

YEAST (Home Made) (3)

30g hops • 1 cup flour • 2 tablespoons sugar • 6 cups water •
1 medium raw potato

Boil hops for a few minutes in a small quantity of water. Drain and add sufficient water to make 6 cups. Add sugar. When tepid shake in flour. Never mind if it seems lumpy. Grate in potato. Bottle. If you have a little yeast in the bottle to start working, it can be used the same night. With home-made yeast, it takes longer for bread to rise than with compressed yeast. Divide into 3 bottles and leave enough room to work.

CHUTNEYS, PICKLES AND SAUCES

It is always desirable to put in a little less salt and mustard than stated until you taste the mixture. It is easy to add more seasoning, but impossible to take out once added.

To prevent home-made pickles from shrinking, cover with wax after bottling.

If pickles become shrunk and crusted, mix equal parts boiling water and vinegar, and a little sugar. Put on top of chutney. Do not take the dry crusty part off, but push it down in several places with a wooden skewer, and leave it for a while. Every now and then stir with the skewer. It should be as good as new.

APPLE CHUTNEY

900g tomatoes • 1.8kg apples • ~~⬛⬛⬛⬛~~ • 450g sugar •
60g salt • 15g ground ginger • ¼ teaspoon cayenne pepper •
7g allspice • 4 cups vinegar • 450g seedless raisins

Skin tomatoes, mince apples ~~⬛⬛⬛⬛~~. Tie spices in a muslin bag. Boil all together in a saucepan for 1 or more hours, until brown and cooked. Half a cup of finely chopped mint leaves added makes an interesting flavour.

APPLES (Cloved)

1.8kg apples • 1.6kg sugar • 2 cups water • 12 cloves

Peel and core apples and divide into quarters. Boil sugar, water and cloves to a syrup. Add apples and bring to the boil. Simmer gently until all the apple is cooked but not broken. Lift out carefully into small hot jars. Seal immediately. If done properly they should keep well, and are delicious with cold meat, cheese or salad.

APRICOT CHUTNEY

2.7kg apricots • ~~[illegible]~~ • 790g sugar • 1 dessertspoon salt • 1 teaspoon cloves • 1 teaspoon peppercorns • 1 teaspoon ground mace • 1 teaspoon curry powder • ½ teaspoon cayenne pepper • 4 cups vinegar

Cut up apricots ~~[illegible]~~ Put in a pan with the remaining ingredients. Boil for 1 hour. Nice in sandwiches for supper.

BEAN RELISH

12 cups vinegar • 2 tablespoons salt • 2 small teaspoons pepper • 3 cups sugar • 1.8kg sliced beans (scarlet runners are good) • ~~[illegible]~~ • 2 tablespoons flour • 2 tablespoons mustard • 2 heaped teaspoons turmeric • a little cold water

Boil vinegar, salt, pepper, sugar, beans ~~[illegible]~~ together for 1 hour, or until tender. Mix flour, mustard and turmeric with water. Stir into beans and boil a few minutes longer. Cover when cold. A small piece of finely chopped garlic is an improvement.

BEETROOT CHUTNEY

1.4kg beetroot • 680g apples • ▆▆▆▆ • 2 cups vinegar •
½ teaspoon ginger • 1 teaspoon salt • juice of 1 lemon • 340g sugar

Boil beetroot until tender. Cut into cubes when cold. Cut apples ▆▆
▆▆▆▆ small and boil for 20 minutes with vinegar and remaining ingredients. Add to beetroot and boil another 15 minutes.

BEETROOT RELISH (Uncooked)

3 medium beets, washed, scraped and skinned • ½ cup sugar •
a little cinnamon • salt and pepper • 1 cup vinegar • a few cloves

Grate beets on a carrot grater, more finely than a piece of horseradish. Add sugar, cinnamon, and salt and pepper. Boil vinegar with cloves, and strain. When cold, mix with beets. Leave about a week before using.

BLACKBERRY PICKLE

2 cups blackberries • 450g white sugar • 1 cup vinegar •
15g ground ginger • 30g allspice

Steep blackberries and sugar for 12 hours. Bring vinegar to the boil. Add blackberries and boil for 30 minutes. When cold, add ginger and spice, and mix well. Put in jars and cover.

CABBAGE PICKLE (Uncooked)

cabbage or cauliflower • salt • allspice • best vinegar

Cut up cabbage (or cauliflower), sprinkle with salt and leave overnight. In morning wash off salt and drain for half a day. Put into jars with allspice sprinkled on the bottom. Sprinkle allspice in the middle and on top. Cover with vinegar, filling the jars. Cover tightly and keep in a cool place.

RED CABBAGE PICKLE

1 fresh dry red cabbage, finely cut • salt • vinegar — to every
4 cups vinegar allow: 30g peppercorns • 30g ginger •
30g allspice • 1 tablespoon sugar

Bring cabbage to the boil. Strain and press into jars. Boil vinegar mixed with peppercorns, ginger, allspice and sugar. Pour hot vinegar over cabbage. Ready in a week.

CABBAGE PICKLE (White)

1 large white cabbage, finely cut • ▮▮▮▮▮▮▮ • salt •
4 cups vinegar • 1 cup flour • 1 cup sugar • 2 cups vinegar

Sprinkle cabbage ▮▮▮▮▮▮ with salt and leave to stand 24 hours. Drain water off and boil vegetables slowly for 15 minutes in 4 cups vinegar. Mix flour, sugar and 2 cups vinegar. Add to vegetables and boil for 10 minutes. Put in jars, and cover when cold.

CAPERS, PICKLED

capers • vinegar — to each 2 cups vinegar add: 1 teaspoon mace •
1 bay leaf • 2 whole peppercorns • 1 teaspoon brown sugar

Pick capers when ripe. Put in the sun for 1 day to dry. Put in large jars with vinegar and let stand 3 or 4 weeks. Drain, and pack closely in jars. Bring vinegar, mace, bay leaf, peppercorns and sugar to the boil. Strain, and fill jars. Cover closely and store in a cool dark place. Best kept 2 months before using.

CAULIFLOWER PICKLE

1 cauliflower, cut up fine • ████████, cut fine • salt •
4 cups vinegar

Sprinkle vegetables with salt and leave overnight. Strain. Boil for 20 minutes in vinegar.

Thickening:

½ cup flour • 1½ teacups golden syrup • ½ tablespoon
curry powder • ½ tablespoon turmeric • 2 dessertspoons
mustard mixed with 2 cups vinegar

Heat all ingredients until thick. Stir in to vegetables. Boil all for 5 to 6 minutes. Bottle when cold.

CAULIFLOWER AND PINEAPPLE PICKLE

████████████ • 1 large cauliflower broken into little florets •
handful of salt • vinegar • 1 large tin pineapple, cut small •
½ cup flour • 1 tablespoon mustard • 2 tablespoons curry powder

Sprinkle ████████ cauliflower with salt and leave overnight. Next day, strain, and cover with vinegar. Boil for 30 minutes. Add pineapple. Mix flour and remaining ingredients to a paste with a little water. Stir into the pickle. Boil for 10 minutes. Bottle.

CELERY PICKLES (With Tamarillos)

18 ripe tamarillos • 5 good heads of celery • 2 cups brown sugar •
1½ cups vinegar • 2 tablespoons salt (or less) • 1 teaspoon cloves •
1 teaspoon allspice • 1 teaspoon cinnamon • 1 teaspoon mustard

Bring gradually to the boil and simmer for about 1½ hours. Fill warm jars and seal while still warm.

CHOKO CHUTNEY

10 large chokos • 680g stoned dates • 680g sugar • 3 large cooking apples • ▬▬▬ • 220g preserved ginger • 85 to 115g salt • 1 teaspoon cayenne pepper • 450g sultanas • 6 cups vinegar • 450g raisins

Cut up chokos finely overnight. Next morning boil all ingredients together until tender.

CHOKO PICKLE

8 fair-sized chokos, washed • 450g beans, washed • salt and water brine • 1 dessertspoon peppercorns • 1 level teaspoon cloves • 1 cup sugar • 4 cups vinegar • a little mace • 1 salt spoon cayenne • ▬▬▬ • 1 teaspoon ginger • 1 teaspoon curry powder • 1 dessertspoon flour • 1 tablespoon mustard • 1 dessertspoon turmeric

Dice chokos and beans, and stand in weak salt and water for 12 hours. Strain. Tie spices in a bag. Boil all ingredients in vinegar (except flour, mustard and turmeric) for about 15 minutes. Add mustard, turmeric and flour blended with a little vinegar. Boil until tender. Bottle when cold.

CHOW CHOW

1.4kg beans • ▬▬▬ • 3 or 4 cucumbers • 220g salt • 8 cups vinegar • 450g brown sugar • 30g cloves • 30g spice • 30g peppercorns • 85 to 115g mustard • ½ teaspoon cayenne • 1 tablespoon turmeric • 4 tablespoons flour

Cut up vegetables and sprinkle with salt. Stand overnight. Drain. Add 5 cups of the vinegar and boil, only until vegetables are tender. Add sugar and all spices. Mix flour with remaining vinegar. Add to vegetables and boil until thick. Bottle.

CUCUMBER PICKLES (Small)

24 small cucumbers, washed and wiped • salt • water • vinegar •
~~██████~~ • 5 whole cloves • 1 tablespoon mustard seed •
2 blades mace

Place cucumbers in a jar. Boil salt and water brine, made strong enough to bear an egg [fresh eggs will float in brine if it contains enough salt]. Cover cucumbers with boiling brine. Leave for 24 hours. Take out and wipe dry. Place in clean jars. Cover with hot vinegar spiced with ██████, cloves, mustard seed and mace. Leave for 2 weeks before eating. If white vinegar is used, they will be a much better colour.

CUCUMBER RELISH

450g apples (peeled before weighing) • 2 cups vinegar •
450g sugar • 30g salt • 1 teaspoon pepper • ██████ •
680g cucumbers (unpeeled), minced • 1 dessertspoon curry
powder • 2 tablespoons turmeric

Mince apples and cook in vinegar. When soft, add sugar, salt, pepper ██████ Cook until soft. Add cucumber and curry powder. Boil about 5 minutes. To colour, add turmeric.

PICKLED CUCUMBERS (Jewish Method)

salt • sugar • grape leaves • whole cucumbers, unpeeled

Put a thin layer of salt, sugar then grape leaves in a small barrel or stone jar. Add cucumbers whole. Repeat until jar is full. Seal well. Ready in about 2 months.

SWEET PICKLED CUCUMBERS

1.8kg large, full-grown cucumbers, peeled • salt • 4 cups boiling
vinegar • 1 cup sugar • cloves • cinnamon • ginger

Scrape out inside of cucumbers. Cut into pieces. Sprinkle with salt
and leave overnight. Strain the next day. Add boiling vinegar. Let
stand 1 day. Pour off vinegar and boil it with sugar, cloves, cinnamon
and ginger (to taste). When cool, pour over pickle. Put into screw top
jars. In 2 weeks, pour off vinegar. Reboil and return to pickle when
cool. Make airtight.

ECONOMY PICKLE

leftover vinegar from pickled onion bottles • 1 cup dates •
1 cup raisins • 1 cup figs

Boil vinegar with fruit for about 20 minutes. Press through a sieve.
Put in jars and seal.

FIG CHUTNEY

680g fresh figs • 80g dates • 60g preserved ginger • 2 cups
vinegar • 170g brown sugar • 80g raisins • ▬▬▬▬ •
½ teaspoon salt • ¼ teaspoon cayenne pepper

Cut figs into rings. Cut dates and ginger into cubes. Boil vinegar and
sugar. Pour over all other ingredients. Leave overnight. Next day
boil until thick and dark, about 3 hours.

PICKLED FIGS (Fresh)

cloves • 2.7kg figs, unpeeled • 4 cups vinegar • 1.4kg sugar •
1 tablespoon mixed spices (allspice, mace, cinnamon, etc.)

Stick 2 or 3 cloves into each fig. Boil vinegar, sugar and spices together. Add figs. Boil slowly until figs can be pierced with a straw. Put fruit into hot jars. Boil syrup for 5 minutes. Pour over figs, and seal while hot.

FRUIT CHUTNEY (With Quinces)

450g tomatoes • 450g apples • 450g quinces • ▓▓▓▓▓▓ •
220g raisins • 110g preserved ginger (or bruised whole ginger) •
220g brown sugar • 30 to 60g salt • 15g ground ginger •
½ teaspoon cloves • ½ teaspoon cayenne pepper • 2 cups vinegar

Chop fruit and vegetables finely. Boil all ingredients for 2 to 3 hours.

PICKLED GHERKINS

gherkins • salt and water brine • spiced vinegar (allspice, mace, cloves, etc.) (see page 227)

Easy way: place gherkins in brine and leave until yellow. Drain and put into jars. Cover with hot spiced vinegar. Put in a warm place until gherkins are green again. Pour off vinegar. Add a fresh supply of spiced vinegar, and seal jars.

GREEN GOOSEBERRY CHUTNEY

900g green gooseberries • 450g chopped prunes • 450g raisins or sultanas • ▓▓▓▓▓▓▓ • 60g ground ginger • a good pinch cayenne pepper • 1 small teaspoon salt • 4 cups vinegar • 450g brown sugar

Boil all ingredients except sugar until fruit is pulpy. Add sugar. Stir until dissolved. Boil 1 minute. Bottle.

GOOSEBERRY MINT JELLY

green gooseberries, washed • cold water • 2 cups sugar • stalks of fresh mint, tied in a bundle

Put gooseberries in a pan and nearly cover with water. Cook until pulpy. Strain through a sieve and add sugar. Add mint and boil until setting stage. Remove mint. Bottle jelly. Eat with cold meat.

INDIAN CHUTNEY (With Gooseberry)

900g green gooseberry pulp • 450g sultanas • 450g dates, cut small • 2 cups vinegar • 30g garlic cut small • 450g brown sugar • 450g white sugar • 115g preserved ginger • 2 teaspoons cayenne pepper • 60g salt

Boil all ingredients together for 15 minutes. Bottle in wide-mouthed jars.

MANGO CHUTNEY

2.25kg half-ripe mangoes • 4 cups vinegar • 2.25kg sugar • 4 small red peppers • 115g garlic • 220g raisins • 220g reserved ginger • 1 tablespoon salt • 2 tablespoons whole cloves

Peel mangoes and cut in slices 12mm thick and 25mm long. Bring vinegar and sugar to the boil. Add other ingredients and cook until mangoes are transparent. Put fruit in jars and pour syrup over. Leftover syrup may be used to pickle fresh or canned peaches, pears or apricots.

MINT AND APPLE CHUTNEY

2.25kg sugar • 2.25kg skinned and chopped tomatoes •
▆▆▆▆▆▆▆▆▆▆▆▆▆▆▆▆ • 2.25kg peeled and sliced apples •
8 cups vinegar • 900g raisins • pinch of cayenne pepper •
4 tablespoons salt • 3 tablespoons mustard • 2 cups chopped mint

Have all ingredients well pressed down in a large pan. Simmer gently
for about 45 minutes.

MINT SAUCE (Preserved)

225g sugar • ½ cup vinegar • ½ cup water • 1 teacup finely
chopped mint • salt and pepper to taste

Put sugar, vinegar and water in pan and bring to the boil. Boil for
5 minutes. Cool. Add mint and seasoning. Pour into small bottles and
use as required. You may need a little extra hot water when using sauce.

MIXED PICKLE

1.4kg green tomatoes, sliced • ▆▆▆▆▆▆▆▆▆▆ peeled •
2 or 3 cucumbers with ends removed, cut into small pieces •
3 small cauliflowers, separated into small florets • 1 small cabbage,
shredded • salt and water brine to cover • 8 cups vinegar •
220g sugar • spices to taste

Put all vegetables in a large basin. Cover with brine and leave
overnight. Drain and rinse well with cold water. Dry. Pack in jars or
bottles. Cover with vinegar boiled with spices and sugar. Cover and
store. This is ready in several weeks. A little golden syrup may be
boiled with the vinegar and spices.

MOTHER'S PICKLE

1 cabbage, cut up very fine • 1 white cauliflower • 1 large cucumber •
900g tomatoes • ~~450g onions~~ • 1 small marrow • 675 to 900g
scarlet runner beans • sprinkling of salt • 1 cup water •
vinegar to cover vegetables • 1 small tin golden syrup •
½ cup vinegar • mixed spice to taste • ground cloves to taste •
nutmeg to taste • cinnamon to taste • curry powder to taste •
1 level teaspoon mustard • 2 tablespoons turmeric for colouring •
flour

Cut all vegetables up fine. Leave in a china bowl overnight with a
sprinkling of salt. Next day, sprinkle with water. Strain off brine. Put
vegetables in a pan and cover with cold vinegar. Bring to the boil. In
a separate saucepan, heat golden syrup with ½ cup vinegar. Pour into
hot vegetables. When cooked, thicken with the spices and enough
flour mixed with water to make a paste. Put in boiling mixture. Cook
not more than 6 minutes. Bottle when cool. Cover with brown paper
and make airtight.

MUSHROOM KETCHUP (1)

freshly picked mushrooms • salt • black peppercorns • a little
cayenne pepper • cloves • a little mace

Put mushrooms in an earthenware basin and sprinkle with salt.
Leave overnight or longer. Bring slowly to the boil, and simmer 30
to 40 minutes. Strain through muslin. Put liquid on again, add other
ingredients, and boil another 30 to 35 minutes. Strain all. Bottle
when cold. Should keep for about 2 years.

MUSHROOM KETCHUP (2)

fresh mushrooms, wiped • salt • 4 cups mushroom juice (when cooked) • 30g peppercorns • 30g allspice • 1 blade of mace or a little powdered mace • 15g root ginger

Sprinkle mushrooms with salt. Put in a large crock, covered with a damp cloth, and leave in a warm place for 24 hours. Mash well and strain. To each 4 cups juice, add 30g peppercorns. Boil for 30 minutes. Add allspice, mace and ginger. Simmer another 15 minutes. Remove from heat and let get cold. Boil again for 15 minutes, and cool again. Reboil for 15 minutes, then strain, bottle and seal. This is a very old recipe, and the repeated boiling is a special feature — it makes the best ketchup. Boiling may be repeated as many as 6 times.

MUSHROOMS — Pickled

mushrooms • salt • vinegar • pepper • spice

Cook mushrooms in their own juice with sprinkling of salt for 30 minutes. When nearly all liquid has boiled away, cover with vinegar. Add pepper and spice to taste. Boil for a few minutes. Pot and seal.

SWEET MUSTARD PICKLE

about 4kg cut up mixed vegetables (tomatoes, cucumber, ███████, cauliflower) • salt • 8 cups vinegar • 220g treacle or golden syrup • 900g sugar • 30g mustard • 15g ground ginger • ¼ teaspoon cayenne pepper • cornflour to thicken • curry powder to thicken

Put vegetables in an earthenware jar, add a handful of salt to each layer and leave overnight. Next day, drain off liquid, and wash vegetables in water. Put all other ingredients in a pan. Boil and add vegetables. Boil for 5 minutes, or longer. Thicken with cornflour and curry powder. Cover while hot.

NASTURTIUM SEEDS

Spread nasturtium seeds in sun for 2 or 3 days to dry. Put in jars, and sprinkle with salt. Fill jars with boiled, spiced vinegar (see page 227), and seal when cold. Leave 2 months before using.

Put green seeds in salt and water for 2 days; then in cold fresh water for 1 day. Pack into jars, cover with boiling vinegar seasoned with mace, peppercorns and sugar. Cork.

PICKLED ONIONS

1 cup salt • 8 cups vinegar • 900g light brown sugar • 900g golden syrup • 30g peppercorns • 30g cloves • a few small chillies

Peel onions and keep dry. Sprinkle onions with salt and leave overnight. Next day, wipe onions. Boil vinegar and other ingredients. When cold, pour over onions.

VARIATIONS
• Peel onions and place in jars. Add 1 teaspoon sugar and 3 peppercorns (or spices) to each jar. Fill jar with cold vinegar. Cork. Ready in 2 weeks.
• Peel and wipe 2.7kg onions. Add 8 cups vinegar to a saucepan with a piece of salt the size of an egg (or less), and 450g white sugar. Bring to the boil. While boiling, add onions. Stir carefully for 5 minutes. No spices; onions stay nice and light.

PICKLED ONIONS WITH HONEY

4 cups vinegar • 1 cup honey • onions

Mix vinegar and honey well. Put onions in jars, pour over liquid. This is ready in about 4 days.

PICKLED PEACHES

2 cups vinegar • 1 teaspoon cinnamon • 1½ cups sugar • ....
peaches, stoned and halved • a few cloves

Put vinegar, cinnamon and sugar in a pot and boil for 10 minutes.
Add peaches. Boil until tender. Lift peaches into hot jars. Boil syrup
again and pour over peaches. Add cloves to each jar and seal tight.
White vinegar may be used.

PEACH CHUTNEY

2.7kg peaches, stoned and cut up • vinegar • 1.4kg brown sugar •
2 tablespoons salt (or as desired) • 1 small teaspoon cayenne
pepper • 60g garlic • 10g whole ginger, bruised and put in a
muslin bag • 4 cups sultanas

Cover peaches with vinegar. Add all other ingredients. Boil all to
pulp.

PEACH AND PLUM CHUTNEY

900g ripe but firm peaches, stoned • 900g ripe but firm plums,
stoned • salt and pepper • 4 cups vinegar • 1 cup brown sugar •
6 tablespoons preserved ginger • 4 tablespoons cloves •
....

Put layers of fruit in a dish. Sprinkle with salt and pepper. Leave
24 hours. Drain. Put fruit in a pan with vinegar, brown sugar, ginger,
cloves and onions. Boil slowly until peaches are tender. Strain
through a sieve. Fill small jars and make airtight.

PEARS (Pickled with Onion)

~~900g onions, sliced~~ • salt • 2.7kg pears • 3 bottles vinegar
(9 cups) • 680g sugar • ¼ teaspoon cayenne pepper •
1½ tablespoons curry powder • 1½ tablespoons mustard •
2 tablespoons flour

~~Sprinkle onions with salt and leave overnight. Strain off brine~~. Cut
up pears. Put in a pan with vinegar, ~~onions~~ and sugar. Boil until
tender. Add other ingredients, wet with a little vinegar, and boil a
few more minutes. Bottle and tie down.

PICCALILLI

1.4kg prepared marrow • 450g (medium) cauliflower •
450g French or runner beans • 220g onions • ½ large or 1 small
cucumber • salt • 8 cups vinegar • 50g mustard • 50g ground
ginger • 15g turmeric • 30g flour • 170g sugar

Quantities of vegetables may be varied but should be a total weight
of 2.7kg. Cut prepared vegetables into uniform pieces. Sprinkle well
with salt and leave for 24 hours. Drain thoroughly. Mix a little vinegar
with spices and flour. Boil vegetables with remaining vinegar and
the sugar for about 20 minutes. Stir in flour and spices and boil for
3 minutes. Bottle and cover.

SWEET PICCALILLI

900g green tomatoes • ~~900g onions~~ • 900g green beans •
1 medium cauliflower • 6 small cucumbers • brine of 1 cup salt to
4 cups water • 10 cups vinegar • 2 cups sugar • 1 cup flour •
4 tablespoons mustard • 1 tablespoon turmeric

Wipe vegetables and cut up neatly. Cut cauliflower stalks and put in. Break cauliflower into little florets. Put all vegetables in brine, cover, and leave 48 hours. Bring to scalding point in brine. Strain carefully. Pour on 8 cups vinegar and bring to the boil. Mix up sugar, mustard, flour with the remaining 2 cups vinegar, and add. Cook 10 minutes more.

PLUM CHUTNEY

2.7kg plums • 3 cups vinegar • 1.4kg apples, peeled, cored and quartered • ~~900g onion cut up fine~~ • 900g sugar • 110g salt • 1 level teaspoon pepper • 1 level teaspoon mustard • small piece of garlic, cut finely • 220g dates • 220g raisins • 220g preserved ginger, chopped • 1 dessertspoon whole allspice • 1 dessertspoon pickling spices

Boil plums in vinegar then put through a sieve. Add apples, ~~onions~~ and other ingredients, with spices in a muslin bag. Stir well, and boil for 2 hours. Remove spice bag before bottling.

PLUM SAUCE

2.7kg dark plums • 6 cups vinegar • 900g sugar • 1 teaspoon cayenne pepper • 6 teaspoons salt • 2 teaspoons ground cloves • 2 teaspoons ground ginger • 1 teaspoon black or white pepper • 1 teaspoon ground mace • 30g garlic

Boil all together until pulpy. Strain through a colander. Bottle when cold. Should keep well.

PRUNE PICKLE

900g prunes, washed • 3 cups vinegar • 110g sugar • 30g chillies

Prick prunes with a fork. Leave overnight soaking in water. Strain off water next morning. Put prunes in jars. Boil vinegar, sugar and chillies. Allow to cool. Pour over prunes. Stand 1 week before using.

QUICK CHUTNEY

3 tablespoons plum jam • 1 tablespoon Worcestershire sauce • 1 tablespoon vinegar • salt to taste

Mix all together. Then ready for use.

QUINCE CHUTNEY

6 large quinces • 450g ripe tomatoes • 900g apples • 4 large onions • 900g brown sugar • 60g salt • 30g ground ginger • 6 chillies • ¼ teaspoon cayenne pepper • 1 teaspoon mustard • 1 teaspoon curry powder • 220g seeded raisins • about 6 cups vinegar

Peel and cut up quinces, tomatoes, apples and onions. Add all other ingredients except vinegar. Mix then cover with vinegar. Boil slowly for 3 to 4 hours. Bottle while hot.

RHUBARB CHUTNEY

900g rhubarb • 2 finely cut lemons • 900g sugar • 30g bruised whole ginger

Boil all together until thick and dark. Remove ginger. Bottle.

RHUBARB RELISH

2 cups chopped rhubarb • ████████████████ 1 cup vinegar •
2 cups brown sugar • ½ tablespoon salt • cinnamon • ginger •
cayenne pepper

Mix all ingredients in an enamel saucepan. Boil 20 to 30 minutes, or until a jam consistency. Bottle and seal.

PICKLED SHALLOTS (1)

████████████ • 4 cups boiling water • 1 small cup salt • 4 cups
vinegar • ¼ cup pickling spices • 2 cups honey (or 3 cups sugar)

Add shallots to boiling water and salt, cool. Leave overnight. Dry shallots with clean muslin and put into jars. Boil vinegar with pickling spices and honey for 5 to 10 minutes. Pour over shallots in jars.

PICKLED SHALLOTS (2)

shallots, peeled • a little salt • a few cloves • allspice •
4 teaspoons sugar

Put shallots in a big basin and sprinkle with salt. Leave overnight. Remove shallots, lay on a cloth and remove any skin. Quarter fill a jar, adding some cloves and some allspice. Repeat until jar is full. Pour on cold vinegar. Add sugar to top and leave.

TAMARILLO CHUTNEY

1.4kg tamarillos, skinned and cut up • ████████████ • 680g apples •
2 cups vinegar • 1.1kg brown sugar • half a packet of mixed spice •
1 tablespoon salt • ¼ to ½ teaspoon cayenne pepper

Boil for about 1 hour. Will make about 2.5kg chutney.

TAMARILLO SAUCE

3.6kg tamarillos • ▆▆▆▆▆▆▆ • 900g apples •
900g brown sugar • 110g salt • 60g black pepper •
30g allspice • 15g cayenne pepper • 4 cups vinegar • 30g cloves

Boil all for 4 hours and strain.

TOMATO CHUTNEY (Red)

24 large ripe tomatoes • 85g salt • 6 good-sized tart apples •
▆▆▆▆▆ • rind of 1 lemon • 5 cups vinegar • 30g garlic •
400g light brown sugar • 60g ginger • 170g finely cut raisins

Slice tomatoes, sprinkle with salt and leave to drain overnight. Add apples, ▆▆▆▆, lemon rind and vinegar. Boil until tender and put through a colander. Add remaining ingredients. Boil for 3 or 4 hours.

TOMATO KETCHUP (No Spice)

5 to 6kg ripe tomatoes • ▆▆▆▆▆▆▆ • ½ cup salt •
1 teaspoon cayenne pepper • 3 cups sugar • 2½ cups vinegar •
3 tablespoons cornflour

Cut up tomatoes ▆▆▆▆▆. Sprinkle with salt and leave overnight. Boil until soft and put through a sieve. Bring to the boil again with cayenne, sugar and vinegar. Boil about 1½ hours. Thicken with cornflour mixed with a little of the cooled mixture. Boil another 3 or 4 minutes. Bottle and seal.

TOMATO RELISH (Quite Hot)

900g tomatoes • ~~large onions~~ • salt • 2 cups vinegar •
2 cups sugar • 10 small chillies • 1 tablespoon curry powder •
1½ teaspoons mustard • 2 tablespoons flour

Cut tomatoes ~~and onions~~ in slices. Sprinkle with salt and leave overnight. Drain next day. Boil in vinegar for about 10 minutes. Add sugar and chillies. Add other ingredients mixed to a paste with a little cold vinegar. Boil for 1½ hours. Bottle while hot.

TOMATO SAUCE

pinch cayenne pepper • 80g whole spice • 15g cloves •
15g ground ginger • 3.6kg sliced tomatoes • ~~3 large onions, sliced~~ •
3 large cooking apples, unpeeled, cored and cut up • 80g salt •
900g light brown sugar • 4 cups vinegar

Put all spices in a muslin bag. Boil all ingredients together for 3 hours. Strain and boil again for 30 minutes. The second boiling is absolutely necessary. Cork or seal tightly.

TOMATO SAUCE WITHOUT VINEGAR

4.5kg tomatoes • 450g apples • ~~3 onions~~ • juice of 5 or 6 lemons •
110g salt • 340g white sugar • 20g whole cloves • 30g allspice

Cut tomatoes and apples in pieces without peeling. ~~Peel onions and cut into cubes.~~ Add other ingredients. Boil for 2 hours. Rub through a fine sieve. Boil up again. Put into sterilised bottles. Cork tightly.

BRIGHT RED PURE TOMATO SAUCE

5.4kg ripe tomatoes, washed and cut up • 80g allspice •
1.4kg brown sugar • 3 cups vinegar • 80g salt

Put all ingredients (with spices tied up in muslin) in a pan and boil for 3 hours. Stir frequently. When cooked, put through a colander and bottle. Cork when cold.

GREEN TOMATO SAUCE

3.6kg tomatoes • 900g apples • ▓▓▓▓▓▓ • 5 cups vinegar •
900g sugar • 110g salt • ¼ teaspoon cayenne pepper • 30g each
of peppercorns, allspice and cloves, tied in muslin

Cut up and boil tomatoes, apples ▓▓▓▓▓▓ with half the vinegar and other ingredients for 45 minutes. Strain. Add remaining vinegar and boil another 45 minutes. Bottle and cork when cold.

GREEN TOMATO CHUTNEY

1.4kg green tomatoes • 2 small cucumbers • 4 large apples •
▓▓▓▓▓▓ • 170g sultanas • 450g brown sugar •
2 tablespoons mustard • 1½ teaspoons ground ginger •
½ level teaspoon cayenne pepper (or to taste) • 1½ tablespoons salt •
a little more than 2 cups vinegar

Peel, slice and cut up all vegetables. Put all ingredients in a pan and gradually bring to the boil. Simmer for 2 to 3 hours, stirring often. Seal in jars.

GREEN TOMATO PICKLE

2.7kg green tomatoes • 2 tablespoons salt • 4 cups vinegar •
████████████████ • 1 teaspoon allspice •
1 teaspoon cayenne pepper • 2 tablespoons curry powder •
1 cup golden syrup • flour to thicken

Cut up tomatoes and sprinkle with salt. Stand for 6 hours. Strain
and cover with vinegar. Bring to the boil. Add ███████ spices and
golden syrup. Simmer 1 hour and thicken with flour. Bottle hot.

VINEGAR (Spiced)

4 cups vinegar • 10g cinnamon • 10g whole cloves • 10g mace •
10g root ginger • 3 or 4 peppercorns • pinch of cayenne pepper

Heat vinegar in a pan, covered. When it cools, add spices in a muslin
bag. Cool, and remove spice bag. Cold vinegar is best for crisp pickles
such as onions and cabbage. Hot vinegar should be used for softer
pickles, such as walnuts, plums, beetroot or mushrooms.

WALNUTS (Sweet Pickled)

Gather walnuts in early December — prick well with a fork.

walnuts • water • 4 cups boiling water • 1 tablespoon cloves •
1 tablespoon allspice • piece of stick cinnamon (or ½ teaspoon
powdered cinnamon) • 2 cups vinegar • 450g sugar

Put walnuts into jar and cover with water. Change water every day
for a week. Strain and put in boiling water with spices. Boil until
tender. Pour off water and spices. Boil vinegar and sugar and add to
walnuts. Stand for 1 week. Strain off vinegar and bring to the boil.
Put walnuts in bottles, pour over boiling vinegar, and screw down.

PICKLED GREEN WALNUTS

Pick walnuts early in the season.

about 100 walnuts, pricked all over • 4 cups water • 170g salt •
8 cups vinegar • 60g black pepper • 80g ginger • 80g cloves •
60g mustard seed

Place walnuts in brine of the salt and water. Change brine every
3 days and keep stirring about. This takes about 9 days until they
go black. Boil up vinegar and remaining ingredients for about
10 minutes. Strain and pour over walnuts in glass bottles.

WORCESTERSHIRE SAUCE (Quite Hot)

16 cups vinegar • 1.35kg apples (pulpy) • 900g brown sugar •
6 cloves garlic • 2 teaspoons cayenne pepper • 2 tablespoons
ground ginger • 4 tablespoons salt • 2 tablespoons cloves • peel
of
1 orange, grated fine

Boil for 2 hours. Strain and bottle. This is a good sauce. It keeps well
and can be recommended.

JAMS AND JELLIES

Jam Hints:

- When making plum jam always put in plenty of stones as they help the jam to set.
- Boil fruit and water well before adding sugar. Add the sugar warm, stir until dissolved, and then give the jam a good rolling boil.
- When jam sets too thick, add enough boiling water to the pot to make the right consistency. Or empty pot into a saucepan and add boiling water. It sets right when cold.
- When making blackberry jam, put the berries through the mincer, making sure all the juice is caught and saved. Makes nice even jam, with no lumps.
- Sugar must be well dissolved before the jam is brought back to the boil again.
- Making jam from pulp — allow ¾ to 1 cup sugar for each cup of pulp, and add the juice of 1 or 2 lemons.
- Put about ½ teaspoon salt to 2.7kg (say) of jam about 15 minutes before taking up. Helps to settle scum, and clears the jam.
- When mildew forms on top — scrape off mildew, brush top of jam with vinegar, then fit in rounds of paper brushed in vinegar, and screw down. Vinegar discourages growth of mould.
- Jam gone sugary — stand jar in warm oven, until melted. Then stir in a little boiling water, to make sure that sugar is thoroughly dissolved.
- A packet of jelly crystals will help set obstinate jam. Or a little gelatine. Or the juice of 1 or 2 lemons added before jam comes off the boil. Or 1 teaspoon citric acid.
- Jelly-jams should cool a little in the pan before being bottled, and then there should be no settling of the thick part in bottom of the jars.
- Japonica apples added to jelly help it set, and give a nice flavour.

- When jam has burnt, try stirring in a little peanut butter. Or reboil with a small teaspoon of baking soda.
- Stir jam with a wooden or silver spoon.
- Jam made from over-ripe fruit will not keep.
- A knob of butter put in just before dishing up jam will help it set, and remove scum.
- Pack jams and pickles at the bottom of the cupboard, as the top is hotter.
- Jam from jelly pulp — After straining for fruit for jelly, to each cup of pulp add ¾ cup of sugar and about 3 tablespoons of water. Stir well and boil for 10 minutes.
- If cellophane labels stick together, hold them over the steam from a kettle and they will curl apart.

STANDARD JAM METHOD

An experienced and successful home-maker uses this recipe for all jam making — 2.7kg fruit (not too ripe), 12 cups water, 225g of sugar. The fruit may all be of one kind, or mixed, say 1.8kg plums, 900g raspberries, etc. Boil fruit slowly in water until tender, and have the sugar warmed. Stir in sugar, continue stirring until thoroughly dissolved, and then boil hard, a rolling boil, until it will set when tested; sometimes 45 minutes, sometimes less, or more, according to the fruit. If desired, jam can be strained to get out seeds or skins.

APPLE JELLY

2.7kg unripe apples, cut into small pieces, with skins and cores •
water • 1 cup sugar to each 1 cup liquid from cooked fruit •
juice of 2 lemons • 1 teaspoon salt • 1 tablespoon butter •
1 bottle raspberry essence (or strawberry, or lime with a
little food colouring)

Barely cover apples with water. Boil for about 30 minutes. Leave until cool. Strain through a jelly bag overnight. Next day, measure and bring to the boil. Add sugar to liquid, the lemon juice, salt and butter. Take off heat, and stir in raspberry essence. Stir well and bottle hot.

APRICOT GINGER

This is a lovely refreshing jam that can be made any time of the year, as apricot pulp is used.

grated rind of 3 or 4 lemons • 1 cup water • 3.4kg tinned apricot pulp • 3kg sugar • juice of 3 or 4 lemons • 220g finely chopped preserved ginger

Cook lemon rinds in the water for about 1 hour. Put apricot pulp, sugar, lemon juice, cooked rind and preserved ginger in a preserving pan. Bring to the boil and keep boiling until thick, about 15 minutes.

APRICOT AND LEMON JAM

450g dried apricots • 10 cups boiling water • 2.25kg sugar • 450g lemons

Pour boiling water over the apricots, and soak overnight. Boil lemons until tender. Drain well. When cold slice very thinly, removing the pips. Boil apricots until pulpy, add lemons and sugar and boil until jam sets, about 1 hour.

APRICOT AND ORANGE JAM

900g washed and dried apricots • grated rind of 5 oranges • pulp of 5 oranges, sliced • 14 breakfast cups water • 3.6kg sugar

Soak apricots with grated rind and sliced orange pulp in water for 24 hours. Next day, bring to the boil, and boil for 30 minutes. Add sugar, and boil another 30 minutes, stirring constantly, until it jellies.

APRICOT AND PINEAPPLE

900g dried apricot • 10 cups hot water • a little baking soda •
3kg sugar, warmed • 2 tins crushed pineapple

Wash apricots in hot water and a little baking soda. Soak all night
with the water. Next day, boil for 30 to 40 minutes. Add sugar and
pineapple. Boil until it will set, about 30 to 45 minutes, stirring
constantly. Half quantities may be used.

APRICOT JAM (Fresh)

450g apricots, weighed once cut in half and stones removed •
450g sugar

Wipe fruit with a damp cloth. Lay in a pan, with layers of sugar,
and stand overnight. Next day, bring slowly to the boil, stirring
constantly for 30 to 45 minutes, until it will set. Can be made in
larger quantities.

BLACKBERRY JAM

450g blackberries • ½ cup water • 570g sugar

Boil fruit and water together for 30 minutes. Break up berries with
a potato masher. Add sugar and boil until it jellies, 20 to 30 minutes.
This makes excellent jam. Can be made in larger quantities.

BLACKBERRY AND APPLE JELLY

900g apples • 2.7kg blackberries • water •
1 cup sugar to each cup juice

Chop apples, including skins and cores. Place in a preserving pan with blackberries and water to cover. Cook until soft. Strain through a jelly bag. Measure juice and bring to the boil. Stir in sugar gradually. When sugar is dissolved, boil fast until a little jellies when tested on a saucer, about 30 to 45 minutes.

BLACKBERRY AND CRAB APPLE JELLY

Roughly equal quantities of fruit.

crab apples, halved and quartered • blackberries, crushed • water •
450g preheated sugar to each 2 cups liquid

Put fruit in a pan with water and simmer for 1 hour with lid off. Strain through a flannel for not more than 24 hours. Measure the liquid and bring to the boil. Add sugar gradually, stirring all the time to completely dissolve sugar. Bring quickly back to boil and boil fast until it will set, probably about 5 to 10 minutes.

BLACKBERRY AND ELDERBERRY JAM

Equal quantities of fruit.

blackberries, stalks removed • elderberries, stalks removed •
340g sugar for every 450g fruit

Put fruit in a preserving pan. Squeeze slightly and bring to the boil. Boil for 20 minutes. Put sugar in a dish and warm in the oven before adding to the fruit. Add sugar and bring to the boil again. Boil again for 20 minutes or until jam will set when tested on a plate.

BLACKBERRY AND PLUM JAM

900g plums • 2 cups water • 2.25kg blackberries • 2.5kg sugar, warmed • tartaric acid or citric acid

Stew plums and water. Add blackberries and boil until soft, about 15 minutes. Stir. Add sugar and stir until dissolved. Ten minutes before taking up add 1 small teaspoon tartaric acid or citric acid.

BLACK CURRANT JAM (1)

For every 450g black currants, allow 1½ breakfast cups juice from stewed rhubarb and 680g sugar

Boil black currants and rhubarb juice together for 10 minutes. Add sugar and stir until dissolved. Boil for about 5 minutes. Test before bottling.

BLACK CURRANT JAM (2)

1.4kg black currants • 3 cups water • 2kg sugar • juice of 1 lemon

Boil fruit in water for 10 minutes. Add sugar and lemon juice, and boil fast for 45 minutes. Test before bottling.

CAPE GOOSEBERRY JAM

2.25kg cape gooseberries • 2.25kg sugar • 4 cups water

Boil sugar and water for 10 minutes. Add berries and boil hard until jam sets when tested. Bottle when cool.

CAPE GOOSEBERRY AND LEMON JAM

2.25kg sugar • 2 cups water • juice of 5 lemons • 2.25kg cape
gooseberries, shelled

Boil sugar and water in a pan. Add lemon juice. When syrup is quite
clear add gooseberries. They may be pricked with a needle. Boil for
about 1½ hours, or until will set when tested.

CHERRY AND RED CURRANT JAM

1.8kg cherries • 2 cups red currant juice (fruit boiled in a little water
until mushy, then strained) • 2 cups sugar to every 2 cups cherries
when cooked

Simmer cherries until soft. Add equal measured quantity of sugar.
Stir until sugar is dissolved. Boil until jam will set when tested.
Bottle when it has cooked a little.

CHINESE GOOSEBERRY JAM

Chinese gooseberries [kiwifruit] • 1½ cups sugar to every 2 cups pulp

Cut gooseberries in half and scoop out pulp. Cover the bottom of a
pan with water. Add fruit pulp and boil until cooked. Add sugar to
measured fruit pulp. Stir until dissolved. Boil again until it will set
when tested. Vary by cooking in lemon juice and water.

CHINESE GOOSEBERRY AND ORANGE JAM

2kg Chinese gooseberry [kiwifruit] pulp • 2.25kg sugar •
juice and grated rind of 2 lemons

Boil all together until it sets.

CHOKO AND PASSIONFRUIT JAM

3.6kg chokos, peeled and sliced • 3.2kg sugar • 1 cup boiling water • juice of 6 lemons • 36 passionfruit

Cut up chokos. Add 6 cups of the sugar and stand for 24 hours. Next day, add boiling water and boil until clear. Add lemon juice and remaining sugar. Stir until dissolved. Cool rapidly until it will set. Add passionfruit. Boil about 3 minutes. Seal cold.

CRANBERRY JELLY

1.8kg cranberries • 4 cups water • 1½ to 2 cups sugar for each 2 cups juice

Put cranberries in a pan with water. When tender, strain off juice. Measure and put back in the pan. Add sugar. Stir and skim until sugar has dissolved. Simmer, not hard boil, and take up as soon as it will set.

DAMSON JAM (Without Stones)

3.6kg damsons • water • 2.7kg sugar

Boil damsons with very little water until tender. Strain through a sieve. Add sugar and stir until dissolved. Boil until it will set when tested.

ELDERBERRY JELLY

Gather berries while dry.

elderberries • ⅓ quantity of apples (or jelly apples) to 1 quantity elderberries • water • 1 cup sugar to 1 cup liquid from berries and apple

Pick off elderberry stems and clean. Leave smaller stems on. Cut up apples as for apple jelly and add. Barely cover with water and leave overnight. Next day, boil up until soft and pulpy. Strain through muslin. Leave again overnight. Next day, add sugar, and stir until dissolved. Boil up until set.

ELDERBERRY AND APPLE JAM

1.8kg cooking apples, cored and cut up • 1.4kg elderberries, stalks removed • 340g (1½ cups) sugar to each 900g fruit

Boil together apples and elderberries until soft. Add sugar. Stir until dissolved and boil until it will set, about 30 minutes.

FEIJOA JAM

Do not peel feijoas.

2.25kg feijoas, cut into thin slices • 8 cups water • 2.7kg sugar

Put feijoas and water in a pan. Cook until soft. Add sugar gradually, stirring all the time. Bring carefully to the boil, still stirring; keep at a fast rolling boil until jam sets when tested. Feijoa jam must be watched, as it jellies quickly.

FEIJOA, GUAVA AND APPLE JELLY

1.4kg feijoas • 450g ordinary red guavas • 900g small apples •
1 cup sugar to each 1 cup juice

Cut up fruit roughly and boil until well pulped (about 1 hour). Strain well. Boil the juice with sugar until a little jells, about 10 minutes.

FIG CONSERVE (Fresh)

3.6kg peeled figs • 2.7kg sugar • 450g preserved ginger • juice of 4 or 5 lemons

Cut figs in halves or quarters. Put in a pan with sugar and ginger. Pour over lemon juice. Heat slowly until sugar is dissolved, stirring gently. Boil fast for 1½ hours, or until sets when tested.

FIG JAM (Fresh)

1.2kg figs, tailed and cut up small • 220g apples, peeled and cut up small • ¼ cup preserved ginger, cut small • 1.4kg sugar • ½ breakfast cup lemon juice • 2½ breakfast cups water

Add all ingredients to a preserving pan. Bring slowly to the boil. Boil about 40 minutes. Test before taking up. A lovely amber colour.

FIVE-MINUTE BERRY JAM

Suitable for strawberries, loganberries, raspberries, gooseberries, or red or black currants.

2.7kg fruit • 2.7kg sugar • pinch of salt

Put fruit in a pan. Sprinkle over 2 cups of the sugar. Boil for exactly 5 minutes. Add remaining sugar, and stir until dissolved. Bring to the boil again. Boil fast for exactly 5 minutes (work by the clock). When cold, should be a beautiful firm jam.

FRUIT SALAD JAM (Fresh) (1)

900g peaches • 900g apricots • 10 bananas • 1 tin crushed pineapple • 1 lemon, no skin or pips • pulp of 4 or more passionfruit • 2 oranges, no skin or pips • 2.25kg sugar

Cut up peaches, apricots and bananas. Add pineapple, lemon and orange pulp, passionfruit pulp and sugar. Boil for about 20 minutes, until fruit is cooked and jam will set when tested.

FRUIT SALAD JAM (Fresh) (2)

900g apples • 900g plums • 900g pears • 900g apricots • 4 cups water • 3.6kg sugar • 2 oranges • 2 lemons

Peel and stone fruit. Put peel and stones in the water and boil for 30 minutes. Strain, and put liquid back into the pan with sugar. Bring to the boil, stirring all the time. Add juice and a little pulp of oranges and lemons. Add cut-up fruit. Boil about 45 minutes, or until it will set.

GOOSEBERRY JAM

450g gooseberries • 2 cups water • 900g sugar

Boil fruit and water together for 20 minutes. Add sugar, dissolve, and boil fast for about 40 minutes, or until it will set when tested. Three times this amount of gooseberries makes a lot of jam by this recipe. May be made in larger quantities.

GRAPE JELLY

freshly picked grapes • 2 cups sugar to each 2 cups juice

Put grapes, stalks and all, into a pan. Nearly cover with water. Boil until mashed. Strain through a jelly bag. Bring juice to the boil, and boil for a few minutes. Add sugar, and boil until it will set.

GREEN GOOSEBERRY AND CHERRY PLUM JAM

1.4kg green gooseberries • 1.4kg cherry plums •
12 cups water • 2.5 to 3.5kg sugar, warmed

Boil fruit and water for 30 minutes, or until soft. Add sugar and dissolve, stirring. Boil quickly until will set when tested.

GREEN GOOSEBERRY MARMALADE

2 lemons • 2 small breakfast cups boiling water •
1.4kg green gooseberries • 3 small breakfast cups
cold water • 2.7kg sugar, warmed

Shred lemons as for marmalade. Cover with the boiling water and leave overnight. Next day, boil up with gooseberries and the cold water, for 1 hour. Add sugar and stir until dissolved. Bring to the boil and hard boil for not more than 10 minutes. Delicious. Green in colour. Test for setting.

GREEN GRAPE JAM

900g grapes • 1 teacup water • 790g sugar • ¼ teaspoon citric acid

Put grapes and water in a pan. Press and cook until soft. Add sugar and boil until it will set. Strain through a strainer to get out skins and seeds. Add citric acid. Essence may be added if liked.

GUAVA JELLY

8 cups guavas • 2 lemons • water • sugar, warmed

Cut guavas and lemons. Put in a preserving pan and cover with water. Simmer about 2 hours then strain through a jelly bag. Measure the liquid obtained. Add 1 cup sugar to each 1 cup juice. Bring juice to the boil, and stir until dissolved. Boil hard until it will set. Pour into heated jelly jars and allow to cool. Pour melted wax over then cover the jars. Store in a cool dark cupboard. A beautiful red jelly which can be served in the usual way or as a condiment with cold lamb or veal.

HAWTHORN JELLY

hawthorn berries • cold water • 1 cup sugar to each 1 cup liquid • juice of 1 lemon to each 2 cups liquid

Wash and put hawthorn berries into a big preserving pan. Add enough water to three-parts cover them. Cover and simmer gently for 1½ hours. Leave overnight. Next day, bring to the boil then strain through a jelly bag. Measure the liquid, bring to the boil and add sugar. Add lemon juice. Boil briskly for 1 hour or until it will set when tested. Bottle hot, seal cold.

JAPONICA AND APPLE JELLY

900g japonica apples • 900g cooking apples • 1 cup sugar to each 1 cup fruit pulp

Cut up fruit. Cover with water and boil until soft. Leave until cold. Strain through a jelly bag. Next day, measure juice and bring to the boil. Gradually add sugar and boil until it sets when tested, about 20 minutes.

JAPONICA JELLY

japonica apples • cold water • 1 cup sugar to each 1 cup juice • juice of 1 lemon to each 1.35kg japonicas

Cut up apples, put in a pan. Add cold water, but not enough to cover. Cover and cook until tender. Strain overnight. Next day, measure juice and bring to the boil. Add sugar and boil until it will set. Sets quickly. Lemon juice improves the flavour of this jelly.

LAUREL BERRY AND APPLE JAM

1.4kg laurel berries • 1.2kg cut up apples • water •
1 heaped cup sugar to each 1 cup juice

Cover fruit scantily with water in a pan. Boil to a pulp and strain through muslin bag. Leave overnight. Bring to the boil. Add sugar. Boil quickly for 30 minutes or until jam will set.

LOGANBERRY JAM

Do not have fruit too ripe.

450g loganberries • 1 cup water • 570g sugar, warmed

Boil fruit and water. Add sugar, dissolve, and boil until it will set, about 15 minutes. Can make in larger quantities.

LOGANBERRY AND PLUM JAM

2.7kg plums • 900g loganberries • 12 cups sugar, warmed

Boil plums with a little water. Add loganberries and cook until soft. Add sugar and boil until it will set.

MARMALADE (Dundee)

1.4kg sweet oranges • 2 lemons • 12 large cups water •
4kg sugar, warmed

Slice or mince the fruit. Leave to soak in water for 24 hours. Boil for 20 minutes. Leave 34 hours again. Boil again, add sugar and boil again until will set when tested, about 20 minutes. Bottle while hot.

MARMALADE (Easy)

oranges, lemons or grapefruit • 2 cups water for every
piece of fruit • 450g sugar for every piece of fruit

Cut up fruit, cover with correct amount of water. Leave 12 hours. Next day, boil slowly until soft. Add sugar and boil quickly until it sets.

MARMALADE — NZ Grapefruit (Johnny's)

450g grapefruit • 6 cups water • 1 cup sugar to each cup of pulp

Cut fruit very finely. Weigh. Add water. Let stand for 36 hours. Bring quietly to the boil and boil 1½ hours. Take off and leave overnight. Weigh again and add sugar. Boil until it will set when tested. Can be made in larger quantities.

MARMALADE (Prize)

6 New Zealand grapefruit (or 4 grapefruit and 2 sweet oranges) •
12 breakfast cups water • 4kg sugar

Cut up fruit very finely. Add water and leave for 12 hours. Bring to the boil and boil until soft. Leave overnight. Boil for 30 minutes. Add sugar, and boil for 45 minutes to 1 hour, or until it will set. Makes good jelly — not too sweet and not too bitter.

MARMALADE WITH GREEN TOMATOES

2.7kg green tomatoes • 6 lemons, minced, skins and all •
2.7kg sugar • water

Slice tomatoes, add lemon juice and very little water. Cook until tender and soft. Stir in sugar and boil fast until it will set when tested.

MARROW JAM

1.4kg vegetable marrow, peeled and pips removed •
juice of 2 lemons • rind of 2 lemons cut finely • 1.4kg sugar •
30g ground ginger • ginger tied in a muslin bag

Cut marrow into pieces about 5cm long. Put into a pan. Add lemon juice and rind. Add sugar and ginger. Boil until clear and soft, about 1 hour. Seal cold.

MARROW AND QUINCE JAM

2.7kg marrow, peeled and minced • 2.7kg sugar • 1.8kg quinces, minced • 2kg sugar

Cover marrow with 12 cups sugar and leave overnight. Next day, add quinces and the remainder of sugar. Boil together for about 3 hours until set.

MEDLAR JAM

1.4kg medlars, washed • 1 cup water • juice of 2 lemons •
1.4kg sugar

Put medlars into a preserving pan with water and lemon juice. Stand over a slow heat, and simmer for 1 hour. Strain with a dish underneath. Mash with a wooden spoon, taking care no pips pass through. Put back into pan and add sugar. Boil fast for about 45 minutes. Put in jars and cover as usual.

MELON JAM

1 small melon • 2 cups sugar for each cup of fruit • 1 cup water to each 1 cup melon • juice and rind of 1 lemon for every 450g melon (or ½ an orange, or 1 medium pineapple, cut up)

Cut up melon small. Sprinkle half the sugar right through melon and leave overnight. Next day, add water and simmer gently until soft — may be 2 hours. Add remaining sugar, stir until dissolved. Then boil rapidly. Flavour with lemon juice and rind.

MELON JAM (Never Fails)

Do not let the cut fruit stand.

5.4kg melons • juice and grated rind of 6 oranges •
4 cups water • 4kg sugar • 220g finely cut preserved ginger

Cut melon into cubes. Add orange juice and rind, and water, and boil. Stir carefully for 30 minutes until tender. Add sugar and ginger. Boil until golden brown.

MELON AND PASSIONFRUIT JAM

2.7kg pie melon, cut up • 450g sugar • pulp of 48 passionfruit, tied in muslin • 450g sugar

Put melon in a basin with sugar. Leave overnight. Put melon, passionfruit and sugar in a preserving pan. Boil for 2½ to 3 hours. Excellent.

MELON AND TAMARILLO JAM

1.4kg yellow tamarillos • boiling water • 4.5kg pie melon, cut up •
juice and rind of 3 lemons (if liked) • 450g sugar to each 450g fruit

Pour boiling water over tamarillos. Skin and cut up. Add melon. Put all in a pan, bring to the boil, and add about half the sugar. Boil again, adding remaining sugar. Boil until will set when tested.

MINT AND APPLE JELLY

900g windfall apples, quartered (unpeeled) • water • 4 tablespoons chopped green mint • ½ cup sugar to each 1 cup of juice

Almost cover apples with water. Boil for 10 minutes. Add mint. Boil 20 minutes, then strain. Add sugar and boil until it will set when tested.

MOCK RASPBERRY JAM (Or Strawberry)

The recipe is extremely popular and very delicious.

1.8kg tomatoes • 1.4kg sugar • juice of 1 lemon •
1 tablespoon raspberry or strawberry essence

Skin tomatoes and cut up fairly fine. Add sugar and lemon juice. Boil gently for about 2 hours. Stir in essence. Do not boil after essence is added, or flavour is lost. Test for setting.

MULBERRY JAM

2.7kg mulberries • 2.25kg sugar • 1 small teaspoon citric acid

Boil fruit without sugar for 15 minutes. Crush a few to start juice flowing, or add 1 tablespoon water. Heat sugar for browning. Pour in sugar, which should be hot enough to keep jam boiling. Boil quickly for 45 minutes. Add citric acid a few minutes before taking off heat.

NECTARINE JAM

2.7kg stoned nectarines, washed but not peeled • 2 cups water •
juice of 2 lemons • 1 dessertspoon butter • kernels of about ¼ of
the fruit • 2kg sugar, warmed

Cut nectarines into pieces. Put into a pan with the water, butter, lemon juice and kernels. Boil until soft. Add sugar, about 2 cups at a time. Boil, stirring well, for about 1 hour. Test before taking up.

PARSLEY JELLY

450g fresh parsley • water • juice of 1 or 2 lemons • 1 cup sugar to each 1 cup liquid from parsley

Press parsley down and barely cover with water. Simmer 1 hour. Add lemon juice and simmer for 10 minutes. Strain through muslin. Bring to the boil, add sugar, and simmer until it jells.

PASSIONFRUIT JAM

passionfruit • ¾ cup of warmed sugar to each 1 cup pulp

Wash passionfruit well, cut in halves, scoop out the pulp. Put skins on to boil for about 30 minutes or until tender. Scoop out the soft part, leaving skins like thin paper. Discard skins. Add pulp to the seed pulp. Add sugar. Boil until it will set, about 1½ hours. Or may be added to melon jam.

PASSIONFRUIT AND APPLE JAM

passionfruit • 1 cup grated apple to each 2 cups fruit • 340g sugar to each 450g mixed fruit

Cut passionfruit and scoop out insides. Boil skins until tender. Remove pulp inside the skins. Add to the seeds with apple. Boil. When fruit is cooked add sugar. Boil until it will set, as usual.

PASSIONFRUIT AND TOMATO JAM

15 to 20 passionfruit • 2.7kg tomatoes, skins removed by putting into hot water • 2kg sugar

Scoop seeds from passionfruit. Boil skins in water until soft. Add pulp to the seeds. Cut up tomatoes and boil with sugar until melted. Add passionfruit pulp. Boil for 20 minutes, or until it will set.

PEACH JAM (1)

2.7kg peaches • butter • 2kg sugar • 1 to 2 cups water

Slice peaches, remove stones, and put in a well-buttered preserving pan with water. Bring to the boil and cook 5 minutes. Add sugar. Boil swiftly until a little will set when tested.

PEACH JAM (2) (Good)

1.4kg peaches • 6 cups water • 2.25kg sugar •
1 tablespoon butter • juice of 1 lemon

Cut up peaches and boil in water until soft. Add sugar, butter and lemon juice. Boil very hard, stirring frequently, until a lovely golden colour and will set — about 45 minutes. Not too stiff. These proportions may be used for plums, apricots and nectarines.

PEACH JAM (3)

peaches • 340g sugar to each 450g stoned fruit • water •
a few pieces root ginger (if desired)

Peel peaches and cut into thin slices. Cover with some of the sugar and leave overnight. Next day, boil with a little water for 30 minutes or until tender. Add remaining sugar, heated in the oven so that boiling continues. This is improved by adding ginger. Take ginger out before bottling.

DRIED PEACH JAM

450g dried peaches, cut up • 2 lemons, sliced finely •
8 cups water • 2.25kg sugar

Soak peaches and lemons overnight in water. Next day, boil up. Add sugar and boil until it sets, about 20 minutes.

PEACH AND PASSIONFRUIT JAM

2.7kg peaches (not too ripe), peeled and stoned • 2.7kg sugar •
24 or more passionfruit • juice of 2 lemons • 1 extra cup sugar

Cut peaches into pieces. Sprinkle with a little of the sugar. Leave a while. Scoop out pulp of passionfruit. Boil skins until soft. Scoop out pulp from inside skins and add to seed mixture. Boil peaches until soft. Add remaining sugar and boil for 1 hour. Add passionfruit mixture, lemon juice and extra sugar. Boil until it will set when tested.

PEAR AND PASSIONFRUIT JAM

1.4kg sugar • 2 cups water • 1.8kg pears, peeled and cut up • 1½
cups passionfruit pulp

Boil sugar and water for 5 minutes. Drop in pears and simmer for about 1 hour. Add passionfruit pulp and simmer until a good colour and consistency. If preferred without the passionfruit seed, the pulp should be whisked well with an egg beater, then strained.

PEAR GINGER (With Lemon Juice)

2.7kg pears • 2kg sugar • 2 lemons, minced • 1 cup finely cut preserved ginger

Peel and cut pears into eighths. Sprinkle with half the sugar. Leave 24 hours covered over. Add remaining sugar, lemons and ginger. Boil about 2 hours and test before taking up.

PERSIMMON JELLY

Use ripe fruit.

persimmons, skinned • water • juice of 1 strained lemon to each 2 cups juice • 2 cups warmed sugar to each 2 cups juice

Put fruit in a pan. Cover lightly with water. Boil briskly for 2 hours. Strain through muslin. Measure juice and add lemon juice. Boil. Add sugar and stir until sugar is dissolved. Boil rapidly until jelly will set when tested.

PINEAPPLE AND PEACH JAM

1 large ripe pineapple • 3.2kg peaches • juice of 3 lemons • 115g warmed sugar to each 450g prepared fruit

Peel and mince pineapple, removing hard core. Peel and stone peaches. Put into a preserving pan with lemon juice and bring slowly to the boil. Cook gently for 30 minutes. Add sugar and boil until it will set when tested.

PLUM JAM (Good)

1.4kg plums • 3 breakfast cups water • 5 breakfast cups sugar

Put fruit and water in a pan and cook until plums are soft. Add sugar and boil swiftly until a little tried will set firmly. Remove stones as they rise to the surface. Let cool a little before bottling.

PLUM AND BLACK CURRANT JAM

1.8kg plums, peeled, halved and stoned • 1.4kg black currants •
4 cups water • 3.2kg sugar

Boil fruit in water until soft. Rub through a colander. Put into a pan, and bring to the boil. Slowly add sugar and boil for 40 minutes, or until it will set when tested. Raspberries can be done the same way.

PLUM AND RASPBERRY JAM

1.4kg red plums • water • 3.2kg raspberries •
4.5kg sugar • pinch of salt

Cover plums with water. Boil for 1 hour then strain through a colander. Put raspberries in a preserving pan. Add plum pulp and cook for a few minutes. Add sugar slowly. Add salt. Bring to the boil and boil quickly for 30 minutes or until it will set.

PRUNE AND RHUBARB JAM

3.6kg rhubarb • 4.5kg sugar • 1.8kg prunes •
6 lemons, cut in quarters

Cut rhubarb small and cover with 4 cups of the sugar. Leave overnight. Wash prunes and soak overnight in enough water to cover. Next day, put rhubarb in a preserving pan with prunes, water and lemons. Add remaining sugar. Boil fast for 30 minutes, or until it will set when tested. Remove the lemons. Pour jam into hot jars, and seal.

PUMPKIN JAM

2.25kg pumpkin, cut into 1cm cubes • 2kg sugar •
2 oranges • 1 lemon • 1 teaspoon ground ginger • pinch of
cayenne pepper • ½ teaspoon citric acid

Cover pumpkin with some of the sugar and leave overnight. Put oranges and lemon through mincer, catching the juice. Add fruit, juice and ginger to pumpkin. Boil slowly until clear. Add remaining sugar and stir until dissolved. Bring to the boil. Add cayenne and citric acid and boil until it will set.

QUINCE CONSERVE

3.2kg quinces • 14 cups water • 4kg sugar

Wipe quinces well, put in a pan with water and boil until soft. Take out, peel and core, and cut into suitable pieces. Add half the sugar to the water. Add quinces and boil for 30 minutes. Add remaining sugar. Cook until a bright colour and will set when tested, about 45 minutes after last sugar is added.

QUINCE HONEY

6 large quinces, peeled, cored and minced (peel and core retained) •
hot water • 8 cups sugar to each 2 cups quince juice • juice of
1 lemon • ½ cup boiling water

Boil peel and cores, strain and make up to 2 cups with hot water. Make a syrup with this liquid and sugar as above. Add quinces. Boil for about 2 hours, or until it will set when tested. Add lemon juice and the boiling water before taking up. Should be a fine red colour.

QUINCE AND PINEAPPLE HONEY

2 cups water • 12 cups sugar • 5 large quinces, peeled and minced • 1 large pineapple, peeled, hard core removed, and minced

Boil water and sugar for 10 minutes. Add fruit to the syrup. Boil for 30 minutes or until will set. Do not over boil. This is a golden-coloured jam.

QUINCE JAM

quinces • 1 cup sugar to each 1 cup chopped quinces

Wipe quinces. Peel, core and cut into quarters. Put peels and cores in pot, just cover with water, bring to boil. Boil gently till pale pink. Cut fruit into small pieces. Sprinkle quinces with sugar and leave overnight. Put in a pan with the water that the skins and cores were boiled in. Do not add more sugar or water. Boil hard for about 1 hour. Then boil gently until nice and red, and will set.

QUINCE JELLY

quinces, cut fairly small (including cores and skins) • 1 cup warmed sugar to each 1 cup juice

Barely cover quinces, skins and cores with water. Bring to the boil and simmer until it is a thick, soft pulp. Strain through a cloth overnight. Sugar can be warmed in a meat dish in the oven. Bring juice to the boil and add sugar gradually. Stir continually over a moderate heat until sugar is dissolved. Bring to the boil again, and boil very fast at a rolling boil, until it will set when tested.

QUINCE AND TOMATO JAM

900g quinces, peeled, cored and minced, catching every drop of juice • 1.4kg ripe tomatoes, skinned and cut up roughly • 2.25kg sugar

Put quinces and tomatoes in a preserving pan and heat. When hot, add sugar, stirring until dissolved. Boil until jam is cooked and will set when tested. Tastes like rich raspberry jam.

RASPBERRY OR STRAWBERRY JAM (3 Minute)

raspberries or strawberries • 2 cups sugar to each 2 cups fruit when boiled

Bring berries to the boil. Add sugar and boil hard for only 3 minutes. Retains bright colour and natural flavour.

RASPBERRY AND RED CURRANT JAM

raspberries and red currants • 1 cup sugar to each 1 cup cooked fruit

Pick over fruit and wash very gently. Do not leave in the water. Drain, and put in a preserving pan. Crush a little fruit to start the juice. Bring to the boil quickly. Add sugar. When dissolved, boil rapidly until it will set, about 8 to 10 minutes. Red currants may be strained before adding sugar.

RASPBERRY AND RHUBARB JAM

2.7kg rhubarb, cut up small • 3.6kg sugar • 1.8kg raspberries

Sprinkle rhubarb with sugar and leave overnight. Bring to the boil and cook until soft. Add raspberries, and boil until it will set when tested.

RED CURRANT JELLY

4.5kg fruit • 2 cups water • 2 cups warmed sugar to each 2 cups
juice • 1 knob of butter • lemon juice (if desired)

Simmer fruit until soft. Strain through a jelly bag for 24 hours. Add
sugar. Bring to the boil and boil until it will set when tested. Add
butter. A little lemon juice is nice.

RHUBARB JAM

3.6kg rhubarb, cut into short pieces, with coarse parts of skin
removed • 340g sugar to each 450g fruit • 900g tin strawberry or
raspberry jam

Put rhubarb and sugar in a bowl and leave overnight. Boil until jam
sets when tested. Add tin of jam.

RHUBARB AND LEMON JAM

rhubarb • 450g sugar to each 450g rhubarb • juice and rind of
2 small lemons to each 1.8kg to 2.25kg rhubarb • 1 walnut-sized
knob of butter

Cut rhubarb into small pieces and cover with sugar. Leave overnight.
Add lemon juice and rind, and boil. Boil for about 1 hour, or until it
will set. Drop in the butter before taking off the boil. Rhubarb jam
is always fairly liquid.

RHUBARB AND PINEAPPLE JAM

1.8kg rhubarb • 1 large tin pineapple, juice retained • 1.4kg sugar

Cut up rhubarb and pineapple. Add sugar and leave overnight. Next day, boil until it will set when tested. Just before bottling, add the pineapple juice and stir well. Bottle in usual way. A lovely pink colour.

ROSEHIP JAM

Hips are red fruits or seed pods which form when wild rose blooms have dried off. Make jam same day they are gathered. Work with all stainless steel utensils.

rosehips • 2½ cups water to each 900g rosehips • 1 cup sugar to each 2 cups purée • sugar to add when jam is made

Add water to rosehips and boil until tender. Strain through a fine sieve, then through a double thickness of butter muslin to remove sharp hairs on seeds. Add sugar and stir until thoroughly mixed and smooth. Bring to simmer carefully and cook 10 minutes. Put into jam jars. When cold, put a layer of sugar on top to help keep the flavour.

STRAWBERRY CONSERVE

2.7kg strawberries • 2.7kg sugar • 3 cups red currant juice or gooseberry juice

Put strawberries in a basin and sprinkle with half the sugar. Leave overnight. Put currant or gooseberry juice in a pan with the remaining sugar and juice from the strawberries. Boil for 8 to 10 minutes, stirring all the time. Add strawberries and boil until set, about 20 minutes. Skim. Fill warm jars. Cover when cold. Whole strawberries in a heavy jelly.

STRAWBERRY JAM

1.8kg strawberries • juice of 4 lemons • 1.8kg sugar

Cook fruit and lemon juice, simmering gently until soft. Add sugar and stir until dissolved. Boil until it sets when tested. Pot when half cold. Stir before bottling.

STRAWBERRY AND GOOSEBERRY JAM

2.25kg gooseberries • 7 cups water • 4kg sugar •
900g strawberries

Boil gooseberries in the water for 20 minutes. Add sugar and stir until dissolved. Add strawberries and boil for 45 minutes, or until it will set when tested.

STRAWBERRY AND RHUBARB JAM

220g rhubarb • 450g strawberries • 680g sugar

Cut rhubarb to the size of a strawberry. Cover rhubarb and strawberries with half the sugar. Leave overnight. Next day, bring to the boil. Add remaining sugar and boil until it will jell.

TAMARILLO JAM

1.4kg tamarillos • 450g green apples, peeled and minced •
2 teacups water • 1.8kg sugar • juice of 1 or 2 lemons

Scald tamarillos to peel. Cut up. Put apples in a pan with tamarillos and the water. Bring to the boil. Add sugar, and boil until it will set, about 1 hour. Add lemon juice, and bottle hot.

THREE FRUIT JELLY

900g black currants • 900g red currants • 450g raspberries •
1 cup sugar to each 1 cup juice

Put fruit in a pan with just enough water to cover. Bring slowly to the boil. Simmer gently until thoroughly cooked. Put in a jelly bag and leave to drip overnight. Next day, add sugar, dissolve and bring quickly to the boil. Boil slowly for 15 minutes, or until it will set.

TOMATO AND APPLE JAM

2.25kg ripe tomatoes • 2.25kg apples, peeled, cored and cut up •
450g preserved ginger, cut up • 3.6kg sugar

Crush tomatoes in a preserving pan. Boil with other ingredients for 30 minutes. Add sugar and stir until dissolved. Boil 1 hour on a low heat, until it sets. No water needed.

TOMATO AND PASSIONFRUIT JAM

1.8kg ripe tomatoes • 1½ cups passionfruit pulp • 2.25kg sugar

Skin tomatoes. Boil half the passionfruit skins until inside is soft. Scoop them out with a spoon. Add this pulp to tomatoes and passionfruit pulp. Add sugar and stir until dissolved. Boil together until it will set when tested.

TOMATO AND PINEAPPLE JAM

2 large pineapples • 2.25kg tomatoes • sugar (340g for every 450g fruit pulp)

Peel and cut up pineapples. Skin and cut up tomatoes. Boil pineapple and tomatoes together until pineapple is soft. Add sugar to mixture, stirring frequently, for about 30 minutes or until mixture sets. Remove hard core of pineapple.

GREEN TOMATO JAM (With Apples)

2.7kg green tomatoes, cut up • 900g apples, cut up • 225g preserved ginger, cut up • 1 cup water • 3.6kg sugar

Put fruit and ginger in pan with water. Boil, stirring frequently, for about 30 minutes. Add sugar and stir until dissolved. Boil until it will set.

GREEN TOMATO JAM (With Lemon Juice)

1.4kg tomatoes • juice of 6 lemons • 115g shredded preserved ginger • 1.8kg sugar

Slice tomatoes. Add lemon juice, ginger, and very little water to prevent sticking. Boil for 30 minutes until soft. Add sugar and boil until will set when tested, about 45 minutes.

PRESERVING

Two main points are essential in successful preserving —
1. Sufficient processing or cooking at sufficiently high temperature to kill all bacteria, moulds and yeasts.
2. Complete sealing so that no air can get into jars afterwards. If fruits go mouldy, or ferment, while the seal appears to be airtight, it must be because the fruit was too ripe when preserved, or not sufficiently cooked, or the jars were not properly sterilised. If using open-pan (or stewing method), each jar must be taken one at a time from a hot oven, or hot water, filled right to the top, and sealed immediately, before any air has time to get in. Run a hot knife round the side of the filled jar very quickly to make sure no air bubbles have been trapped among the fruit. Store jars in a cool, dry, dark place.

Enzymes are the substances in all fresh fruit and vegetables which cause normal ripening. If the ripening process is not checked, it will go on until decays set in. Extreme heat will check the growth of enzymes, as in preserving, or extreme cold, as in deep freezing.

Fermentation sometimes occurs in jars of preserved fruit. The seal may not be perfect or air bubbles may have been trapped among the fruit when filling the jars, or air might have got inside in some other way. Or the jars may have been stored in too warm a place. Fermentation causes a gas to be produced which forces loose the seals on the jars.

Acid foods are fruits, including tomatoes and rhubarb. They are processed safely at boiling point.

Non-acid foods are vegetables, meat and fish. These must be processed at a higher temperature than boiling point, and should be done in a pressure canner by applying 4.5kg to 6.75kg of steam pressure. If non-acid foods are processed in a water-bath, they need

3 to 4 hours at boiling point, and even then should be boiled for 10 to 15 minutes before using or even tasting.

Do not use salicylic acid or other chemical preparations in bottling.

Preserve only good fruit just ripe. Damaged or bruised fruit can be cut and the good parts used for pulping.

THE STEWING METHOD

This is easy, and safe for fruit only. Make a syrup using 2 cups water to each cup sugar — or less sugar if desired. Boil sugar and water, and stir, over a low heat, until sugar is dissolved. Boil for 5 minutes. Prepare the fruit — whole, halved, or sliced. Drop fruit into boiling syrup and cook gently until soft but not mushy. Have jars hot and sterilised. Have a board ready beside the boiling pan of fruit, and put one hot jar at a time on the board. Fill quickly with fruit, using a perforated spoon (also hot and sterilised), cover with the syrup right up to overflowing and seal. Stand out of draught and test after 24 hours according to directions given with the seal. The pan of fruit must be kept boiling gently all the time you are bottling. Store in a dry, cool, dark place. The jars may be wrapped round with brown paper to keep them dark.

WATER-BATH METHOD
(For Acid Foods Only)

This is very easy and safe. Pack the prepared fruit into clean jars. Fill up to neck of jar with syrup (or water, but the syrup gives the fruit a much better flavour). Cover with whatever type of seal you are using, according to the directions. Place the jars on a rack (or folded cloths) in a deep pan and completely cover with cold water. Bring slowly to simmering point, taking 1½ hours to do this. It is this slow heating that results in all bacteria, moulds and yeasts being killed throughout the whole of the contents of each jar; it also keeps the fruit a good colour and shape. Maintain the boiling for 10 to 15 minutes for most fruits, but 30 minutes for pears and tomatoes. Lift out of water and cool on a wooden surface, out of draughts.

To save time you can pack the fruit into hot jars, cover with hot syrup, and lower the jars gently into a hot water-bath. Use the method as above. The processing time is shorter.

THE OVEN METHOD

Only fruits and tomatoes may be preserved in the oven. Many people object to this method because jars have been known to burst. Have hot, sterilised jars, fill with the prepared fruit (whole or halved or sliced), put in very little liquid, and in the case of strawberries and raspberries no liquid at all is necessary; cover loosely with a patty pan or saucer or something similar. Have oven at 120°C, and leave for 45 minutes to 1 hour until the fruit shrinks and is partly cooked. Tomatoes and pears generally need 30 minutes longer. If the fruit has shrunk very much (as berries and rhubarb do), you can fill up the jars from 1 or 2 of the others, but return them to the oven again for a few minutes. Have ready a saucepan of boiling syrup (or kettle of boiling water), take out one jar at a time, fill quite full with boiling syrup and seal immediately. Stand on a wooden surface out of draughts. This method is popular because you can process a few kilograms of fruit at any time without any trouble. Especially good for tomatoes and berries.

PULPING FRUIT (No Sugar)

This is an excellent way for preserving fruit ready for making into jam, or sauce, or for use in pies and tarts later on. By pulping it is preserved until you need it, and you can make up a little at a time. Simply boil the fruit until soft and pulpy, using only enough water to prevent the fruit from burning. Soft berry fruit and tomatoes should be crushed against the sides of the pan to draw sufficient juice to commence cooking, and no water will be needed at all. For tomatoes, boil up again after straining, for 10 minutes. Harder fruits will need a little water, according to the kind. When all is pulpy, have ready hot sterilised jars and take up one at a time to fill to overflowing with the boiling pulp, sealing each one immediately, before any air can get in.

When making into jam, bring pulp to boil, add cup for cup of sugar, stir until dissolved, and boil fast until jam will set when tested. Less perfect, or even bruised fruit can be used for pulping, provided it is not over-ripe, and the bruised or damaged parts are cut away.

PRESERVING NON-ACID FOODS
(Vegetables, Meat, Fish)

Vegetables are safest if preserved by pressure-cooking. The makers of pressure cookers and pressure saucepans also often supply their own instructions for preserving. Non-acid foods, if not preserved under pressure, can only be done safely in a water-bath. Even then, they should be boiled for 15 minutes before using or even tasting.

BLANCHING

All vegetables should first be blanched — to clean the surface properly, to make them flexible so that they pack better, to reduce the loss of vitamin C, and to help the heat penetrate better during the processing. The easiest way is to put the peas (or other vegetables) into a piece of butter muslin, plunge into boiling water for 3 to 5 minutes, then into cold water for 1 minute to make them easy to handle. Vegetables need a little salt — 1 teaspoon to a 1 litre jar. A little sugar and vinegar may also be added to peas, beans, beetroot, corn and tomatoes.

PRESERVING BEANS BY SALT AND SUGAR METHOD

To 1.2kg beans allow 2 cups salt and 1 cup sugar. Cut beans as for the table and put in a bowl. Mix sugar and salt well, sprinkle over and through beans, and leave overnight. Next day, pack jars, cover with the brine which formed. Keep in a cool place. Do not screw airtight. Wash and cook as usual.

PRESERVED BEETROOT (1)

Peel and dice the beetroot. Cook in boiling salted water until tender. Take equal portions of vinegar and the liquid that the beet was boiled in. Bring to the boil and pour over the beet in jars. Overflow and seal down. This keeps very well and is like fresh cooked beet.

PRESERVED BEETROOT (2)

Three-parts cook beet, then dip in cold water and rub off skins. Slice beet and pack at once into hot containers. Add 1 teaspoon salt (not iodised) to each 1 litre jar. Fill with fresh boiling water and sterilise 1 hour after adjusting lids. Or if done under pressure, 30 minutes to 4.5kg pressure.

BEETROOT (Spiced)

Cook beetroot in the usual way. Skin and slice into preserving jars. Make a spiced vinegar as follows: 4 cups water, 15g peppercorns, 8 cloves, 30g sugar. Bring to the boil for a few minutes, pour over beetroot in jars, and close down immediately.

BERRY JUICE — OR JUICE OF ANY SOFT FRUIT

Crush fruits and allow to stand a little. Add very little water, and place on the warm part of the stove to make juices flow. Remove and strain through a cloth. Bring to the boil, add 115g sugar to each 2 cups juice. Boil steadily for 5 minutes then strain through muslin. Pour into sterilised bottles while boiling hot and put 1 teaspoon olive oil on top of each bottle. Put in corks tightly. To use, soak up oil with cotton wool.

CANDIED CHERRIES

Make a very heavy syrup in the proportions of 450g sugar to 1 teacup of water. Let it simmer until the sugar is dissolved. Put cherries into the boiling syrup, and simmer very slowly until quite clear. Pour off syrup, place fruit on flat dishes, and let dry in the sun or slow oven. Will take several hours. When thoroughly dry, dust over with sugar, and store in paper-lined tins.

CANDIED VIOLETS AND ROSE PETALS

Wash and rinse the flowers. Drain and spread out to dry. Make a syrup of 2 cups sugar and ½ cup boiling water. Stir constantly over a gentle heat until it reaches boiling point. Then stir in ⅛ teaspoon cream of tartar. Allow to cook rapidly undisturbed until the 'soft ball' stage, tested by dropping a little syrup into cold water. It should be taken up and formed into a soft ball between thumb and forefinger. Add flowers to boiling syrup, press them well under, and let it boil up once. Pour gently, without shaking, into a meat platter rinsed in cold water, and leave to stand until next day. Drain flowers from syrup, add another 1 cup of sugar to the syrup, and again bring to the soft ball stage. Add flowers again, and leave until next day. Repeat the process once more, and after the pot is removed from the heat, stir until the sugar turns grainy. Separate flowers, and dust off any superfluous sugar. Pack into boxes between sheets of waxed paper.

CANDIED PEEL

Cut citrus skin into quarters and soak in salt and water for 4 days. Drain and boil in fresh water until tender. Make syrup with 1 cup sugar and 1 cup water. Put peel into this and boil until soft. Leave until next day. Remove peel and add to syrup the juice of 1 lemon and 1 cup sugar. Boil until thick. Pour over peel, and gradually dry off in oven. Orange peel is very nice done this way.

TO CRYSTALLISE FRUIT

Make a syrup with 450g sugar and 1 cup water. Stir until dissolved, and when just at boiling point add ¼ teaspoon cream of tartar. Leave off stirring, and allow to boil quickly for 3 to 4 minutes. Test syrup by dropping a little into cold water — if it forms a soft ball between thumb and forefinger, it has reached desired stage. Drop in fruit to be crystallised, a few at a time. Lift out gently, and drain free from syrup. Place fruit on wire cake trays, and put in sun to dry. When dry, make syrup as before, and when at 'soft ball' stage drop in fruit. Put on wire trays, sift over coarse granulated sugar, and leave again in sun to dry. When dry, pack in boxes between sheets of waxed paper. Keep in a cool dry place.

FIGS, TO DRY

Make a strong syrup in the proportion of 450g sugar to 2 cups water. When boiling, drop in whole figs and boil gently for 30 minutes, or until the fruit becomes clear. Enough citric acid to cover half a ten cent piece may be added if the intense sweetness is not liked. Drain clear figs and dry outdoors in the usual way. If conditions are dusty or the sun not strong enough, use a warm oven. Leave door ajar. When dry, but still quite pliable, pack fruit in paper-lined boxes or airtight jars.

Spread ripe figs in a netting frame in the sun and leave to dry. The air must be able to circulate freely all round them. When dry, store in boxes.

PICKLING FISH

Scale and clean fish and cut into fillets. Pack into mason jars not too tight. Cover with vinegar, 1 teaspoon salt and a little pepper. Screw down top lightly and process in boiling water for 2 to 3 hours. Lift out and fill to the top with boiling vinegar. Screw down until airtight.

Oysters may be done in the same way, only sterilise 1 hour. Crayfish also — cook crayfish first and take out of the shell; put in jars and cover with vinegar and sterilise 1 hour.

GRAPE JUICE

1 cup grapes (170g), 1 cup sugar and boiling water. Thoroughly clean a 1 litre jar (preferably with glass top). Wash grapes, put into the jar and add sugar. Fill jar with boiling water and close tightly. The juice is ready for use in 6 weeks.

PRESERVED GRAPES

Take all fruit off stalks and pack in clean jars. Stand jars in a warm oven and slowly increase the heat to about 180°C. Cook until they change colour, then remove from oven, and re-fill jars, making 2 full ones out of 3 (when cooked they sink down). Have your syrup boiling, overflow the jars and seal in the usual way.

PRESERVED GUAVAS

Make a syrup of 1 cup sugar to 2 cups water. Wipe guavas and pack them in jars. Cover with hot syrup and adjust lids according to their type. Process the jars in a boiling water-bath for 15 minutes for 500ml jars and 25 minutes for 1 litre jars. Leave jars to stand and then test the seals.

LEMONS, TO PRESERVE

Take large, firm lemons, and run a thread through the hard nib at the end of the lemon. Tie ends of the string, and hang in a dry, airy place. Do not let lemons touch each other, or anything else.

Put a layer of sand in a box. Lay clean lemons in a row, not touching each other. Cover with more clean sand and continue layers until the box is full. Keep in a cool place.

Coat each lemon with Vaseline or a paste egg preservative. Wrap each in tissue paper. Do not use skins.

TO PRESERVE LEMON JUICE

Strain pure uncooked juice into small sterilised bottles, nearly filling the bottle. Fill remaining space with olive oil, which excludes the air. Cork. Keep in a cool place. When needed, drain off oil with cotton wool.

MEATS — TO KEEP

Bacon, to Cure, in One Week

To every 11.25kg meat take 670g salt, 110g pepper, 220g brown sugar and 30g saltpetre. Mix well and divide into 3 parts. Take 1 part daily for 3 days, heat in the oven as hot as the hand can bear, and rub both sides of the meat vigorously, keeping the mixture hot. Turn meat daily, take out on the eighth day. Rinse in warm water and hang to dry. Hams may be left 2 days longer.

Bacon, to Cure

3.5kg coarse salt, 1.4kg sugar, 1 heaped teaspoon saltpetre, 1 heaped teaspoon bicarbonate of soda, 1 heaped tablespoon mace and 1 tablespoon pepper. Mix well together. Sprinkle over bacon evenly, and leave to cure for 14 days, turning often. Wash, swish with vinegar, and hang up.

Beef Pickle (1)

670g common salt, 80g saltpetre, 1 teaspoon black pepper, and 1.8kg brown sugar. Mix all together and rub over beef. Rub and turn every day.

Beef Pickle (2)

560g common salt, 450g coarse brown sugar, 60g saltpetre, 4 cups water. Boil all ingredients in the water for 10 minutes. When cold, pour over meat. Turn every day for a week.

Mutton, Ham, to Cure

For 1 hind-quarter of mutton, take 450g salt, 170g brown sugar, 30g saltpetre, 1 grated nutmeg and 15g pepper. Cut mutton into shape of a ham. Mix other ingredients and rub well into the ham every day until the mixture is rubbed in. Then press with a heavy weight. Let it lie about 14 days, turning every 3 days, and rubbing well with the pickle. Take it out, let it drain, and hang up. If you have the means for smoking it, do so. When wanted to boil, soak for a few hours in water. Put in cold water and boil for about 2 hours after it comes to the boil.

Mutton, to Pickle

Pour boiling water over common salt, about 2 litres to 450g salt. Stir until dissolved. Leave until cold, and see if it will float a potato. Add 2 or 3 tablespoons sugar to the brine. Mutton can be kept in this for a week or two.

Mutton, Spiced Shoulder (Boned)

110g coarse brown sugar, 1 dessertspoon powdered cloves, 1 teaspoon pepper, 1 teaspoon ground mace, 1 salt spoon ground ginger and 80g salt. Mix all but the salt, and rub into the shoulder. Next day, rub in the salt. Turn twice a day, and rub occasionally with the mixture for 8 or 9 days. Then roll up and tie.

Tongues, Pickle

2.7kg salt, 900g sugar, 12 litres water and 80g saltpetre. Put this on the cooktop, stirring occasionally, and skim when it begins to boil. Boil for at least 30 minutes. Strain into a tub, and let cool. Add tongues. A fortnight is the average time for pickling, or longer or shorter time according to the size and saltiness required.

MUSHROOMS — PRESERVED

If possible, preserve on the day they are picked — in any case, not longer than the following day. Peel and place in a pot or preserving pan. Sprinkle each layer lightly with salt. When juice flows, put over a gentle heat, stirring occasionally with a wooden spoon. When sufficient juice is there, increase the heat and boil until cooked. Turn into a basin, and when cool pack firmly into jars. Fill with their own juice to within 12mm of the top. Seal. Put in a water-bath and sterilise at boiling point for 2 hours. Take out, and store. If there is more juice than needed for the jars, add mace, peppercorns, salt and ginger to taste. Boil for 30 minutes, and thus make ketchup.

PRESERVED PASSIONFRUIT (1)

Allow ¾ cup sugar to each 1 cup passionfruit pulp. Mix and put aside for 24 hours, stirring frequently until sugar dissolves, and to remove air bubbles. Cork down. Use small jars.

PRESERVED PASSIONFRUIT (2)

One cup passionfruit pulp and 1 cup sugar or honey. Bring to boiling point. Bottle in sterilised bottles and cork. Cool a little and dip in wax. Less sugar may be used, in which case the pulp and sugar should be boiled for 1 to 2 minutes, then filled into sterilised bottles.

TOMATO PUREE

Have good tomatoes, not over-ripe and bursting. Cut up into a can (which may be lightly buttered). Add no water, but a little salt (say 2 teaspoons for every 1.8kg to 2.25kg tomatoes), and a few peppercorns. Bring slowly to the boil, stirring gently. Cook until soft and thick. Strain through a sieve to remove seeds and skins. Bring back to the boil for 8 to 10 minutes. Fill sterilised jars to overflowing, sealing each one immediately as you work, so each is sealed while boiling. Many cooks add 1 tablespoon sugar as well as the salt when cooking — not enough to sweeten but it does enhance the flavour.

TO PRESERVE TROUT

Skin and fillet trout. Cut into suitably sized pieces and sprinkle with salt and a little sugar. Pack into jars with a generous lump of butter to each jar. No moisture. The butter makes a covering for fish when cooked. Stand jars in a vessel of water and sterilise as for fruit. Screw lids on tightly as soon as cooked, and leave to cool in vessel. Next day sterilise again without loosening the lids. Cool again in the vessel. Tighten lids as much as possible. Use new rubbers always. Excellent. Tastes like salmon.

HOW TO PRESERVE A HUSBAND

Be careful in your selection. Do not choose too young. When once selected, give your entire thoughts to preparation for domestic use. Some insist on keeping them in a pickle, others are constantly getting them into hot water. This may make them sour, hard and sometimes bitter. Even poor varieties may be made sweet, tender and good by garnishing them with patience, well-sweetened with love and seasoned with kisses. Wrap them in a mantle of charity. Keep warm with a steady fire of domestic devotion and serve with peaches and cream. Thus prepared, they will keep for years.

BEVERAGES AND CONFECTIONERY

APPLE CIDER

apple peelings and cores, any amount • handful of hops •
1 large cup sugar

Put apple peelings and cores in a 6 litre enamel saucepan with hops and sugar. Fill saucepan with water. Bring to the boil and leave in a warm place all night. Strain through muslin, and bottle, tying the corks tightly. Store bottles in a cool place. Windfall apples may be used.

BOSTON CREAM

6 cups boiling water • 1.2g sugar • 60g citric or tartaric acid •
1 good dessertspoon lemon essence • pinch of baking soda

Pour boiling water over sugar. Add citric acid. Stir well, and when cool add lemon essence. Bottle when cold. To drink, use one tablespoon and a pinch of baking soda to a glass of water.

CLARET CUP

1 bottle claret or other red wine • 2 tablespoons sugar • juice of
1 sweet orange • juice of 1 lemon • rind of half a lemon • 1 slice
cucumber • 2 tablespoons brandy • 1 cup crushed ice • 2 bottles
soda water

Pour wine over sugar and allow to soak for 1 hour. Add other ingredients except soda water. Add soda water immediately before serving. Sufficient for 6 persons.

ELDERBERRY WINE

elderberries • water • for every 1 gallon (4.5 litres) of juice use
1.6kg sugar • 60g bruised ginger • 15g cloves • a little allspice •
creamed yeast on toast

Gather fruit on a dry day. Put in a clean tub and barely cover with water. Let stand about 3 days, occasionally stirring and pressing out juice. Strain through a fine sieve or cloth. Measure juice.

Add ingredients as above, except for yeast on toast. Boil all together for 1 hour. Pour back into tub or jar, which has been well scalded out. When cooled to lukewarm, add creamed yeast on toast in the proportion of 15g per 4.5 litres up to 23 litres. If over 23 litres take 7.5g per 4.5 litres. Let work for 3 full days. Keep well covered with a heavy cloth or blanket. Skim off froth and pour into a clean cask. Paste a piece of brown paper or muslin over the bung hole for 1 or 2 days. Securely bung and leave 2 or 3 months. Half wine and half water at bedtime is good for a cold.

FRUIT CUP

12 lemons • 12 oranges • 1 x 500ml bottle each strawberry,
raspberry and pineapple syrup • 4 cups unsweetened grape juice •
12 cups water • 1 large or 2 small bottles dry ginger ale •
banana slices to serve

Strain juice of lemons and oranges into a bowl. Add fruit syrups, grape juice and water. Chill for 2 hours. Add dry ginger ale and garnish with slices of bananas. Serve at once.

FRUIT PUNCH

juice of 18 grapefruit • juice of 6 lemons • pulp from 12 passionfruit •
sugar • water • 2 large tins pure orange juice • 2 large tins pure
pineapple juice • 6 bottles ginger ale • 6 bottles lemonade •
lemon and orange slices to serve • ice cubes to serve

Put all the juice in a bowl. Add sugar to taste and a little water
(about half as much as juice in the bowl). Dissolve all the sugar
before adding canned juice. Just before serving, add ginger ale and
lemonade. Stir well. Put slices of lemon and orange to float on top
and a few ice cubes. If grapefruit is not in season, use 2 large tins
canned grapefruit juice.

MINTED FRUIT PUNCH

4 cups hot strong tea • 6 tablespoons finely chopped mint •
1½ cups lemon juice • 2½ cups orange juice • 1 cup grapefruit
juice • ¼ cup lime juice • ½ teaspoon salt • rind of 3 cucumbers,
cut in long strips • 4 cups boiling water added to 2 cups sugar,
dissolved • 7 cups grape juice • 6 cups dry ginger ale • 3 cups
soda water • ice to serve • lemon and orange slices to serve

Fruit juice may all be bought. Mix first 9 ingredients. Let stand
until cold, then strain and chill. Just before serving add grape juice,
ginger ale and soda water. Serve with ice and garnish with lemon
and orange slices.

GRAPE WINE

Grapes must not be over-ripe.

4 litres (or 16 cups) grapes • 4 litres (or 16 cups) water •
1.5 to 2kg sugar • ½ cup brandy • 15g bitter almonds
(may be cooking almonds) • 7.5g isinglass

Steep, wash and bruise grapes in a wooden tub. Do not crush seeds. Add water, cover and leave for 1 week, stirring occasionally. Strain through a jelly bag. Add sugar, let dissolve, pour into a cask. Leave bung lightly covered until hissing ceases. Add brandy and almonds. Tie isinglass in muslin, attach to bung, and close cask securely. Keep 6 months before bottling, and 6 months before using.

HOME BREWED ALE

450g best-quality hops • 40 litres water • 3.6kg sugar •
2.25kg malt extract • 1 cup baker's yeast (or ½ tablet
compressed yeast) • 1 packet isinglass, dissolved in
boiling water (or 1 bottle brewer's finings) •
1 salt spoon salt for each large bottle of ale made

Boil hops and water for 1 hour. Add sugar, and boil for another hour. Add malt extract. Stir until thoroughly dissolved. Transfer to cask. When blood heat, add yeast. Leave for several days, skimming every morning. When finished working (6 or 7 days) add isinglass or brewer's finings (instructions on bottle). Leave to clear and then bottle, adding salt to each bottle. Ready in 1 week but better if kept longer.

HONEY MEAD

1.4kg honey • 1 piece root ginger • 16 cups water • 15g hops •
1½ to 2 tablespoons yeast

Boil honey, ginger and water for 1 hour. Add hops. Boil for 30 minutes. When nearly cold, add yeast. Cork lightly as soon as pressure will allow, and tighten later. Can be made in larger quantities.

ICED TEA

2 large teaspoons good tea • 2 cups boiling water • crushed ice •
1 teaspoon sugar • ½ cup orange juice • juice of 1 lemon

Make tea with freshly boiled water. Allow to infuse for 4 minutes. Strain carefully into a jug containing crushed ice. Add sugar and fruit juices. Chill and serve with sugar and thin lemon slices. Orange juice may be omitted.

PARSNIP WINE

1.4kg parsnips, washed • 16 cups water • 1.4kg sugar •
a little yeast, dissolved in lukewarm water

Weigh out parsnips and cut into slices. Boil in water until tender. When cool enough, strain through a muslin bag, taking a small portion at a time to get all the liquid out. When done, make up water to the required amount (some water boils away). Add sugar. When lukewarm, add yeast. Let work for 3 weeks, stirring several times a day for the first week. At the end of the third week strain, being careful not to disturb sediment on the bottom. Let stand for another 3 or 4 days (1 or 2 days longer makes no difference). Strain again as before. Put in a keg, bung tightly and leave for 7 months. Can be made in larger quantities.

PASSIONFRUIT WINE

72 ripe passionfruit • 16 cups water • 1.8kg sugar

Halve and pulp fruit. Add water and let ferment for 6 to 8 days. Drain through a muslin cloth. Add sugar. Let work for 3 weeks then strain. Let stand for a few days. Strain again and keg up tight. Leave for about 7 months. It is then ready for use. To improve the colour, chop up small a lot of the nice ripe skins and add them to the pulp during the first ferment. Stir well several times a day.

PLUM WINE

Use an earthenware or wooden vessel, not tin or any metal. Do not let wine get chilled during fermentation; keep in a fairly warm room. Do not move vessel about.

> 3.6kg to 5.4kg very ripe plums • 16 cups hot water • 1.6 to 1.8 kg sugar (according to sweetness of plums)

Put plums in vessel and mash well. Cover with water and leave for 6 to 8 days while fermentation is active, stirring frequently every day. Strain juice through a muslin bag, measure it, and add sugar. Let this stand and work for as long as it will. Skim daily, keeping some juice to add after skimming so as to keep the same quantity. It may work for 1 or 2 months. When it ceases working, bung tightly, or bottle and cork well. Should be ready in 3 months, but the longer left to mature the better. Wine matures best in a wooden keg. Keep keg covered with a light cloth during fermentation period as it attracts a lot of insects.

TOMATO JUICE COCKTAIL

> 2 cups canned tomato juice • 1 tablespoon lemon juice •
> ½ teaspoon salt • 1 tablespoon sugar • 1 small onion, sliced •
> 1 bay leaf • 1 piece celery, crushed a little • 1 teaspoon minced
> parsley • 1 tablespoon Worcestershire sauce

Combine all ingredients and chill for some hours. Strain and serve.

BARLEY SUGAR

450g sugar • 1 cup water • essence of choice •
½ teaspoon cream of tartar

Boil quickly until a pale golden colour and it will set in water. Add any essence liked and pour into a buttered dish. When cool enough, cut into strips and twist.

BUSHMAN'S BUTTTERSCOTCH

4 cups sugar • 1 tablespoon butter • 1 tablespoon vinegar

Butter a frying pan and two large plates. Heat pan until hot. Add sugar. Make a hole in the centre and add butter and vinegar. Stir until like honey and free from lumps. Pour on to plates. Takes about 10 minutes.

BUTTERSCOTCH

1½ cups butter • 1 cup molasses or golden syrup • 1 cup sugar •
pinch of cream of tartar • 1 teaspoon vanilla essence • ½ teaspoon
lemon essence

Put all except essences in a pot. Stir until just under 150°C or until it will harden in cold water. Take off, add essences, and put in buttered tins. When half cold, mark off; when cold, break up.

CHOCOLATE FUDGE

60g butter • 2 cups sugar • ½ cup milk • 2 tablespoons cocoa •
chopped walnuts • 1 teaspoon vanilla essence

Boil first three ingredients together for 5 minutes. Add cocoa. Boil for 10 minutes. Take off stove. Add a few walnuts and vanilla essence. Beat for a little and pour into a buttered tin.

TOFFEE

225g sugar • 60g butter • ½ teaspoon vinegar •
2 dessertspoons golden syrup

Put all in a saucepan and stir occasionally. Boil about 20 minutes.
Pour into a greased tin.

TOFFEE APPLES

apples

Wash and thoroughly dry apples before making toffee. Carefully
insert skewers into the cores.

Toffee:

3 cups sugar • 3 tablespoons vinegar • 1 tablespoon butter •
⅓ cup cold water • good pinch alum or cream of tartar

Boil, and test by dropping a little into cold water — it should snap.
If apples are greenish, add a few drops of red colouring. When toffee
is ready, turn heat very low, and dip apples in while it is still boiling.
Place apples, skewers upwards, on a greased dish to dry.

TURKISH DELIGHT

4 dessertspoons gelatine • 2 breakfast cups sugar • 1 cup hot water •
very small teaspoon citric acid • red colouring (for pink Delight) •
vanilla essence • almond or lemon essence • icing sugar • cornflour

Put gelatine, sugar, acid and water in a pan and stir until dissolved.
Boil for 20 minutes. Do not stir after it boils. Remove from heat and
allow to cool for 10 minutes. Divide the mixture, and colour one half
pink. Flavour pink half with vanilla, and white half with almond
or lemon. Grease 2 flat dishes and pour mixture in. Leave at least
24 hours. Cut into squares, and roll in mixture of icing sugar and
cornflour.

Index

Index

285